Access 2000

A Tutorial to Accompany Peter Norton's

Introduction to Computers

Glencoe McGraw-Hill

New York, New York   Columbus, Ohio   Woodland Hills, California   Peoria, Illinois

Access 2000
A Tutorial to Accompany
Peter Norton's® Introduction to Computers

Glencoe/McGraw-Hill

*A Division of The **McGraw·Hill** Companies*

Send all inquiries to:

Glencoe/McGraw-Hill
936 Eastwind Drive
Westerville, OH 43081

ISBN 0-02-804923-3
Development: FSCreations, Inc.
Production: MicroPublishing

1 2 3 4 5 6 7 8 9 066 04 03 02 01 00 99

CONTENTS

CONTENTS

CONTENTS

Lesson 4:
Retrieving Data 162

CONTENTS

PREFACE

Access 2000, one of the instructional tools that complements *Peter Norton's®
Introduction to Computers,* covers the basic features of Access 2000. Glencoe and Peter
Norton have teamed up to provide this tutorial and its ancillaries to help you become
a knowledgeable, empowered end user. After you complete this tutorial, you will be
able to create and modify Access databases and use Access 2000 to explore the World
Wide Web, including creating and using hyperlinks and creating Web pages from
Access objects.

STRUCTURE AND FORMAT OF THE *ACCESS 2000* TUTORIAL

Access 2000 covers a range of functions and techniques and provides hands-on oppor-
tunities for you to practice and apply your skills. Each lesson in *Access 2000* includes
the following:

- **Contents and Objectives.** The Contents and Objectives provide an overview of the
  Access features you will learn in the lesson.

- **Explanations of important concepts.** Each section of each lesson begins with a
  brief explanation of the concept or software feature covered in that lesson. The
  explanations help you understand "the big picture" as you learn each new Access
  2000 feature.

- **Access in the Workplace.** This marginal element provides a brief overview of how
  the Access concepts presented in the lesson can help you succeed in the workplace.

- **New terms.** An important part of learning about computers is learning the termi-
  nology. Each new term in the tutorial appears in boldface and italic and is defined
  the first time it is used. As you encounter these words, read their definitions carefully. If you encounter the same word later and have forgotten the meaning, you can
  look up the word in the Glossary.

- **Hands On activities.** Because most of us learn best by doing, each explanation is
  followed by a hands-on activity that includes step-by-step instructions, which you
  complete at the computer. Integrated in the steps are notes and warnings to help
  you learn more about Access 2000.

- **Access Basics.** This element appears in the margin next to Hands On activities.
  Access Basics lists the general steps required to perform a particular task. Use the
  Access Basics as a reference to quickly and easily review the steps to perform a task.

- **Hints & Tips.** This element appears in the margin and provides tips for increasing
  your effectiveness while using the Access 2000 program.

- **Another Way.** This element appears in the margin and provides alternate ways to
  perform a given task.

- **Did You Know?** Read each Did You Know?, another element that appears in the
  margin, to learn additional facts related to the content of the lesson or other interesting facts about computers.

- **Web Note.** Web Notes that appear in the margin contain interesting facts and Web addresses that relate to the content of the lesson and to your exploration of the World Wide Web.

- **Illustrations.** Many figures point out features on the screen and illustrate what your screen should look like after you complete important steps.

- **Using Help.** Each lesson contains one or more Using Help activities in which you access the Microsoft Access Help feature to explore lesson topics in more depth.

- **Self Check exercises.** To check your knowledge of the concepts presented in the lesson, a self-check exercise is provided at the end of each lesson. After completing the exercise, refer to Appendix D: Answers to Self Check to verify your understanding of the lesson material.

- **On the Web.** At the end of each lesson, an On the Web section teaches you how to use Access to explore the World Wide Web. Various activities show you how to insert a hyperlink into an Access database object, navigate the Web, use the Search page, create a Web page, and more.

- **Summary.** At the end of each lesson, the Summary reviews the major topics covered in the lesson. You can use the Summary as a study guide.

- **Concepts Review.** At the end of each lesson, there are five types of objective questions: a true/false exercise, a matching exercise, a completion exercise, short-answer questions, and an identification exercise. When you complete these exercises, you can verify that you have learned all the concepts that have been covered in the lesson.

- **Skills Review.** The Skills Review section provides simple hands-on exercises to practice each skill you learned in the lesson.

- **Lesson Applications.** The Lesson Applications provide additional hands-on practice. These problems combine two or more skills learned in the lesson to modify Access 2000 databases.

- **Projects.** The Projects provide additional hands-on practice to apply your problem-solving skills. Each project allows you to create a new database or modify an existing database to incorporate one or more skills learned in the lesson. In each lesson, the Projects section contains an *On the Web* project, which reinforces the skills learned in the On the Web section, as well as a *Project in Progress* that builds from one lesson to the next.

- **Case Study.** The Case Study is a capstone activity that allows you to apply the various skills you have learned throughout the *Access 2000* tutorial to plan, create, and modify an Access database.

- **Portfolio Builder, Command Summary, Toolbar Summary, and Answers to Self Check.** These appendices provide a wealth of information. The Portfolio Builder gives an overview of portfolios and provides tips on creating your personal portfolio. The Command Summary and Toolbar Summary review both mouse and keyboard techniques for completing Access 2000 tasks. Answers to Self Check exercises found throughout each lesson are provided in the last appendix.

- **Glossary and Index.** A Glossary and an Index appear at the back of the tutorial. Use the Glossary to look up terms that you don't understand and the Index to find specific information.

- **Access Data CD.** Attached to the inside back cover of this tutorial you will find the Access Data CD. This CD contains Access 2000 files for you to use as you complete the hands-on activities and the end-of-lesson activities. You must copy the files from the Access Data CD to a Zip disk, to a folder on the hard drive, or to a folder on a network drive to create the Student Data Disk. (Instructions for copying files from the Access Data CD are provided on pages xv-xvi of this tutorial.)

MOUS CERTIFICATION PROGRAM

The Microsoft Office User Specialist (MOUS) program offers certification at two skills levels—"Core" and "Expert." *Access 2000* is approved courseware for the MOUS program that will aid you in fully understanding the skills required for the Microsoft Access 2000 "Core" certification exam. Obtaining MOUS certification can be a valuable asset in job searches and workplace advancement. For more information about the Microsoft Office User Specialist program, visit www.mous.net.

ABOUT PETER NORTON

Peter Norton is a pioneering software developer and an author. *Norton Utilities, AntiVirus,* and other utility programs are installed worldwide on millions of personal computers. His books have helped countless individuals understand computers from the inside out.

Glencoe teamed up with Peter Norton to help you better understand the role computers play in your life now and in the future. As you begin to work in your chosen profession, you may use this tutorial now and later as a reference book.

REVIEWERS

Many thanks are due to the following individuals who reviewed the manuscript and provided recommendations to improve this tutorial:

Carol Hernandez
Davenport College
Merrillville, Indiana

James Johnson
Valencia Community College
Orlando, Florida

Sandra Lehmann
Moraine Park Technical College
Fond du Lac, Wisconsin

Patsy Malavite
The University of Akron—Wayne College
Orrville, Ohio

COPYING FILES FROM YOUR ACCESS DATA CD

CD-ROMs can hold hundreds of megabytes of data. As their name implies (Compact Disc-*Read-Only* Memory), you cannot modify the data they contain. Hard and floppy disks are the media generally used as personal data storage devices. To complete the lessons in this tutorial, you must copy the files from the Access Data CD to a Zip disk, to a folder on the hard drive, or to a folder on a network drive. You'll use these files, called the Student Data Disk, throughout the rest of this tutorial.

1. **Turn on the computer you are using.**

2. **Insert the Access Data CD in the CD drive of your computer.**

3. **Click Start** [Start]**, point to Programs, and click Windows Explorer.**

The Exploring window opens.

4. **In the Folders pane of the Exploring window, find and click the drive icon that represents your CD drive.**

The contents of the CD drive will appear in the Contents pane, as shown in Figure 1.

5. **Click the Edit menu and click Select All, then click Copy** [Copy]**.**

6. **Scroll up, if necessary, and click the appropriate drive icon (and folder, if necessary) where you want to store your Access files.**

Copy button

Paste button

The Folders pane

Folders

Files

The CD drive is selected.

The contents of the CD drive appear in the Contents pane.

Figure 1 ◀
The contents of the
Access Data CD

 Note If you are copying the Access Data CD folders and files onto a Zip disk, be sure to write Access Student Data Disk *on the disk label and insert the disk into the Zip drive. Then, go to step 7.*

If you are copying the Access Data CD folders and files onto the hard drive or network drive, navigate to the drive and folder if necessary where you want to store the files. To create a folder for the Access Data CD folders and files, click the drive icon, click the folder name if necessary, click the File menu, click New, click Folder, and type Access Student Data Disk*. Click this newly created folder in the Folders pane of the Exploring window; then go to step 7.*

7. Click Paste.

A Copying box will appear on the screen to indicate the progress of the copying process. To use and save changes to the files copied from the Access Data CD, you must remove the read-only attribute and add the archive attribute to each of the files in *each* of the folders.

8. In the Folders pane of the Exploring window, click the appropriate drive icon and folder, if necessary, where the Access Student Data Disk files are stored. Click **Edit** and click **Select All**. Then, right-click one of the selected files in the Contents pane, and click **Properties** on the shortcut menu that appears.

9. In the Attributes area on the General tab of the Properties dialog box, click the **Read-only box** until the check mark disappears. Then, click the **Archive box** until a check mark appears in the white box, as shown in Figure 2. Finally, click **OK**.

Now you must change the file attributes of the files in each of the folders.

10. In the Folders pane, double-click the drive icon and folder if necessary where the Access files are stored.

Each of the five subfolders appears in the Folders pane.

11. In the Folders pane, click the **Lesson Applications folder**. Click **Edit** and click **Select All**. Right-click one of the selected files in the Contents pane, and click **Properties**. On the General tab of the Properties dialog box, deselect **Read-only**, select **Archive**, and click **OK**.

12. Repeat step 11 for each of the other folders on the Access Student Data Disk: *Projects, Skills Review, Supplemental Activities*, and *Tutorial*.

13. Close Windows Explorer. Remove the disk from the drive, if necessary. Remove the Access Data CD from the CD drive.

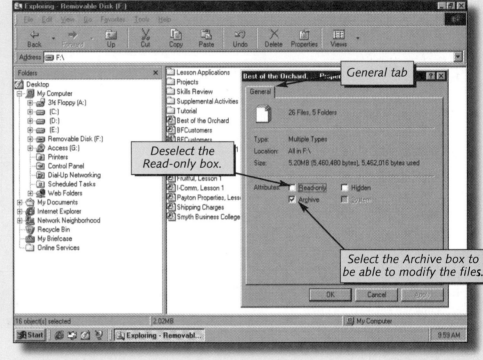

You are now ready to begin working with *Access 2000!*

Figure 2 ◀
The General tab of the
Properties dialog box

Access 2000

Managing the "Infoglut"

Data warehousing and data mining offer a new approach

For many corporations, data is their lifeblood. For years, companies have collected, sorted, stored, and spit out vast amounts of data about their customers, products, inventories, employees, sales, and stores. They also store external data about their competitors and their industry. This data is crucial for managers, employees, and executives to better understand their organization and industry.

All this collected data—this *infoglut*—raises two major issues that affect companies all around the world: Where's the best place to store all this data? And once we have it stored, how can we access it efficiently? The usual approach to managing infoglut is to maintain well-designed databases. At some point, however, the law of diminishing returns comes into play—there is just too much information, and it simply is not practical to create a new database or a new database management system (DBMS) for each new situation that comes along.

The newest approach to solving the problem of infoglut is to build a *data warehouse* and then *data mine* the warehouse for critical information. A data warehouse is a massive collection of corporate information, often stored in gigabytes or terabytes of data. It can include any and all data that is relevant to running a company. All this data is stored in databases spread among many storage devices on computers running tens or even hundreds of central processing units. However, setting up a data warehouse is much more complicated than simply dumping all kinds of data into one storage place. You should consider the following factors when setting up a data warehouse:

What type of processing scheme will be used? Generally, two types of technologies, Symmetrical Multiprocessing (SMP) or Massively Parallel Processing (MPP), are used. For smaller storage needs, such as between 50 GB to 300 GB, companies use SMP. For data warehouses larger than 300 GB, many companies opt for MPP because of the ability to scale (or add) additional processors as their storage needs grow.

How much storage space is needed and what type of backup plan is needed? One of the most popular storage schemes is RAID (Redundant Array of Independent Disks). RAID is a storage system that links any number of disk drives to act as a single disk. In this system, information is written to two or more disks simultaneously to improve speed and reliability and to ensure that data is available to users at all times. RAID's capabilities are based on three techniques: (1) mirroring, (2) striping, and (3) striping-with-parity:

- In a *mirrored* system, data is written to two or more disks simultaneously, providing a complete copy of all the information on a drive, should one drive fail.

- *Striping* provides the user with speedy response by spreading data across several disks. Striping alone, however, does not provide backup if one of the disks in an array fails.

- *Striping-with-parity* provides the speed of striping with the reliability of parity. Should a drive in such an array fail, the system administrator can use the disk that stores the parity information to reconstruct the data from the damaged drive. Some arrays using the striping-with-parity technique also offer a technique known as *hot swapping,* which enables a system administrator to remove a damaged drive while the array remains in operation.

What type of data scrubbing will be set up? Whenever a lot of data is collected, it will, no doubt, contain some errors. *Data scrubbing* means sifting through data and performing such tedious tasks as eliminating duplications and incomplete records and making sure that similar fields in different tables are defined in exactly the same ways.

After a data warehouse has been set up, a company can perform targeted data mining to solve complex business problems, such as determining better ways to serve the needs of customers, outsmarting the competition, discovering trends in the market, and developing new products. To be successful, a company must mine its vast storehouse of information effectively to find out exactly what it knows, how to get to it, and what to do with it. By understanding and using the full capability of the Microsoft® Access 2000 program, you will be well on your way to building effective databases to manage the infoglut!

Photo: Richard Morrell/The Stock Market

LESSON 1

Access Basics

CONTENTS

OBJECTIVES

After you complete this lesson, you will be able to do the following:

- Understand databases and how they work.
- Use your mouse to point, click, double-click, right-click, select, and drag.
- Start and exit Microsoft Access.
- Name the main features of the Database window.
- Select an object using the Objects bar.
- Switch between object views.
- Open and close a database.
- Identify the basic components of an Access database.
- Enter records using a form.
- Find a record.
- Preview and print database objects.
- Use the Office Assistant.
- Get help from ScreenTips.
- Understand and use hyperlinks.
- Backup and restore a database.
- Compact and repair a database.
- Connect to and disconnect from the Internet.
- Explore the Web toolbar and access a Web site.

Access is a powerful database program that enables you to organize and manipulate data, perform selection queries, develop reports and convert files for use on the Web. Access does much of the work automatically and offers help with more complex tasks.

Lesson 1 teaches you basic database terms, shows you how to launch Microsoft Access, and introduces the Access window. You will open and close databases and print reports—essential skills that you will use whenever you work with Access. In addition, you will explore the online Help system, which you can use to learn more about the features of Access and to help you solve problems you may have as you use the Access program.

INTRODUCING MICROSOFT ACCESS

This tutorial teaches you how to use the database program Microsoft Access. A *database* is an organized collection of data about similar things—such as employees, customers, or inventory items. A database is like a computerized Rolodex, paper filing system, or telephone book. As you begin to work with databases, you may encounter the term *DBMS,* for *database management system.* A DBMS is a system for storing and manipulating the data in a database.

Databases are useful any time you have to store, retrieve and manipulate information. You can use databases to store massive amounts of data in a very small space; to manipulate data with ease, sorting to the desired order; and to extract required information. As an example, the database table in Figure 1.1 contains customer information.

Last Name	First Name	Address	City	State	ZIP Code
Kenber	Fra *Field*	1777 Lois Ln.	Rock Creek	NC	28333-1234
Reid	Alyson	7374 Backwoods Rd.	Sebastopol	CA	97777-1111
Turlow	Will	1 Oak Place	Providence	RI	02900-2338
Zheng	Anne	25 Forest Knoll	Santa Rosa	CA	99887-2355
O'Hara	Joan	2234 Hanley Place	Baltimore	MD	21122-5634
Quinonez	James	32123 Overlook Ave.	Portland	OR	99876-2389
Bechdel	Mason	75 Grizzly Peak Blvd.	Orinda	CA	94700-5412
Isherwood	Emma	1314 23rd Ave.	Biddeford	ME	57432-6034
Smith	Christine	5457 Park Pl.	New York	NY	10001-8763
Jackson	Jacqueline	6633 Dallas Way	Houston	TX	47532-7843
Everett	Richard	1310 Arch St.	Berkeley *Record*		98765-3368
Wintergreen	Shelly	21 Barbary Ln.	Omaha	NE	66332-9004
Menendez	Erica	303 Hollywood St. #15	Los Angeles	CA	99887-3489
Zheng	Alicia	32 B St.	Ashland	OR	97998-5098
Ng	Patrick	1112 Spruce St.	Shaker Heights	OH	45678-7842
Apfelbaum	Bob	81 Hacienda Blvd.	Santa Fe	NM	55554-3449
Hatfield	James	15A Vine St.	Ashland	OR	97998-6907
Marais	Jean-Luc	1379 Montgomery Ave. #3	Boston	MA	02101-3930
Savallis	Jordi	100 Riverside Dr. #10B	New York	NY	10025-8035
Yates	Lily	999 35th Ave.	Oakland	CA	94602-8532
Criton	Molly	71 Panoramic Way	Seattle	WA	99981-9532

Figure 1.1
Sample table from a database

The customer information in Figure 1.1 is arranged in well-marked columns and rows and is easy to read. In Access, data is stored in *tables.* Tables organize information into a series of *fields* (columns) that contain categories of data and *records* (rows) that contain the set of fields for one particular entity. The table shown in Figure 1.1 includes fields for each customer's last name, first name, address, city, state, and ZIP Code. In this case, a record consists of all fields that apply to a single customer.

Most Access databases will actually contain one or more tables that you can use together when the need arises. If you have more than one general category of information—such as customer addresses and customer orders—you should place the data in separate tables. While you work, you may require data from multiple tables; for example, you might want to list both customer addresses and orders on an invoice form. You can do this easily in Access, provided that the tables include common fields by which they can be linked.

To use two tables together, you must first define the relationship between them. For instance, Access lets you link two tables that contain a common field. For example, if both your customer address and order tables include a field that contains customer ID numbers, Access can find each customer's orders by scanning the order table for records with the matching customer ID number. This arrangement saves you from having to store copies of the customer name and address data in several places, streamlining your database by eliminating the duplication of data and at the same time reducing the risk of data entry error. (If you enter a name only once, you are less likely to make a mistake.) Database programs that let you link, or relate, two tables in this manner are known as *relational databases.* You will learn more about working with multiple tables in future lessons.

USING THE MOUSE

Microsoft Access is just one of many programs, or *applications,* that requires *operating system* software such as Windows 95 or Windows 98. Soon after you turn on your computer, several *icons* or pictures appear. The icons represent items on a disk, and the screen is the *desktop.* The *taskbar,* the bar across the bottom of the desktop, contains *buttons* that you can click to perform various tasks. The Start button is the one you click to show the Start *menu.* On the Start menu, you can click to open any program installed on your computer, including Microsoft Access.

You will use the *mouse* extensively in Microsoft Access. The mouse is the key to the graphical user interface because it lets you choose and manipulate on-screen objects without having to type on the keyboard. Although the mouse is the most popular pointing device, you may also use several other pointing devices. *Trackballs* have buttons like the mouse, but instead of moving the mouse over the desktop, you spin a large ball. Laptops often employ either a small *joystick* in the middle of the keyboard or a *touch-sensitive pad* below the keyboard. Each of these devices, however, lets you point to items on the screen and click buttons to perform actions on those items.

Your mouse probably has two or three buttons. Whenever the directions in this tutorial say *click,* use the left mouse button. If you must use the right mouse button, the directions will say *right-click* or *click the right mouse button.* You can perform several actions with the mouse:

- On your screen, you should see an arrow pointing toward the upper left. This arrow is called the *mouse pointer,* or more simply, the *pointer.* Moving the mouse to position the pointer on the screen is called *pointing.* Table 1.1 shows several shapes you may notice as you point to objects on the screen.
- To *click* the mouse, point to an object and quickly press and release the left mouse button.
- To work with an object on the screen, you must usually *select* (or *choose*) the item by clicking the object—pressing and quickly releasing the mouse button.
- To *double-click,* point to an object and click the left mouse button twice in rapid succession without moving the pointer.
- To *right-click,* point to an object, press the right mouse button, and then quickly release it.

The mouse was not widely used until the Apple Macintosh computer became available in 1984. The mouse is an indispensable tool for every computer user today.

TABLE 1.1	COMMON POINTER SHAPES
Pointer Shape	**Description**
▨	Normal Select (arrow)
+	Crosshair pointer
▨?	Help Select (What's This? pointer)
▨▨	Working in Background
⧖	Busy
+	Drawing
I	Insertion Point
✋	Drag Box
🖌	Format Painter
⊘	Unavailable
↕	Vertical Resize
↔	Horizontal Resize
↖	Diagonal Resize 1
↗	Diagonal Resize 2
✛	Move Object
🖑	Hyperlink Select

■ To *drag* (or *drag-and-drop*), point to an object you want to move, press and hold the left mouse button, move the mouse to drag the object to a new location, and then release the mouse button.

STARTING MICROSOFT ACCESS

Before you can start Microsoft Access, both Microsoft Access and Windows 95 or Windows 98 must be installed on the computer you're using. The figures in this tutorial use Windows 98; if you are using Windows 95, the information appearing on your screen may vary slightly.

You must create the Student Data Disk for this tutorial from the Data CD located on the inside back cover of this tutorial. If you have not created the Student Data Disk, ask your instructor for help.

Launching Microsoft Access

In this activity, you will start Microsoft Access.

1. Turn on your computer.

If you are prompted for a user name and/or password, enter the information at this time. If you do not know your user name and/or password, ask your instructor for help.

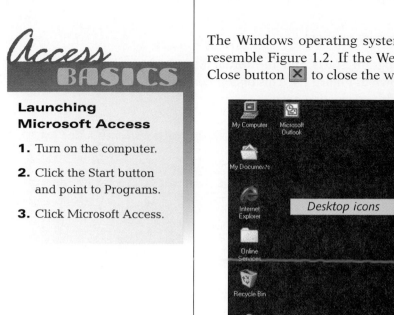

Launching Microsoft Access

1. Turn on the computer.

2. Click the Start button and point to Programs.

3. Click Microsoft Access.

The Windows operating system boots the computer. Your screen should resemble Figure 1.2. If the Welcome to Windows screen appears, click its Close button ☒ to close the window.

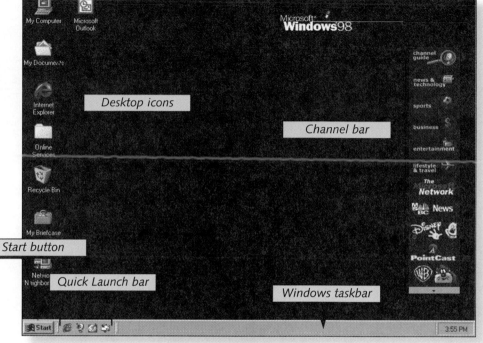

Desktop icons

Channel bar

Start button

Quick Launch bar

Windows taskbar

Figure 1.2 ◄
The Windows Desktop

2. Click the Start button [Start] **on the Windows taskbar.**

3. Point to Programs.

The Programs menu appears, as shown in Figure 1.3. (Depending on the applications installed on your computer, your Programs menu may be different than Figure 1.3.)

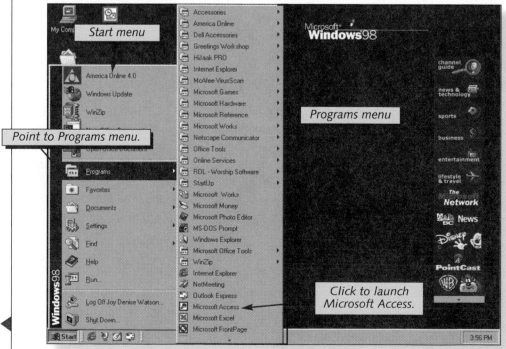

Start menu

Point to Programs menu.

Programs menu

Click to launch Microsoft Access.

Figure 1.3 ◄
The Programs menu

4. Click Microsoft Access.

The Access program starts and the initial Microsoft Access dialog box appears, as shown in Figure 1.4. This dialog box lets you create a new database or work with an existing one.

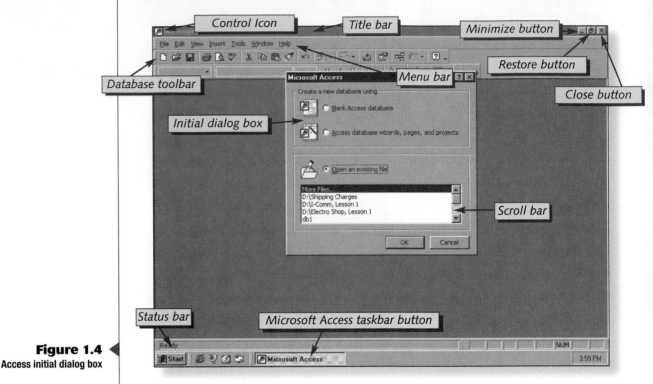

Figure 1.4 ◀
Access initial dialog box

5. For the moment, click the Cancel button to close the dialog box.

You will see the Microsoft Access startup window. In the startup window, many features are not yet available because you haven't opened a database. For example, note that if you click Edit on the menu bar, all the options beneath are grayed (meaning that they're currently disabled). As you will soon find out, the available Access options change depending on what you're doing at the moment.

EXPLORING ACCESS

The Access *application window* (screen) is shown in Figure 1.4. Your window may look slightly different because Access allows users to *customize,* or alter, the Access window to suit their individual needs. The Access window contains many standard Windows elements, including a title bar; the Minimize, Restore, and Close buttons; a menu bar; and the scroll bars. These items should seem familiar if you've used Windows 95, Windows 98, or any other Windows 95 or Windows 98 application. Table 1.2 highlights the main features of the Access window.

An animated character called the Office Assistant is perhaps the most curious object in the application window. In this tutorial, the Office Assistant is a dog named *Rocky.* This character—part of the Help system—represents an Office Assistant for Access users. If the Office Assistant is not on your screen, press F1. When the character gets in your way, drag it to an out-of-the-way location.

TABLE 1.2	THE ACCESS WINDOW
Element	**Description**
Title bar	Contains the Control icon, the name of the program, and the Minimize, Maximize, Restore, and Close buttons.
Control icon	Clicking this icon displays the Control menu, which allows you to manipulate the window. Double-clicking this icon closes Access.
Minimize button	Removes the window from the screen. You will know that the program is still running because a button appears on the taskbar.
Maximize button	Enlarges the window to fill the entire screen.
Restore button	Returns the window to the previous size.
Menu bar	A set of options below the Access title bar that lead to associated menus.
Database toolbar and Formatting toolbar	A series of buttons that contain mouse shortcuts for frequently used commands.
Status bar	Provides information concerning what you are currently doing or where you are in the program. Includes the state of each *toggle key*—a key that turns on and off, such as [Caps Lock] and [Num Lock].

Note *When this tutorial mentions a toolbar button, a picture of the button is displayed within the text. For instance, when a step instructs you to click the Print button , the button will be illustrated as shown here.*

Understanding the Menu Bar

As shown in Figure 1.4, the Access *menu bar* appears below the title bar. The menu bar displays some of the menu names found in most Windows applications, such as File, Edit, and Help.

Menus list the *commands* available in Access. To display a menu's commands, click a menu name on the menu bar. The menu will display a *short menu,* a list of the most-used commands, with an arrow at the bottom. If you keep your pointer on the menu for a few seconds or if you click the double arrow at the bottom of the menu, an *expanded menu* appears. This expanded menu shows all of the commands available on the menu. The most-used commands appear when a menu opens; when the list expands, less common commands appear. Figure 1.5 shows both versions of Access' Insert menu—as a short menu and an expanded menu.

As shown in Figure 1.5, five active commands appear on the initial Insert menu. These five commands are considered to be the commands that users

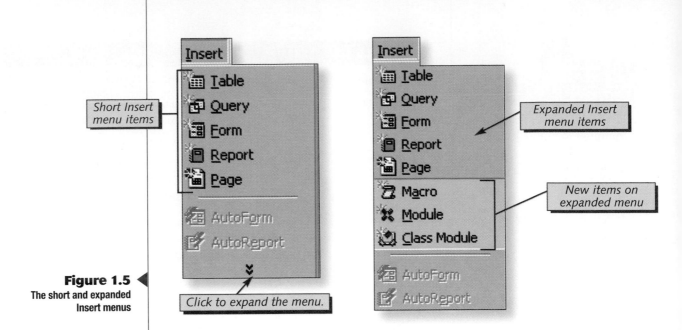

Figure 1.5
The short and expanded
Insert menus

Short Insert menu items

Expanded Insert menu items

New items on expanded menu

Click to expand the menu.

If you prefer to always see the expanded menus, you can click Tools on the menu bar and click Customize. On the Options tab of the Customize dialog box, deselect the *Menus show recently used commands first* option.

issue most often from this menu. The expanded menu shows three additional commands—Macro, Module, and Class Module—which are not used as frequently. The backgrounds of the additional commands are shaded with a lighter shade of gray. After you issue one of these additional commands, the command is added to the short menu. For instance, assume you choose Macro from the Insert menu; the next time you click the Insert menu, the Macro command will be shown on the short menu with a darker gray background. This ***adaptive menu*** feature allows menus to be customized for each user.

After you display a menu, you can choose a command using either the mouse or the keyboard. To choose a command using the mouse, click the command you want. To choose a command using the keyboard, press the underlined letter of the command. For example, to choose the Open command on the File menu, press the letter **O** while the File menu is displayed.

Although the lessons in this tutorial emphasize the mouse method for performing most commands, Appendix B: Command Summary lists the keyboard actions for the commands discussed in this tutorial.

Table 1.3 provides a brief description of the menus available on the Access menu bar. Depending on what you are currently doing in Access, the options on the menu bar can change. For instance, when you open a table, two menus—Format and Records—are added to the menu bar.

Experimenting with Menus

In this activity, you will experiment with the available menus to get a feel for how they work. Since no database is open yet, many of the menu commands will be unavailable for use.

1. Click **View** on the menu bar.

TABLE 1.3	THE ACCESS MENU BAR
Menu	**Contains Commands that Let You ...**
File	Control your databases by opening, saving, and printing them.
Edit	Rearrange the objects within a database by copying, moving, and deleting them.
View	Change the appearance of your screen display, such as displaying or hiding toolbars.
Insert	Insert various objects into a database.
Tools	Access some of Access' specialized tools, such as the spelling checker or database utilities.
Window	Split your screen into several small windows so that you can view more than one object or Database window at once.
Help	Access the online Help system and the Microsoft Office Home Page on the Internet for additional assistance and support.

2. Point to the menu for a few seconds or click the **double arrow** at the bottom of the menu.

Access displays the expanded View menu.

3. Try clicking the **Details option**.

This produces no effect. Menu options that are grayed are disabled (not available) in the current context.

4. Point to the **Toolbars option**.

Access displays the Toolbars submenu. Pointing to or clicking a menu option that has a small triangle to the right leads to an additional menu, called a submenu.

5. Click **Customize** on the submenu.

The Customize dialog box appears as shown in Figure 1.6. Clicking any menu option whose name is followed by an ellipsis (three dots) displays a dialog box that asks for further information.

6. For now, press Esc or click the **Close button** ☒.

Access removes the dialog box from the screen without carrying out any action.

7. Click **File** on the menu bar.

The key combinations Ctrl + N and Ctrl + O appear to the right of the New and Open options at the top of the menu, as shown in Figure 1.7. These are *keyboard shortcuts*—a quick means of using the keyboard to execute commands without going through the menu system.

8. Press Esc or click anywhere outside the File menu.

Access removes the File menu from view; you can use either of these techniques to leave a menu without issuing a command.

Access
BASICS

Using a Menu

1. Click the menu containing the command you want.

2. Click the double arrow to show the expanded menu, if necessary.

3. Click the command you want to issue.

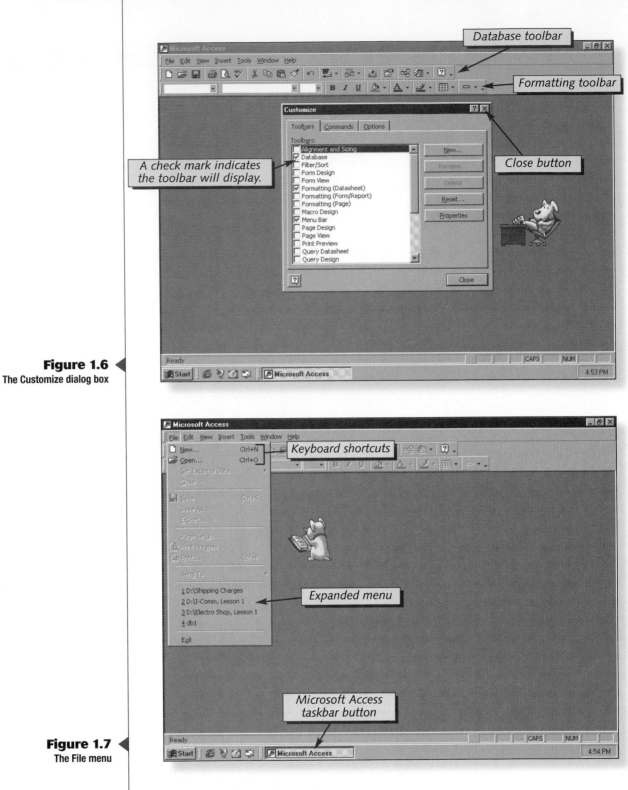

Figure 1.6
The Customize dialog box

Figure 1.7
The File menu

Working with Dialog Boxes

As you learned, menu options followed by an ellipsis lead to dialog boxes. A *dialog box* is a special type of window that requests further information that Access needs before proceeding with the command. Dialog boxes like the one shown in Figure 1.6 can include any number of common items with which you may already be acquainted. Table 1.4 lists some of the features common to dialog boxes.

TABLE 1.4	COMMON DIALOG BOX FEATURES
Feature	**Description**
Check boxes	Boxes that you click to select an option. Clicking a box places a check mark in the box. Clicking again removes the check mark and deselects the option.
Option buttons	Buttons that let you choose one of several options. Clicking one selects the option and deselects the others.
List boxes	Boxes that supply a set of options from which you can choose. The options may become visible after you click a downward-pointing arrow to the right of the box.
Text boxes	Boxes that permit you to type in the desired value.
Command buttons	Buttons that allow you to complete your choices in the dialog box. Most dialog boxes use a command button labeled OK to accept the choices you have made and close the dialog box. A Cancel command button is usually available to close the dialog box without accepting the settings.

Working with Toolbars

Below the menu bar is the Access Database toolbar, as shown in Figure 1.6. A *toolbar* contains buttons for many of the most frequently used commands, such as opening or printing a file. Although you can access these commands by clicking the command on one of the menus, using the buttons on the toolbar as a shortcut is often more convenient. You can quickly identify any command button by pointing to the button and reading the short description that appears.

You may be wondering how you will remember the purpose of each button. The icons themselves often provide a clue—for instance, the button for opening a file features a picture of an open file folder. If you can't guess the button's purpose from the picture, point to the button. Access displays the button name in a small box immediately below the button; this is called a *ScreenTip*. ScreenTips are handy reminders when you can't recall the function of a particular button.

Table 1.5 shows the commands that are available on the Database toolbar.

If it has been activated on your system, the Formatting toolbar (Datasheet) appears directly below the Database toolbar, as shown in Figure 1.6. Access has three Formatting toolbars, one for Datasheet, Form/Report, and Page. The commands available on these Formatting toolbars are listed in Table 1.6 on page 17 and include commands for controlling the appearance of text.

To move a toolbar left or right, point to the handle on the left end. When the four-way arrow appears, drag the toolbar.

 *If you do not see the Formatting toolbar, click View, point to toolbars, and click Customize. Then click Formatting (Datasheet) and click Close.*

TABLE 1.5	**THE ACCESS DATABASE TOOLBAR**	

Button	Name	Action
	New	Creates a new database.
	Open	Opens a database you have already created and saved.
	Save	Saves the layout, design, structure, or content of a database object.
	Print	Prints the selected database object on your printer.
	Print Preview	Allows you to preview how the selected database object will look on the printed page.
	Spelling	Checks the spelling in your database object.
	Cut	Removes and places the selected item on the Clipboard—a temporary storage place for information used by all Windows applications.
	Copy	Copies the selected item and places this copy on the Clipboard.
	Paste	Pastes an element from the Clipboard into the active database object.
	Format Painter	Copies the formatting of one control to another control.
	Undo	Reverses the last action you took that changed your database.
	OfficeLinks	Merges Microsoft Access data with data from another Microsoft Office program.
	Analyze	Analyzes a table and creates a more efficient table design.
	Code	Opens the Visual Basic Editor and displays the code behind a selected form or report.
	Properties	Displays the properties sheet for the selected item.
	Relationships	Displays the relationships between tables and queries.
	New Object: AutoForm	Creates a new object.
	Microsoft Access Help	Displays the Office Assistant, an animated character that can answer your specific questions, offer helpful tips, and provide Help for any Access feature.
	More Buttons	Allows you to customize the toolbar by adding or removing buttons. Also lets you reset the toolbar to display the default buttons.

TABLE 1.6	THE ACCESS FORMATTING TOOLBAR	
Button	**Name**	**Action**
Available on all Three Toolbars		
Abadi MT Condensed	Font	Lists the typeface options available.
10	Font Size	Lists the font sizes available.
B	Bold	Bolds the selected text.
I	Italic	Italicizes the selected text.
U	Underline	Underlines the selected text.
	Fill/Back Color	Adjust the color inside the selected area.
A	Font/Fore Color	Adjusts the color of the font.
	Line/Border Color	Adjusts the color of the border of the selected area.
	Special Effect	Adds special effects to the selected area.
Category ID	Go to Field (Datasheet) Style (Page) Object (Reports and Forms)	Lists the available fields.
Datasheet Only		
	Gridlines	Adjusts the lines in the datasheet view.
Form/Report and Page		
	Align Left	Aligns the selected text at the left margin.
	Center	Centers the selected text between the margins.
	Align Right	Aligns the selected text at the right margin.
	Line/Border Width	Adjusts the width of the lines in the selected area.
Page Only		
	Decrease Indent	Decreases the indent on the selected text.
	Increase Indent	Increases the indent on the selected text.
	Numbering	Inserts auto numbering.
	Bullets	Inserts bullets.

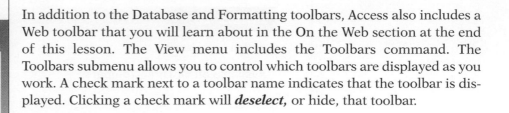

HANDS On

Another Way

To open a file, click Open on the File menu or press Ctrl + O.

In addition to the Database and Formatting toolbars, Access also includes a Web toolbar that you will learn about in the On the Web section at the end of this lesson. The View menu includes the Toolbars command. The Toolbars submenu allows you to control which toolbars are displayed as you work. A check mark next to a toolbar name indicates that the toolbar is displayed. Clicking a check mark will **deselect**, or hide, that toolbar.

OPENING DATABASES

Any time you want to use a database that you or someone else created earlier, you need to **open** the database. Opening a database means copying that file from disk into the memory of your computer so that you can update or view the file. To open any Access file, you can either click the Open button or click File on the menu bar and click the Open command. If you've used a file recently, you may also open a file by choosing the file name from the list of recently opened files that appears near the bottom of the File menu. You can have several files open at the same time. To move between open files, click the appropriate button on the Windows taskbar or use the Windows menu.

Opening a Database

Before you can modify a database, you must open the database. In this activity, you will open a database on your Student Data Disk.

1. Click the **Open button** on the **Database toolbar.**

Access displays the Open dialog box, as shown in Figure 1.8. The Look in box shows the current folder or drive or the last folder used to open a document on your computer.

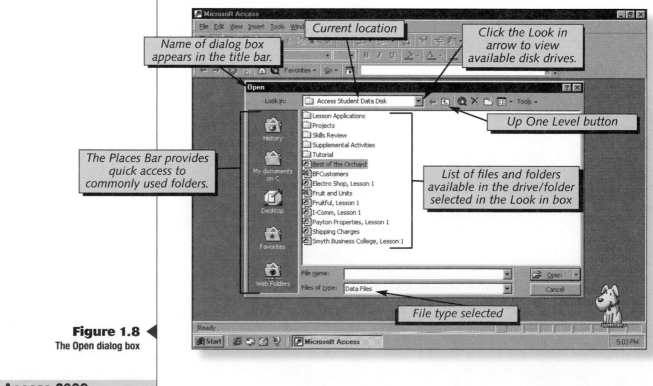

Figure 1.8
The Open dialog box

Opening a Database

1. Click the Open button.

2. Select the appropriate drive from the Look in box.

3. Select the appropriate folder, if necessary.

4. Double-click the file name.

Warning *If you're sharing a computer with one or more users in a lab or school environment, the list of files displayed in the Open dialog box may not contain the file you wish to open. Continue with steps 2 and 3 to properly navigate to your files.*

The Places Bar in various dialog boxes gives you quick access to commonly used folders. For instance, in the Open dialog box, you can click the Favorites folder to see a list of the files stored in this folder. You can access files of different formats by changing the Files of type setting in the Open dialog box.

2. Verify that the Files of type is set to **Data Files** (for any file) or **Microsoft Access Databases** (for only database files).

3. Click the **Look in box arrow** to display a list of the available drives.

If you click the hard drive icon, all of the folders directly under the drive C: root folder appear in the list box. The **root folder** is the main folder on a disk. Within the root folder may be files and other folders—themselves containing files and folders. You can double-click folders in the list box, use the Look in box, or click the Up One Level button 🔼 to find the folder and database file you want to open.

4. Click the drive that contains your Student Data Disk for this tutorial. If necessary, click the folder in which the Student Data Disk files are stored.

A list of files on the Student Data Disk appears in the Open dialog box.

Note *If you copied the Student Data Disk files for this tutorial onto a Zip disk, be sure to insert the disk into the drive.*

5. Click *Fruitful, Lesson 1* in the list of file names, and click the **Open button**.

Access opens the *Fruitful, Lesson 1* database, as shown in Figure 1.9. (The *.mdb* extension may or may not be displayed depending on your computer setup.) Also notice that many more menu and toolbar options become available.

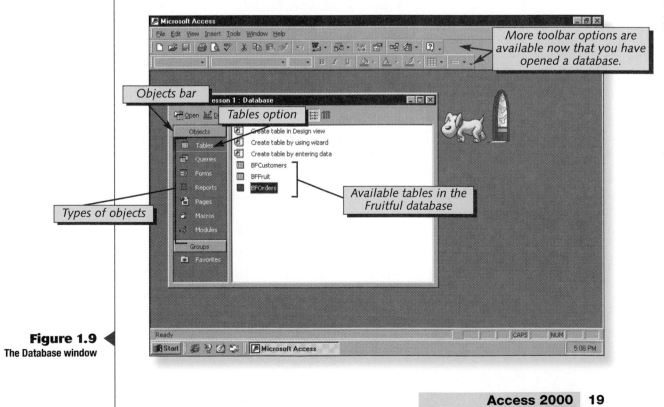

Figure 1.9
The Database window

If no object types appear below the Objects bar, click the Objects bar once.

The Database Window

The *Database window* enables you to gain access to all the tables in your database, as well as to a number of other database objects (or components), such as forms and reports. The Objects bar along the left side of the Database window represents the types of objects available in Access. When you click an option in the Objects bar you see options that allow you to create a new object and an alphabetical list of the existing objects. For instance, the first three options in Figure 1.9 allow you to create new tables. The last three allow you to open existing tables. The Tables option in the Objects bar is selected by default; unless you choose another, you will see a list of the tables in the *Fruitful, Lesson 1* database. Clicking the Reports option would display any reports in the *Fruitful, Lesson 1* database, and so on.

When you're finished working with a particular database, you can close the Database window by clicking File on the menu bar and clicking Close, or by clicking the Close button ☒ in the upper-right corner of the Database window. For now, leave the *Fruitful, Lesson 1* database open so you can explore the various components of Access in the next section.

OBJECTS: THE COMPONENTS OF ACCESS

In Access, the term database means not just the raw data stored in tables, but a collection of *objects.* These objects are the various components of Access—the data, reports, requests, actions, and forms that you use to enter, display, print, and find exactly the information you need in the database. An Access database can contain seven types of objects—tables, queries, forms, reports, pages, macros, and modules.

The Database Table

You've already learned a little about one Access object: the table, which is the holding area for all of your data. The table is like a large sheet of paper divided into columns and rows, which contain the information central to the database. A table has two parts—the information and the structure of the table. The structure controls the kind of information that can be entered into the table. As you are viewing the table, you can edit the data. When you view the design of a table, you can change the structure.

Viewing and Editing Tables

In this activity, you will look at the contents of one of the tables in the *Fruitful, Lesson 1* database. Then you will change the contents of one of the records.

1. With the *Fruitful, Lesson 1* database open, click the **Tables option** in the Database window.

You should see the *Fruitful, Lesson 1* Database window on the screen, as previously shown in Figure 1.9. Notice that the Tables option in the Objects list is selected by default and the names of the three tables in the *Fruitful, Lesson 1* database are displayed under the tab.

Another Way

To open an object, double-click the name.

2. Click the BFCustomers table, and then click the Open button 📇 Open directly below the title bar of the Database window.

The data in the BFCustomers table appears, arranged in a grid of columns (fields) and rows (records), as shown in Figure 1.10.

Figure 1.10
The BFCustomers table

Customer ID	Last Name	First Name	Address	City	State	ZIP Code	Ph
1	Kenber	Franklin	1777 Lois Ln.	Rock Creek	NC	28333-1234	(91
2	Reid	Alyson	7374 Backwoods Rd.	Sebastopol	CA	97777-1111	(41
3	Turlow	Will	1 Oak Place	Providence	RI	02900-2338	(40
4	Zheng	Anne	25 Forest Knoll	Santa Rosa	CA	99887-2355	(70
5	O'Hara	Joan	2234 Hanley Place	Baltimore	MD	21122-5634	(30
	onez	James	32123 Overlook Ave.	Portland	OR	99876-2389	(50
	del	Mason	75 Grizzly Peak Blvd.	Orinda	CA	94700-5412	(51
8	Isherwood	Emma	1314 23rd Ave.	Biddeford	ME	57432-6034	(20
9	Smith	Christine		New York	NY	10001-8763	(21
10	Jackson	Jacqueline		Houston	TX	47532-7843	(50
11	Everett	Richard	1310 Arch St.	Berkeley	CA	98765-3368	(51
12	Wintergreen	Shelly	21 Barbary Ln.	Omaha	NE	66332-9004	(30
13	Menendez	Erica	303 Hollywood St. #15	Los Angeles	CA	99887-3489	(21
14	Zheng	Alicia	32 B St.	Ashland	OR	97998-5098	(50
15	Ng	Patrick	1112 Spruce St.	Shaker Heights	OH	45678-7842	(21
16	Apfelbaum	Bob	81 Hacienda Blvd.	Santa Fe	NM	55554-3449	(80
17	Hatfield	James	15A Vine St.	Ashland	OR	97998-6907	(50
18	Marais	Jean-Luc	1379 Montgomery Ave. #3	Boston	MA	02101-3930	(61
19	Savallis	Jordi	100 Riverside Dr. #10B	New York	NY	10025-8035	(21
20	Yates	Lily	999 35th Ave.	Oakland	CA	94602-8532	(51

Maximize button

Field

Record

Notice table position and size.

Scroll bars

Record: ◀ ◀ 1 ▶ ▶▶ ▶* of 35

Datasheet View

🔊Start | Fruitful, Lesson 1 : Database | 📖 BFCustomers : Table | 5:12 PM

Access
BASICS

Opening and Editing a Database Table

1. Open the database that contains the table you want to open.

2. Click the Tables option in the Objects bar.

3. Click the name of the table you want to open.

4. Click the Open button.

5. To edit a table, type text in a column and row.

3. Click the Maximize button ☐ on the right side of the BFCustomers title bar.

You should see a full screen display of the table.

4. Click and use the *scroll bars*—the shaded bars along the bottom and right side of a window—to view portions of the table not visible on the screen.

5. Press Ctrl + End to move to the end of the table.

6. Press Ctrl + Home to move to the beginning of the table.

7. Press Tab twice.

This action selects the word *Franklin*. Pressing Tab moves the insertion point to the next column (field).

8. Press ↓.

This action selects the word *Alyson*. Pressing ↓ moves the insertion point down one record (row) at a time.

9. With *Alyson* selected, type Alice as shown in Figure 1.11.

You can also use ⇧ Shift + Tab or ← to move back one column or ↑ to move up one row.

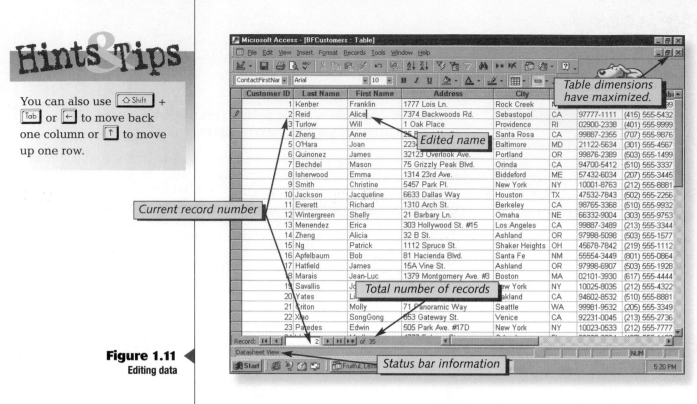

Figure 1.11 ◀
Editing data

The word *Alice* replaces the selected word *Alyson*. (If all capital letters appeared when you typed the name, press Caps Lock to turn off capital letters. Then press Backspace until you remove the capital letters, and type Alice.)

10. Click the Close button ☒ to the right of the menu bar.

Warning *Do not click the Close button ☒ on the Access title bar; this will close the Access program.*

Access removes the BFCustomers table from the screen, returning you to the Database window for the ***Fruitful, Lesson 1*** database. Since you maximized the table, the Database window is now maximized as well. Your change is automatically saved.

HANDS On

Viewing the Table Design

In this activity, you will see the design of the table, rather than the contents. The table's design determines the types of fields it can contain.

1. With the BFCustomers table still selected in the Database window, click the Design button Design.

You will see the BFCustomers table in ***Design view,*** as shown in Figure 1.12. As you will learn in the next lesson, you can set up and modify the layout of a table in Design view.

Looking at the Table Structure

1. Click the View button while viewing a table.

2. Click the View button again to return.

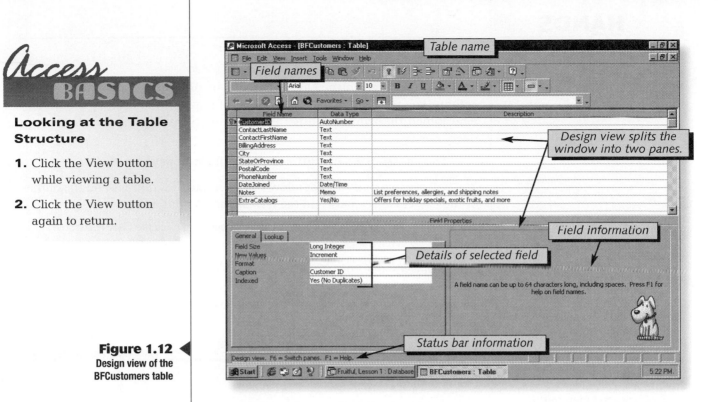

Figure 1.12
Design view of the
BFCustomers table

Another Way

To edit information, click the appropriate pane.

The Design view is split into two panes. The upper pane shows the names and other information about the fields (columns) used in the table. The lower pane further defines the properties used for the field currently selected.

2. Press F6.

Your insertion point moves into the lower pane.

3. Click the Field Size arrow.

You will see the options for the size of the field. In the next lesson, you will learn all about these options.

4. Click File on the menu bar and then click Close.

Again, Access closes the table, returning you to the Database window for the *Fruitful, Lesson 1* database.

Queries: Extracting the Data You Need

A *query* is just what the name implies: a question to the database, generally asking for a set of records from one or more tables that meets specific criteria. For example, you might ask the database to display all the customers in Hawaii or any customers whose bills are past due. Access responds to such queries by displaying the requested data. Because a query is a stored question, rather than the stored response to a question, the results of the query will remain up to date even if the data in your tables changes. Queries are particularly valuable because they enable you both to view and operate on selected subsets of your data.

HANDS On

Access BASICS

Opening a Query

1. Click the Queries option in the Database window.

2. Click the query you want to open.

3. Click the Open button.

4. To view the query design, click the query name and then click the Design button.

Figure 1.13
Query results

Another Way

To display the query in Design view, click the View button on the toolbar while you are looking at the query results.

Viewing Queries

Queries are stored in the Queries option of the Database window. In this activity, you will first display the results of a query that asks for customers who joined the fruit club after 1997. Then you will display and view the query design.

1. Click the **Queries option** in the Objects list in the Database window.

You will see two options that allow you to create new queries and the names of the two existing queries in the *Fruitful, Lesson 1* database.

2. Click the **Post 97 Customers query** and then click the **Open button** 🔲 Open in the Database window.

Access reveals the Post 97 Customer query, as you can see in Figure 1.13. Notice that this query displays selected data from the BFCustomers table that you saw earlier. As you may have figured out, the query asks to display the customers who joined after 1997.

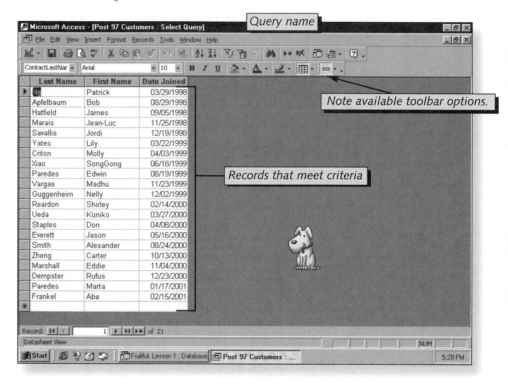

3. Click the **Close button** ☒ at the right end of the menu bar.

Access closes the query results, returning you to the Database window.

4. With the Post 97 Customers query still selected, click the **Design button** 🔲 Design.

Access displays the Select Query window, shown in Figure 1.14. This window lets you choose the fields to be displayed, the order in which they will appear, and the criteria to be used to select records.

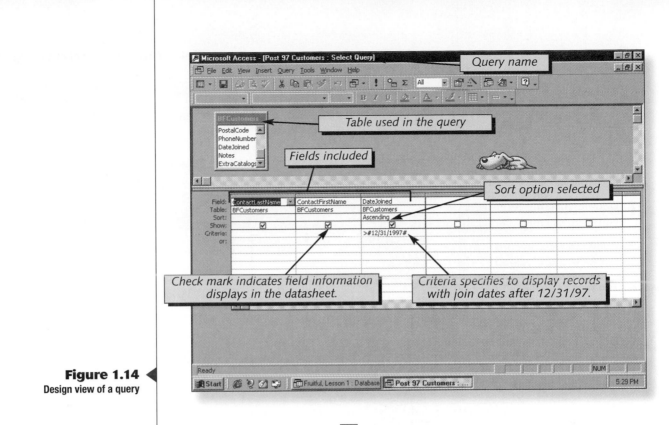

Figure 1.14
Design view of a query

5. Click the **Close button** ✕ at the right end of the menu bar.

Once again, you return to the Database window.

Forms: Viewing, Entering, and Editing Data More Easily

You can view, enter, and edit data in tables (where data is laid out in a series of rows and columns). Often, however, you can more easily use custom forms for this purpose. Access *forms* are the electronic equivalent of paper forms, but electronic forms enable you to create a custom layout for your data—determining how the data from your tables is presented. For example, you could create a form that presents a single record at a time for data entry or editing, or one that displays only certain fields from a particular table. Forms are especially useful when you want to create a more friendly or visually manageable environment for data entry or when you need to control which data is displayed.

HANDS On

Adding a Record in Form View

In this activity, you will open a form that displays all of the fields of the BFCustomers table in a clear format. Then you will add data in a new record.

1. Click the **Forms option** in the Objects list in the Database window.

You will see two options that you can use to create new forms and one option that opens a form that has already been created.

Displaying a Form and Adding Data

1. Click the Forms option in the Database window.

2. Double-click the form you want to view.

3. Click the New Record button to add a record.

4. Type data into each field of the new record.

2. Click the **Columnar Form with All Fields form** and then click the **Open button** [Open].

Access reveals the Columnar Form with All Fields form, as shown in Figure 1.15. Notice that this form displays the first record from the BFCustomers table you saw earlier.

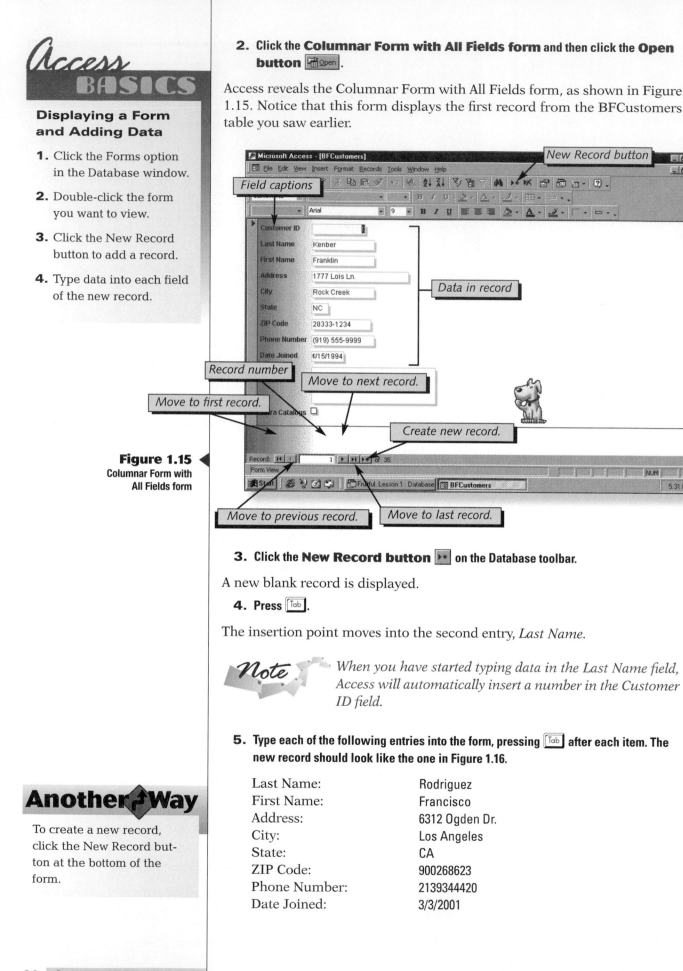

Figure 1.15 ◀
Columnar Form with All Fields form

3. Click the **New Record button** [▶*] on the Database toolbar.

A new blank record is displayed.

4. Press [Tab].

The insertion point moves into the second entry, *Last Name*.

Note   *When you have started typing data in the Last Name field, Access will automatically insert a number in the Customer ID field.*

5. Type each of the following entries into the form, pressing [Tab] after each item. The new record should look like the one in Figure 1.16.

Last Name:	Rodriguez
First Name:	Francisco
Address:	6312 Ogden Dr.
City:	Los Angeles
State:	CA
ZIP Code:	900268623
Phone Number:	2139344420
Date Joined:	3/3/2001

Another Way

To create a new record, click the New Record button at the bottom of the form.

Figure 1.16
New record

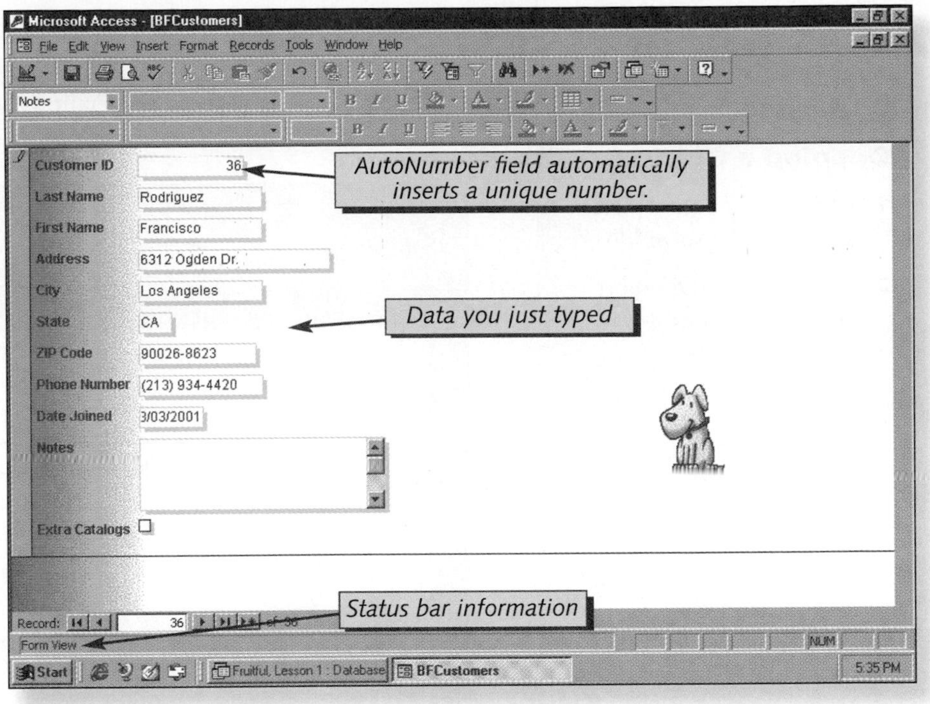

Microsoft Access - [BFCustomers]

File Edit View Insert Format Records Tools Window Help

Notes

Customer ID   36   *AutoNumber field automatically inserts a unique number.*

Last Name   Rodriguez

First Name   Francisco

Address   6312 Ogden Dr.

City   Los Angeles

State   CA   *Data you just typed*

ZIP Code   90026-8623

Phone Number   (213) 934-4420

Date Joined   3/03/2001

Notes

Extra Catalogs ☐

Record: 14 ◄   36   ► ►1 ►* of 36   *Status bar information*

Form View   NUM

Start   Fruitful, Lesson 1 : Database   BFCustomers   5:35 PM

6. Click the **Close button** ☒ to close the form.

Access closes the form, returning you to the Database window. The new record is added. If you opened the BFCustomers table, the new record would be displayed at the bottom of the table.

Reports and Mailing Labels: Generating Printed Output

Often, you will want not only a set of data on the screen but also some type of printed output. Access *reports* are printed output of your data. *Mailing labels* are another kind of printed output—they contain just names and addresses, for easy use with mailings. You can base your reports or mailing labels on data from tables or queries. You can also create reports that show totals and grand totals of the values in a particular field, such as salary or sales. You can print forms, as well as data from tables and queries, but reports enable you to produce presentation-quality output with ease.

HANDS On

Previewing a Report

Before you print a database report, you can preview the report on the screen. In this activity, you will display a database report. You will view a *WYSIWYG* (what you see is what you get) preview that gives you a good idea of what this report will look like when printed.

1. Click the **Reports option** in the Objects list in the Database window.

Access displays two options that help you create reports and one report in the *Fruitful, Lesson 1* database.

Opening a Report

1. Click the Reports option in the Database window.

2. Double-click the report you want to preview.

2. Click the **Fruit Type Summaries report,** and then click the **Preview button** .

In a moment, Access reveals the Fruit Type Summaries report, as shown in Figure 1.17. You can scroll the report to see more.

Figure 1.17
Fruit Type Summaries report

3. Click **File** on the menu bar and then click **Close.**

Access closes the report, returning you to the Database window.

Data Access Pages

Access allows you to post your database data on Web pages. To do so, you can create ***data access pages.*** Data access pages are directly connected to a database and are designed to be viewed in a Web browser—a tool used to navigate the World Wide Web. You will learn more about data access pages in a later lesson.

Macros and Modules

A ***macro*** is an Access object that is composed of a command or series of commands that you can use to automate a task. Each command within a macro is called an ***action.*** Macros are often created to automate tasks that you repeat frequently. Then, instead of issuing several separate actions manually, you can run the macro and the set of actions will be performed automatically. Macros are designed to save time and effort.

Macros are best used for relatively simple tasks, such as opening forms or running reports. For more complex tasks, a module can be programmed. ***Modules*** are sets of programmed statements that are stored together as a unit.

You will learn more about the World Wide Web in the *On the Web* section at the end of this lesson. And you will learn more about creating and publishing Web pages in the *On the Web* section in Lesson 5.

- To activate the Office Assistant, press [F1].

- To temporarily remove the Office Assistant from the screen, click the Help menu and click Hide the Office Assistant.

GETTING HELP WITH ACCESS

While you are using Access, you may need to reference Help. Like many application programs, Access provides an extensive *online Help system*—an electronic manual that you can open with the press of a key or the click of a mouse. Access provides several different Help tools. You can access most of the Help tools through the *Office Assistant,* an animated character that can answer specific questions, offer tips, and provide help for Access features. Through the Office Assistant, you can access various help topics by using the Contents tab, the Index tab, and the Answer Wizard. In addition, you can access ScreenTips—helpful text boxes that provide information on various Access elements—through the Help menu.

While using the Help system, you may find links to other topics in the form of *hyperlinks* within a Help window. Hyperlinks are blue, underlined text; when you point to a hyperlink, the pointer changes to the shape of a hand. Click the hyperlink to jump to a new location. After you've viewed a hyperlink, the color changes from blue to purple. Pictures, graphic elements, and objects may also contain hyperlinks.

Within a Help window, you may also see words that appear in blue with no underlining. These words are also hyperlinks and are called *glossary terms.* When you point to a glossary term, the pointer changes to the shape of a hand. Click a glossary term to display the definition. After you've accessed a glossary term, the color changes from blue to purple. Click anywhere on the screen to cancel a glossary term and return to the Help window.

Using the Office Assistant

If you've used other Microsoft Office 2000 applications, you may have noticed the Office Assistant peeking around the corner of your document. The Office Assistant provides help, sometimes even before you ask. You can activate the Office Assistant by clicking the animated character on your screen, by clicking the Microsoft Access Help button [?], by clicking Microsoft Access Help on the Help menu, or by clicking [F1].

Asking the Assistant for Help

In this activity, you will ask the Office Assistant for help to spell check a database table.

1. Click the **Office Assistant**.

If the Office Assistant is not displayed on the screen, click the Microsoft Access Help button [?] on the Database toolbar.

As shown in Figure 1.18, the Office Assistant asks what you would like to do.

Figure 1.18
Activating the Office Assistant

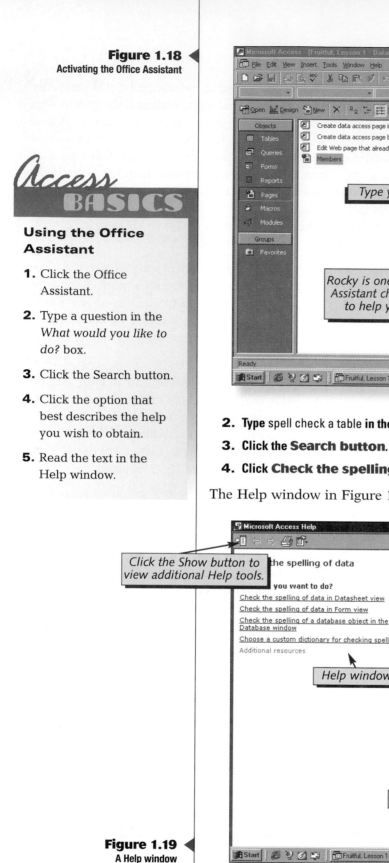

![Access BASICS]

Using the Office Assistant

1. Click the Office Assistant.

2. Type a question in the *What would you like to do?* box.

3. Click the Search button.

4. Click the option that best describes the help you wish to obtain.

5. Read the text in the Help window.

2. **Type** spell check a table **in the *What Would You Like to Do?* box.**

3. **Click the Search button.**

4. **Click Check the spelling of data.**

The Help window in Figure 1.19 appears asking a more specific question.

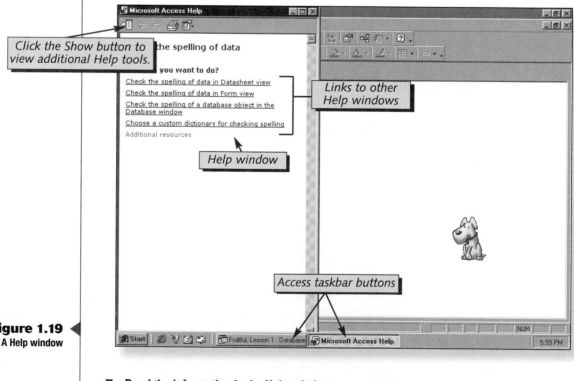

Figure 1.19
A Help window

5. **Read the information in the Help window.**

6. **Click the <u>Check the spelling of data in Datasheet view</u> link.**

7. **Read the step-by-step instructions that describe how to spell check a datasheet.**

If the Office Assistant does not provide an option that answers your question, you may click the *None of the above, look for more help on the Web* option. A new Help window appears that allows you to connect to the Web to obtain further help.

Using the Answer Wizard

1. Click the Answer Wizard tab in the Help window.

2. Type a question or phrase in the *What would you like to do?* box.

3. Click the Search button.

4. Click the topic you want to read.

---

8. Point to the **Spelling button** [ABC] in the Help window.

The pointer changes to the shape of a hand, indicating a hyperlink exists.

9. Click the **Spelling button** [ABC].

A description of the Spelling button appears in a box below the button.

10. Click the description to remove the box.

Using the Answer Wizard, Contents, and Index

You can use the Office Assistant at any time to obtain help with Access. The Office Assistant also contains some other Help tools. You can use the Contents tab to view a listing of general Help topics; this method can be useful if you don't know the name of a feature. The Answer Wizard can answer specific questions similar to the Office Assistant, and the Index tab can find instances of specific keywords within a Help topic.

Using the Answer Wizard

The Answer Wizard is similar to the Office Assistant; you can enter a question or phrase and the Answer Wizard will search the Help system for topics related to your request. In this activity, you will use the Answer Wizard to set up a query.

1. If the Contents, Answer Wizard, and Index tabs are not displayed within the Help window, click the **Show button** [button].

The Help window expands to show the Contents, Answer Wizard, and Index tabs. As shown in Figure 1.20, the Show button changes to a Hide button [button]. You can click this button to display or hide the additional Help tools.

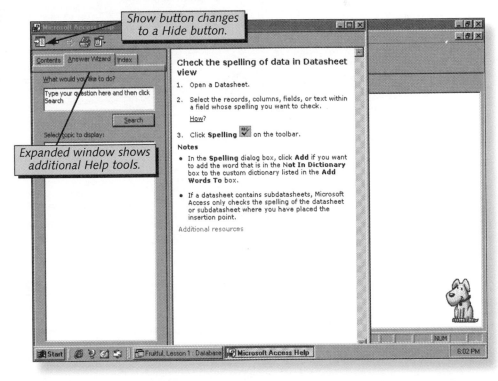

Figure 1.20
Additional Help tools

2. Click the **Answer Wizard tab**, if it is not already selected.

3. Type create a query in the *What would you like to do?* box and then click the **Search button**.

Topics that may answer your question appear in the *Select topic to display* list box; the first topic is selected. The right pane of the Help window displays text that describes how to create a query. Read the text, clicking links as desired.

Using the Contents Tab

The Contents tab lists general categories and subcategories of Help topics. Those categories preceded by a plus sign and a closed book icon contain additional subcategories and/or specific Help topics. You can click the plus sign or double-click the closed book icon to expand the category. Help topics are indicated by a question mark. You can click the question mark to display the Help topic in the right pane of the Help window. In this activity, you will use the Contents tab of the Help window to create a table in Access.

1. Click the **Contents tab** in the Help window.

2. Scroll and click the **plus sign** in front of the **Creating and Designing Tables category**.

The closed book icon changes to an open book icon, and the category expands to show the subcategories as shown in Figure 1.21. Notice that the Help topic displayed in the right pane has not changed.

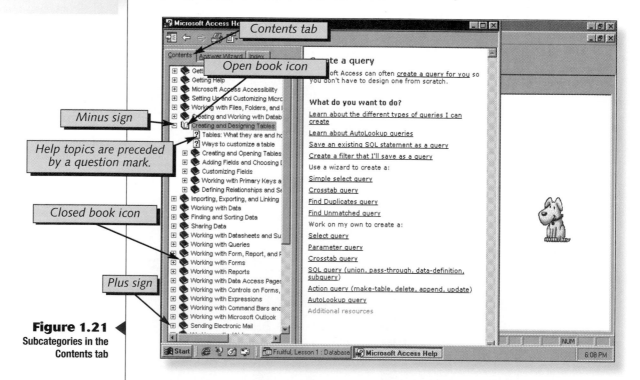

Figure 1.21
Subcategories in the Contents tab

3. Click the **Tables: What they are and how they work topic**.

The text displayed in the right pane of the Help window now changes.

4. Read and explore the text that appears in the right pane of the Help window.

Using the Index

1. Click the Index tab in the Help window.

2. Click or type one or more keywords.

3. Click the Search button.

4. Click the topic you wish to read in the *Choose a topic* box.

Using the Index Tab

The Index tab lists words in alphabetical order. These words, called **keywords,** are contained within the text of various Help topics. You can choose words directly from the keyword list, or you can type keywords in the text box near the top of the window. As you select keywords, the topics that contain those keywords appear in the *Choose a topic* list box. You may then click any topic from the list to view the text in the right pane of the Help window. In this activity, you will use the Index tab to find help on sorting records in a report.

1. **Click the Index tab.**

2. **In the *Type keywords* box, type sort and click the Search button.**

Notice that as you type each letter of the word *sort,* the highlighted word within the *Or choose keywords* box jumps to the next selection that contains the letters that you typed. You may use a combination of the *Type keywords* and *Or choose keywords* boxes to narrow your search.

The topics that contain the keyword you typed appear in the *Choose a topic* box. As you can see in Figure 1.22, nearly 200 topics exist that contain the keyword *sort.*

Figure 1.22
Using the Index tab

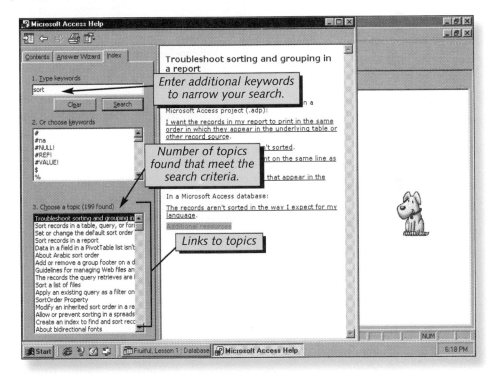

When the Office Assistant is deactivated, clicking the Help button on the Database toolbar will directly access the Help window. To deactivate the Office Assistant, click the Office Assistant, choose the Options button, deselect Use the Office Assistant, and click OK.

3. **Click inside the *Type keywords* list box after the keyword *sort.***

4. **Type the word record so that the words *sort* and *record* appear in the box.**

5. **Click the Search button.**

Help searches for all topics that contain the words *sort* and *record.* The number of topics that meet the search criteria is reduced to around 70 topics.

6. **Scroll the *Or choose keywords* list box to find the word *report.***

7. **Double-click the word *report.***

While using Help, you may discover you need to print a Help topic. You can do this by displaying the topic and clicking the Print button in the Help window.

The keyword is added to the words in the *Type keywords* box, and Access searches Help for the topics that contain all three of the keywords. Figure 1.23 shows the final list of topics that contain the keywords *sort, record,* and *report.* Notice that when using the Index tab, a Help topic that contains your keywords is automatically displayed in the right pane.

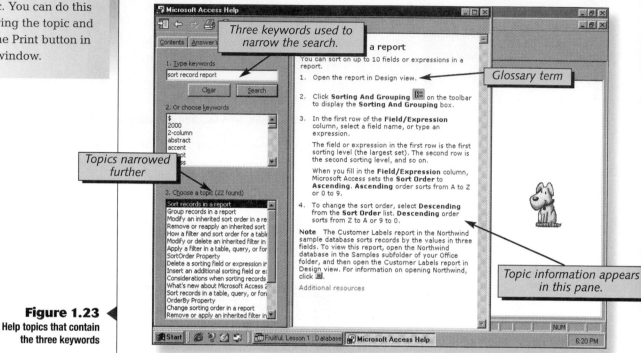

Figure 1.23
Help topics that contain
the three keywords

8. Click **Design view**, a glossary term in the first paragraph of text, as shown in Figure 1.23.

The definition of Design view appears.

9. Read the definition and then click anywhere to remove the definition from the screen.

10. Click the **Close button** ☒ on the Help window.

Regardless of the method you use to get help, once you reach a Help window, you can display the definitions of words or phrases by clicking glossary terms. You can also switch from one Help topic to a related one by clicking links and the Back button ⬅.

Using ScreenTips for Help

ScreenTips are text boxes that show the names and descriptions of different elements on the Access window. When you click *What's This?* on the Help menu, the pointer shows a question mark. While the question mark pointer is displayed, you can click any element on the screen—a menu command, the toolbar, a toolbar button, the database area, or any other element—to see the name and description.

Using ScreenTips

1. Click the *What's This?* option on Help menu.

2. Click the screen element you wish to identify.

Figure 1.24
A ScreenTip

Identifying Screen Elements

In this activity, you will display ScreenTips for various elements.

1. Click Help on the menu bar and click What's This?.

The pointer changes to include a question mark next to the arrow.

2. Click the Relationships button ⊞.

As illustrated in Figure 1.24, the name and description of the Relationships button will appear.

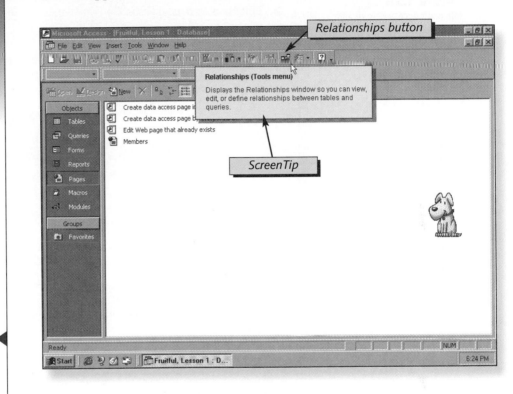

3. Read the ScreenTip. Then, click anywhere on the screen to remove the ScreenTip.

4. Open the BFCustomers table.

5. To use the ScreenTips keyboard shortcut, press ⇧Shift + F1 on the keyboard.

6. When the ScreenTips pointer appears, click any column heading in the frame of the database.

A definition of the field selector appears.

7. Click anywhere on the screen to remove the definition.

8. If time permits, continue to use ScreenTips to explore other parts of the screen.

9. Close the BFCustomers table.

Using HELP

Backing up and Restoring a Database

You can use Microsoft Access Help to learn more about a variety of Access topics. Additionally, you can use Help to back up and restore a database.

1. **Click the Office Assistant.**

Note *If the Office Assistant is not displayed, click Show the Office Assistant on the Help menu.*

2. **Type** Back up a database **in the *What would you like to do?* box.**
3. **Click the Search button.**
4. **Click the Back up a database option to open the Microsoft Access Help window (Figure 1.25).**
5. **Read the information.**
6. **Click the Print button in the Microsoft Access Help window.**
7. **Click the Restore a database from a backup copy option in the *What would you like to do?* box.**
8. **Read the Help information.**
9. **Print the Help information, if desired.**
10. **Click the Close button ☒ to close the Help window, and click the Office Assistant to hide the search box.**

Figure 1.25
Microsoft Access Help window

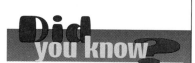

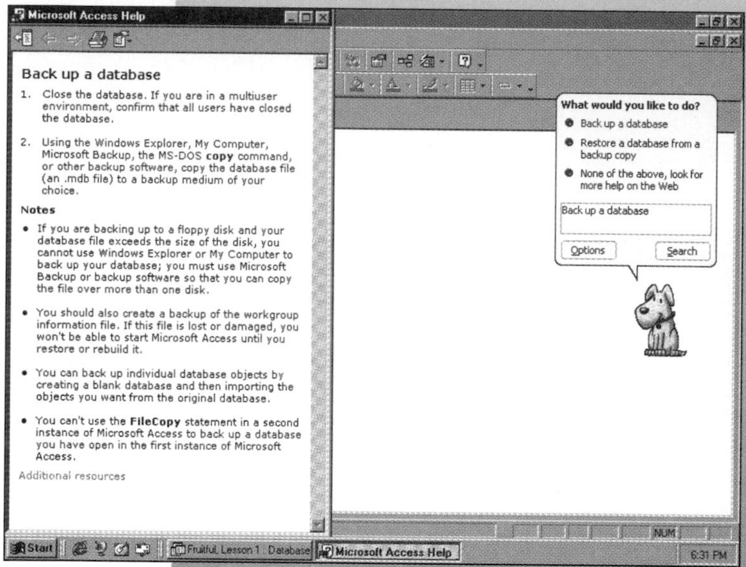

PRINTING OBJECTS

Now that you've explored the Access window and the Help features, you are ready to learn another Access fundamental—printing Access objects. You will need printouts to submit assignments to your instructor, to deliver reports to your boss, to mail information to a client, and much more. You can easily print objects by clicking the database object and clicking the Print button. Tables will print all the information that has been entered in a column and row format. Forms print the information using the layout and design of the selected form, but once again print all the data. Queries can limit the data you print, but a printed query will be in the column and row format. By using reports, you can access the information in the tables and select the layout and design of the information.

Did you know?

You can print a report to a file so you can later print the file on a different type of printer than the one used to create the document.

Printing an Object

1. Click the database object.

2. Click the File menu and click Print.

3. Verify the printing options.

4. Click OK.

Printing a Report

In this activity, you'll print the Fruit Type Summaries report in the Report option in the Database window.

1. **Turn on the printer, if necessary.**

2. **Click the Reports object and click the Fruit Type Summaries report.**

3. **Click the File menu and click Print.**

You'll see the Print dialog box, as shown in Figure 1.26.

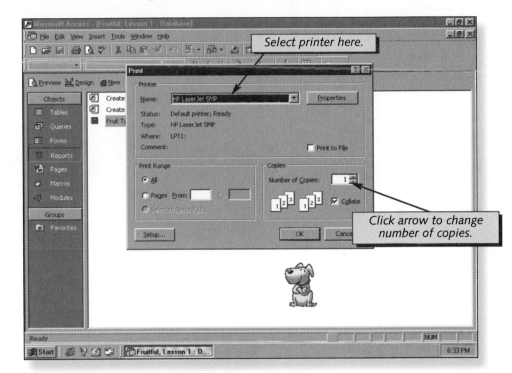

Figure 1.26
Print dialog box

4. **Change the number of copies option to 1, if necessary, and click OK.**

You may have to wait a moment, but Access will generate your report.

COMPACTING DATABASES

As you add, edit, and delete objects, a database changes in size. To minimize the size of a database and to improve performance, you should compact your databases on a regular basis. *Compacting* a database rearranges how a fragmented database is stored on disk. You can use two methods to compact a database. First, you can set Access to compact each database as you close. Second, you can issue a menu command to compact and repair a database at any time.

Another Way

To print, click the Print button 🖨.

Compacting a Database Upon Closing

In this activity, you will instruct Access to compact a database when you close.

1. If any objects are open in the *Fruitful, Lesson 1* database, close them.

2. Click the **Tools menu**, click **Options**, and then click the **General tab** of the Options dialog box, as shown in Figure 1.27.

3. Click **Compact on Close** so that a check mark appears before the option and then click the **Apply button**.

When you close, Access will automatically compact the database.

4. Click **OK** to close the dialog box.

Compacting a Database

Upon closing:

1. Click the Tools menu and click Options.

2. Click the General tab of the Options dialog box.

3. Select Compact on Close.

4. Click OK.

At any time:

1. Click the Tools menu.

2. Point to Database Utilities.

3. Click Compact and Repair Database.

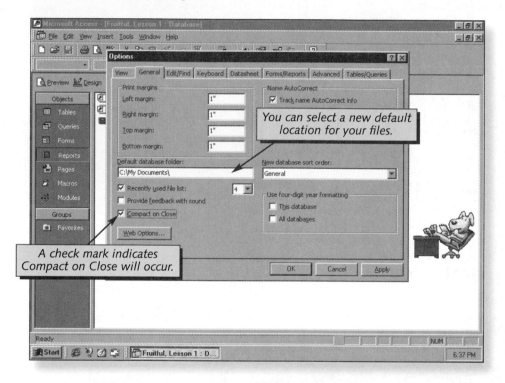

Figure 1.27
The Options dialog box

CLOSING DATABASES AND EXITING ACCESS

When you're finished working with a database, you should *close* the file. Closing the file removes the file from memory, but leaves Access running. When you close a database using the Close button, be sure to click the correct Close button! Clicking the Close button ✕ at the right end of the menu bar in the main database window or clicking the File menu and clicking Close will close the database but will keep Access running. Clicking the Close button ✕ at the right end of the *title bar* in the Access window will close both the database and the Access program.

Databases (or other documents) that you have opened recently are added to a list near the bottom of the File menu. If you need to reopen a database you just closed, you can select the database quickly from that list. By default, Access lists the last four files; a user may choose to list up to nine files on the File menu.

When you close a database, you remove the specific database from memory but leave Access operating. When you're finished working with the Access program, you should exit the program properly. Exiting the program closes any open Access databases and removes Access from the memory of your computer. You can exit Access by clicking the title bar Close button ⊠ or by clicking the Exit command on the File menu. After exiting Access, you will see the desktop if you have no other programs running. From there, you may choose to shut down your computer.

Closing a Database and Exiting Access

In this activity, you will close the *Fruitful, Lesson 1* database.

1. Click the **Close button** ⊠ on the Database window.

The *Fruitful, Lesson 1* database closes. If you watch the left side of the status bar, you may see a brief message indicating that the database is being compacted. Access closes the file, clearing the screen completely—except for the Office Assistant. Since you just closed the only open file, your screen will be blank and will not contain a database window.

2. Click **Exit** on the File menu or click the **Close button** ⊠ on the Access title bar.

If you have not opened any other application, the Office Assistant will close and your screen will return to the Windows desktop.

3. Remove your **Student Data Disk** from the drive, if necessary.

Test your understanding of database objects by matching each of the terms on the left with the definitions on the right. See Appendix D to check your answers.

TERMS	DEFINITIONS
___**1.** table	**a.** A database object meant to be viewed in a Web browser
___**2.** query	**b.** The database object that holds all data
___**3.** form	**c.** A database object that can calculate totals of particular fields
___**4.** report	**d.** To display only the records of employees who earn more than $10 per hour, you could use this database object
___**5.** data access page	**e.** A database object that allows you to design the data in an easy-to-read format; this object is often used to simplify the process of data entry

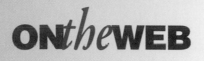

ON the WEB

EXPLORING THE WEB TOOLBAR

Every day, computer users around the world access the Internet for work, play, and research. The **Internet** is a worldwide network of computers that connects each Internet user's computer to all other computers in the network. Vast quantities of infinitely varied information—from simple text in the form of an e-mail message to extremely complex software—can pass through these connections. The Internet organizes information into small parcels, or pages. The most popular tool to access pages is the **World Wide Web** (also called the Web); therefore, a page (parcel) of information is called a **Web page**. Because a page holds a specific place on the Web, it is also called a **Web site** because it organizes information into easy-to-use pages.

If you have a Web **browser**—a software tool used to navigate the Web—you can access most Internet and all World Wide Web sites directly through Access. Using the buttons on the Access Web toolbar, you can navigate to a specific Web site, search the Web, and more. In this activity, you will display the Web toolbar and explore some of the buttons.

1. **Start Access, if it is not running. When the initial Microsoft Access dialog box appears, click** Cancel.

The blank Access screen appears. While using the Web features of Access, you may have either an existing database or a blank screen open.

2. **Click** View **on the menu bar and point to** Toolbars.

3. **From the submenu, click** Web.

Note *If a check mark appears next to Web, the Web toolbar is displayed already. Click outside the menu to leave the Web toolbar selected and close the menu.*

The Web toolbar appears, as shown in Figure 1.28.

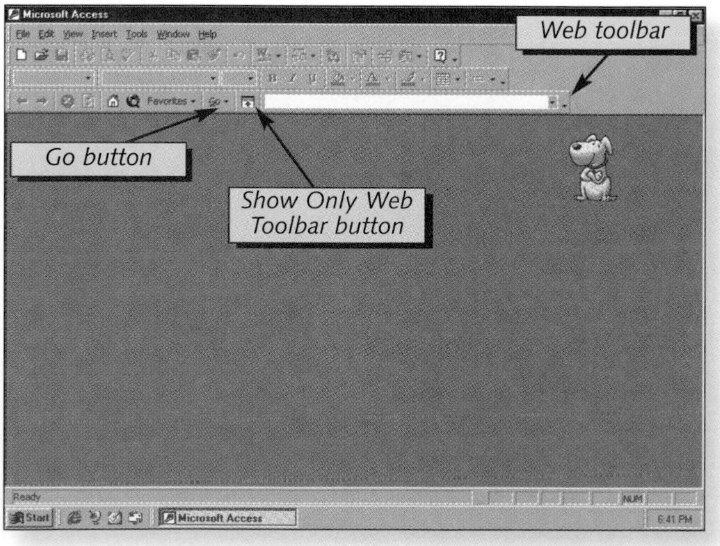

Figure 1.28 ◀
The Web toolbar

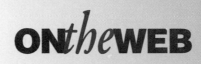

ON*the*WEB

Table 1.7 provides a brief description of each button on the Web toolbar.

TABLE 1.7	THE ACCESS WEB TOOLBAR	
Button	**Name**	**Description**
←	Back	Displays the previous page or site that you visited (up to 10 sites).
→	Forward	Displays the next page or site that you visited (up to 10 sites).
⊗	Stop Current Jump	Stops the connection in progress.
🔁	Refresh Current Page	Reloads the current page.
🏠	Start Page	Loads the Microsoft Start Page or the Web page that you have specified as your Start Page.
🔍	Search the Web	Loads the Microsoft Search Page or the Web page that you have specified as your Search Page.
Favorites ▾	Favorites	Allows you to add and access files and Web sites that you frequently use.
Go ▾	Go	Allows you to access a specific file, page, or Web site by typing the location; also allows you to specify your Start and Search Pages.
⊡	Show Only Web Toolbar	Hides all visible toolbars except the Web toolbar or displays all hidden toolbars.
▭	Address	Allows you to enter the location of a file or Web site to access.
▾	More Buttons	Allows you to customize the toolbar by adding or removing buttons. Also lets you reset the toolbar to display the default buttons.

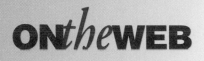
ON*the*WEB

4. Click the **Show Only Web Toolbar button** 🖼.

The Database and Formatting toolbars disappear.

5. Click the **Show Only Web Toolbar button** 🖼 again.

The Database and Formatting toolbars reappear. This button toggles between showing and hiding other open toolbars.

6. Connect to the Internet using your Internet service provider. If necessary, type your user name and password.

> *Note* — *If you are not sure how to connect to the Internet or you do not know your user name and password, ask your instructor for assistance.*

7. If the Access window is not active, click the **Microsoft Access button** on the Windows taskbar.

8. Click the **Go button** Go ▾ and click **Open**.

The Open Internet Address dialog box appears, as shown in Figure 1.29. You can use this box to go to an Internet site or to open a document on your hard drive or on a disk drive.

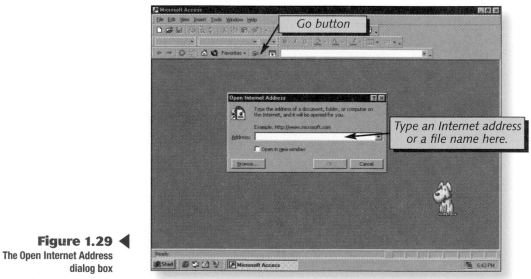

Figure 1.29 ◀
The Open Internet Address dialog box

9. Type www.glencoe.com in the **Address box** and then click **OK**.

Your Web browser launches and connects you to the Glencoe/McGraw-Hill home page, as shown in Figure 1.30. The first of several pages at a Web site is commonly called the **home page.** In a later lesson, you will navigate pages on the Web.

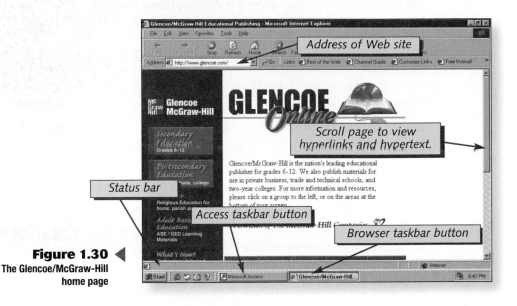

Figure 1.30 ◀
The Glencoe/McGraw-Hill
home page

10. Read the main paragraph; then scroll gradually down the page, noting the hypertext (underlined text in a different color) and other hyperlinks (buttons).

11. To return to Access, click the **Microsoft Access taskbar button**.

12. Click the **Start Page button** 🏠 on the Web toolbar.

Your Web browser reappears and connects you to the Web page designated as your Start Page. Your Internet service provider or your instructor probably designated the Start Page. Start Pages usually provide links to other pages that allow you to explore the Web.

13. Click the **Close buttons** ✕ on all open browser windows.

14. If the Access window is not active, click the **Microsoft Access taskbar button**.

15. Exit Access.

16. Disconnect from the Internet, if your instructor tells you to do so.

Warning

You may proceed directly to the exercises for this lesson. If, however, you are finished with your computer session, follow the "shut down" procedures for your lab or school environment.

Lesson Summary & Exercises

SUMMARY

Databases are used every day, both for business and personal applications. They allow you to present data in an organized form and to maintain and retrieve information electronically. Lesson 1 introduced basic database terms and taught you how to open a database and navigate the Access window. You also learned to print and close a database and exit Access. Access provides several different Help tools to assist you in using Access efficiently. You learned to use the Office Assistant; the Contents, Answer Wizard, and Index tabs; and ScreenTips to answer questions and further your understanding of Access. You learned how to connect to the Internet and use the Web toolbar to access various Web sites.

Now that you have completed this lesson, you should be able to do the following:

- Describe what a database is, explain the use, and give examples of data you can enter. (Access-6)
- Describe the difference between a record and a field. (Access-6)
- Start Microsoft Access and identify parts of the Database window. (Access-8)
- Issue an Access command using a menu or button. (Access-12)
- Provide a brief description of each menu on the menu bar. (Access-13)
- Provide a brief description of each button on the Database toolbar. (Access-16)
- Identify the Formatting toolbar. (Access-17)
- Open a database. (Access-18)
- Move around the database area using the mouse, arrow keys, and keyboard combinations. (Access-19)
- Explain the purpose of the database objects in Access—tables, queries, forms, reports, pages, macros, and modules. (Access-20)
- View and edit tables in Design view. (Access-20)
- Switch between views. (Access-22)
- View queries. (Access-24)
- Use Form view to add records. (Access-25)
- Preview a database object. (Access-27)
- Use the Office Assistant to get help on any Access topic. (Access-29)
- Use the Answer Wizard to access Help. (Access-31)
- Use the Contents tab to access Help. (Access-32)
- Use the Index tab to access Help. (Access-33)
- Use ScreenTips. (Access-35)
- Backup and restore a database. (Access-36)
- Print a database object. (Access-37)
- Compact a database (Access-38)
- Close a database. (Access-39)
- Exit Access. (Access-39)
- Connect to and disconnect from the Internet. (Access-40)
- Name buttons on the Web toolbar and navigate to a Web site. (Access-41)

CONCEPTS REVIEW

1 TRUE/FALSE

Circle T if the statement is true or F if the statement is false.

T F **1.** You can modify the layout of an object in Design view.

T F **2.** A dialog box is a special type of window that requests further information so that the program knows what to do next.

T F **3.** The Database window always first displays the reports in a database by default.

T F **4.** The Contents tab of the Help system allows you to type one or more keywords to narrow the available topics.

T F **5.** A telephone book is an example of a manual database.

T F **6.** Data access pages are best viewed in a Web browser.

T F **7.** You can move to the beginning of a table by pressing ⇧ Shift + Home .

T F **8.** A field in a database contains the set of data for one entity, such as the name, address, and phone number for one customer.

T F **9.** Forms allow you to create a custom layout for the data in a table.

T F **10.** To update the results, you must re-issue a query when the data in a table is changed.

2 MATCHING

Match each of the terms on the left with the definitions on the right.

TERMS

1. DBMS
2. query
3. objects
4. record
5. field
6. relational databases
7. WYSIWYG
8. option button
9. links
10. ScreenTip

DEFINITIONS

a. Database programs that allow you to link tables

b. One of several mutually exclusive options in a dialog box

c. Screen display showing things much as they will be printed

d. Items that permit you to move directly to related Help topics

e. A system for storing and manipulating the data in a database

f. One category of information in a table

g. A text box generated by choosing *What's This?* on the Help menu and clicking a screen element

h. Questions requesting specific information from the database

i. Name for various components of Access

j. Group of fields related to a particular entity

Lesson Summary & Exercises

3 COMPLETION

Fill in the missing word or phrase for each of the following statements.

1. When a menu option is followed by an ellipsis, it leads to a
   _____.

2. You can use the _____ object to automatically
   perform a set of actions.

3. An Access _____ is a question to the database, usually asking for a specific subset of data.

4. When you want presentation-quality hard copy, you
   should print a _____.

5. A _____ is all the fields related
   to a particular entity.

6. A _____ is a set of
   programmed statements that are
   stored together as a unit.

7. In Access, the term
   _____ means a set of related tables, forms, reports, queries,
   pages, macros, and modules.

8. A _____ is a single category of information.

9. When you've finished using Access for the day, you should
   _____ the program.

10. Click the _____ button on the Web toolbar to add or access
    sites that you use frequently.

4 SHORT ANSWER

Write a brief answer to each of the following questions.

1. Name the seven types of Access objects.

2. What is the name of the screen element directly under the Access title bar?
   Does it ever change?

3. When would you use forms rather than tables for data entry?

4. From within a Database window, how would you open a table to change the
   layout?

5. What is the advantage of printing a report rather than printing a form or a
   table?

6. Describe the relationship between tables, records, and fields.

7. Name the different types of Help features in Access.

8. Explain the difference between a listing of items in a database and information provided by a query.

9. Describe the types of elements you find in a typical dialog box.

10. Why is it important to compact a database on a regular basis?

Lesson Summary & Exercises

5 IDENTIFICATION

Label each of the elements of the Access window in Figure 1.31.

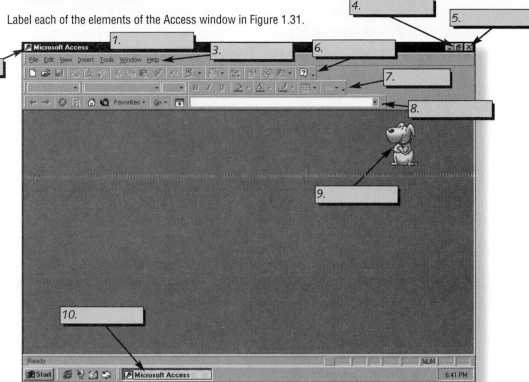

Figure 1.31

SKILLS REVIEW

Complete each of the Skills Review problems in sequential order so that you will review your Access skills to work with menus, toolbars, and dialog boxes; display various views of database objects; and use the Help system.

1 Launch Access and Work with Menus, a Dialog Box, and Buttons

1. Click the **Start button** on the Windows taskbar, point to **Programs**, and click **Microsoft Access**.

2. Click the **Cancel button** to remove the initial Access dialog box.

3. Click **View** on the menu bar.

4. Point to the **double arrow** at the bottom of the menu until Access displays the expanded View menu. Notice the available options and the grayed options.

5. Point to **Toolbars** to show the submenu.

6. Point to the **Tools menu**.

7. Click **AutoCorrect** to display the AutoCorrect dialog box.

8. Click the **Capitalize first letter of sentence option** if a check mark appears in the check box preceding it.

9. Scroll the list of commonly mistyped words and their replacements.

10. Click the **Exceptions button** near the top-right corner of the dialog box; then click the **INitial CAps tab**.

11. Click **Cancel** to close the Exceptions dialog box and click **Cancel** to close the AutoCorrect dialog box without performing the changes you selected.

12. Point to the **Cut button** ✂ until you see the name in a text box.

13. Point to the **Microsoft Access Help button** ? until you see its name.

14. Click the **Microsoft Access Help button** ? to display the Office Assistant. Then click outside of the balloon to remove it from the screen.

2 Open an Access Database and Edit a Table

1. Click the **Open button** 📂 on the Database toolbar.

2. Click the **Look in arrow** in the Open dialog box, and click the drive and folder that contains your Student Data Disk.

3. Double-click *Smyth Business College, Lesson 1*. Click **Tables** (Figure 1.32).

4. Click the **Student Information table** and click the **Open button** 📂Open in the Database window.

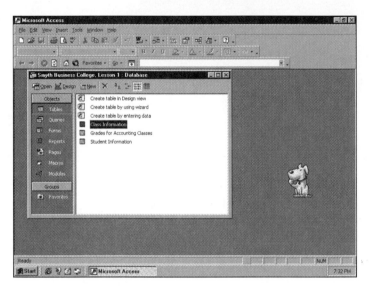

5. Click the **Maximize button** ☐.

6. Press ⎯Tab three times to move to the Address field for George Robinson.

7. Type 1765 Lyle Ave. and press ⎯Tab.

8. In the City field, type Atlanta and press ⎯Tab twice.

9. In the ZIP Code field, type 303371202 and press ⎯Tab.

10. In the Phone Number field, type 4045552969 and press ⎯Tab.

11. Click the **Close button** ☒ to close the table.

Figure 1.32

3 View a Table Design

1. Click the **Class Information table** and click the **Design button** 📐Design.

2. Press F6 to move to the lower panel.

3. Click the **View button** ▦ ▾ on the Database toolbar to display the table in Datasheet view.

4. Click the **Close button** ☒ to close the table.

4 Open and Edit Objects

1. Open the Student Grades for Basic Accounting Classes query.

2. Click the **View button** 📐 ▾ on the Database toolbar to view the query in Design view.

3. Click the query window's **Close button** ☒.

4. Open the Student Information form.

5. Click the **New Record button** ▶* and press Tab.

6. Type each of the following entries into the form, pressing Tab after each item:

Last Name:	Pittinger
First Name:	Rose
Address:	2575 Delk Rd.
City:	Marietta
State:	GA
ZIP Code:	300676584
Phone Number:	7705550737
Major:	Management

7. Click the **Close button** X.

8. Select the Students Listed by Major report.

9. Click the **Preview button** in the Database window.

10. Click the **Close button** X.

5 Use Help

1. Click the **Office Assistant**. Type group data in a report and click the **Search button**.

2. Click the **Group records in a report option** from the results that appear.

3. Read the text in the Help window that appears.

4. Click the **Sorting and Grouping button** in the Help window and read the definition. Then click to remove the definition from the screen.

5. Click the **How?** **link** in the Help window and read the new text that appears.

6. With the Help window still open, click the **Show button** to display the Contents, Answer Wizard, and Index tabs.

7. Click the **Answer Wizard tab**. Type change the design of a report and click the **Search button**.

8. In the *Select topic to display* panel, click **Change the size of a header, footer, or other section on a form or report topic** (Figure 1.33).

9. Click the **Contents tab** and click the **plus sign** in front of the **Working with Data topic**.

10. Open the **Cutting, Copying, and Pasting Items topic**.

11. Click the **Copy or move data from one field to another topic**.

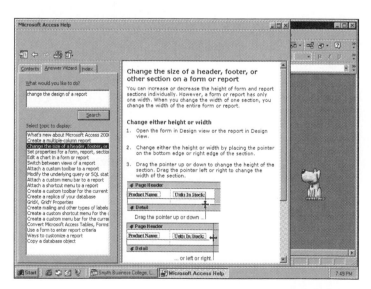

Figure 1.33

Lesson Summary & Exercises

12. Read the new text that appears in the right pane of the Help window.

13. Click the **Index tab** in the Help window. Type hyperlink in the *Type keywords* box and click the **Search button**. Notice the number of results that appear in the *Choose a topic* box.

14. Scroll the *Or choose keywords* box to find the word *create* and double-click.

15. In the *Choose a topic* box, click the **Create a hyperlink on a data access page topic**.

16. Read the text that appears in the right pane of the Help window.

17. Click the **Close button** ☒ on the Help window.

18. Click **What's This?** on the Help menu.

19. Click the **Delete button** ☒ in the Database window.

20. Read the definition of the button and then click anywhere in the window to close the application.

6 Preview and Print a Database Object

1. Click the **Reports option** in the Database window.

2. Click the **Students Listed by Major report**.

3. Click the **Preview button** ▣Preview in the Database window.

4. Click the **Print button** ▤.

5. Close the report.

7 Compact a Database and Quit Access

1. Click **Tools** on the menu bar and click **Options**.

2. On the General tab, click the **Compact on Close option**, if it is not already selected.

3. Click **OK**.

4. Click the **Close button** ☒ on the *Smyth Business College, Lesson 1* Database window.

5. Click the **Close button** ☒ on the Access title bar.

LESSON APPLICATIONS

1 Use Menus and Buttons

Practice using menus, buttons, and dialog boxes with the **Payton Properties, Lesson 1** database stored on your Student Data Disk.

1. Start Access and click the Cancel button when the initial dialog box appears.

2. Click the Open button and open the **Payton Properties, Lesson 1** database on your Student Data Disk.

3. Click View on the menu bar, point to Database Objects and click Reports. Note how many reports are associated with the **Payton Properties, Lesson 1** database.

4. Click Tools on the menu bar and click Options.

5. On the View tab of the dialog box, deselect Status bar. On the Tables/Queries tab, change the default text field size to 40.

6. Click the Cancel button to close the dialog box without saving your changes.

7. Click the Relationships button. Look at the table boxes within the window; you will learn more about relationships in a later lesson. Close the Relationships window without making changes.

2 View and Edit Tables

As a new employee of Payton Properties, Inc., you need to familiarize yourself with the database that the agency uses to track employee information and data on homes available for sale. Start by opening and editing some tables.

1. Open the **Payton Properties, Lesson 1** database stored on your Student Data Disk, if it is not already open.

2. Click the Tables option in the Database window and use the Open button to display the data in the Employees table (Figure 1.34).

3. Read the data. Then change Brian Matthews' phone number to (214) 555-1889 and close the Employees table.

4. Use the Design button to view the design of the Homes for Sale table.

5. Close the Homes for Sale table.

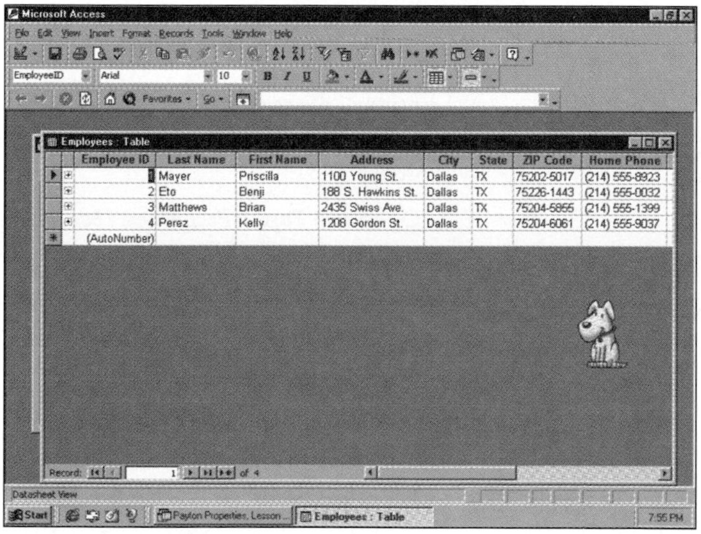

Figure 1.34

3 Work with a Query

One of your clients is looking for a home with four bedrooms. Display the results of a query that asks to view four-bedroom homes available. Then view the design of the query.

1. Open the **Payton Properties, Lesson 1** database stored on your Student Data Disk, if it is not already open.

2. Click the Queries option in the Database window and use the Open button to display the data in the Homes with Four Bedrooms query.

3. Read the data and then close the Homes with Four Bedrooms query.

4. Use the Design button to view the design of the Homes with Four Bedrooms query.

5. Close the query.

4 Add a Record Using a Form

As an employee of Payton Properties, you also need to know how to add records to their database. First, display the homes that Payton Properties has for sale using a form. Then, add a new listing.

1. Open the *Payton Properties, Lesson 1* database stored on your Student Data Disk, if it is not already open.

2. Click the Forms option in the Database window and use the Open button to display the data in the Homes for Sale form.

3. Use the New Record button to add a new, blank record. Type the following data into the new record:

Address:	18 Milikin Dr.
Bedrooms:	3
Baths:	2
Square Feet:	1690
Rooms:	7
Year Built:	1989
Price:	120900
Employee ID:	3

4. Close the Homes for Sale form.

5 Open, Preview, Print, and Close a Report

Your manager has asked you to print a report that shows the basic facts of newly listed homes. Open a report that provides this information and then print a copy for your manager.

1. Open the *Payton Properties, Lesson 1* database stored on your Student Data Disk, if it is not already open.

2. Click the Reports option in the Database window and use the Preview button to display the data in the New Listings by Agent report.

3. Scroll through and read the report.

4. Click the Print button and then close the report.

5. Click Tools on the menu bar, point to Database Utilities, and click Compact and Repair Database. Watch the status bar for an immediate message that the database is being compacted.

6. Close the *Payton Properties, Lesson 1* Database window.

7. Exit Access.

PROJECTS

1 Changing the View of Objects

You work as the retail manager at Electro Shop—a store that sells stereos, televisions, and other electronics. You have created a database to track employee data as well as product data. First open the database called *Electro Shop, Lesson 1* on your Student Data Disk. After you see the Database window, click View on the menu bar and click Large Icons from the expanded menu. Notice that the table options in the Database window change and are represented by large icons. Then use the View menu to switch the display back to List view.

2 Updating a Product Table

Open the *Electro Shop, Lesson 1* database on your Student Data Disk, if it is not already open. Open the Products table. Change the availability date of the RML VCR Model 1200 to 12/3 in the Notes field. Then view the table in Design view. Write down the name and data type of each field in the table, and then close the table.

3 How Many Stereos Did You Sell?

Open the *Electro Shop, Lesson 1* database on your Student Data Disk, if it is not already open. Open the Stereos Sold query and write down the number of records that meet the query. View the query in Design view and notice how the query is structured (Figure 1.35). Can you tell in Design view which field contains criteria to be met? Close the query.

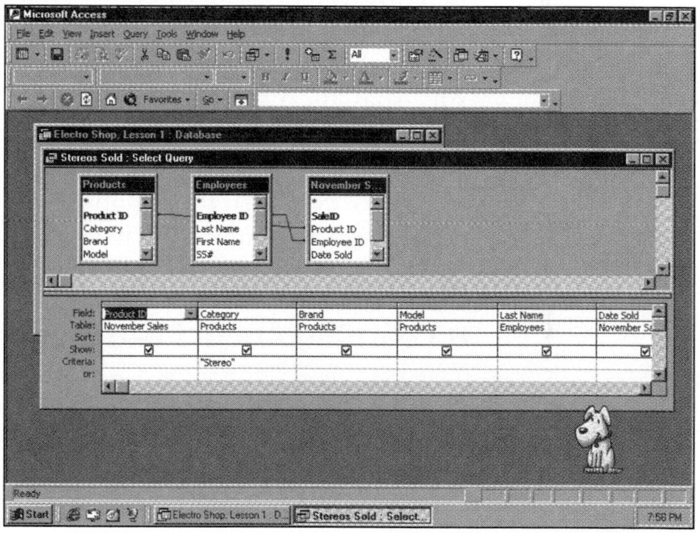

Figure 1.35

4 Adding an Employee

Open the *Electro Shop, Lesson 1* database on your Student Data Disk, if necessary. Open the Employees form. Add the following record in Form view. Then close the form and use the Contents tab of the Help system to learn more about previewing and printing forms.

Employee ID:	*allow the AutoNumber feature to assign a number*
Last Name:	Richards
First Name:	Susan
SS#:	121-21-2121
Hourly Rate:	$7.75
FT/PT:	PT

5 Who Sold What?

Open the *Electro Shop, Lesson 1* database on your Student Data Disk, if it is not already open. Open the Sales by Employee report and use word processing software to describe the information provided in the report. Print one copy of the report and then close the report. Use the Office Assistant to learn more about creating a report with a wizard.

6 Identifying the Parts of a Report

Open the *Electro Shop, Lesson 1* database on your Student Data Disk, if it is not already open. Open the Sales by Employee report in Design view. Display ScreenTips in Design view that identify at least three elements of the report or toolbox buttons. Close the report.

7 Improving the Size and Performance of the Database

Open the *Electro Shop, Lesson 1* database on your Student Data Disk, if it is not already open. Use either of the methods learned in this lesson to compact it. If you share your computer with others and plan to compact the database upon closing it, make sure that the Compact on Close option has not been deselected and then close the database. If you prefer to compact the database immediately, issue the command from the Database Utilities option.

8 Learning About Field Formats

Use the Answer Wizard to learn more about format properties of fields in a table. Using word processing software, list the types of formats available and briefly describe the use of each. Close the Help window. If a Database window is open, close it. Then exit Access.

9 An Online Bookstore

Assume that you are thinking about starting a small business and would like to find some books on financing a business. To help you in your book search, you can use the Internet. Use the Go button to navigate to www.amazon.com. Connect to the Internet. Start Access and display the Web toolbar. Read the information on the Web page. What do you think you would need to do to search for a book? Close the browser and return to Access. Hide the Web toolbar and close any open workbooks. Disconnect from the Internet unless your instructor tells you to remain connected.

Project in Progress

10 Ways to Use Databases in a Communications Business

You own a small business called I-Comm that provides a variety of writing, editing, and training services to other business owners. You facilitate training seminars; write materials such as brochures, training manuals, annual reports, employee handbooks, and newspaper and magazine articles; and create Web pages for small businesses. Think of ways you could use a database in your business. Then start Access and open the *I-Comm, Lesson 1* database on your Student Data Disk. Open each of the three tables in the database and examine the information in them. Open the Writers query and determine the purpose of the query. Open the Projects AutoForm form and add the following information while in Form view (Figure 1.36).

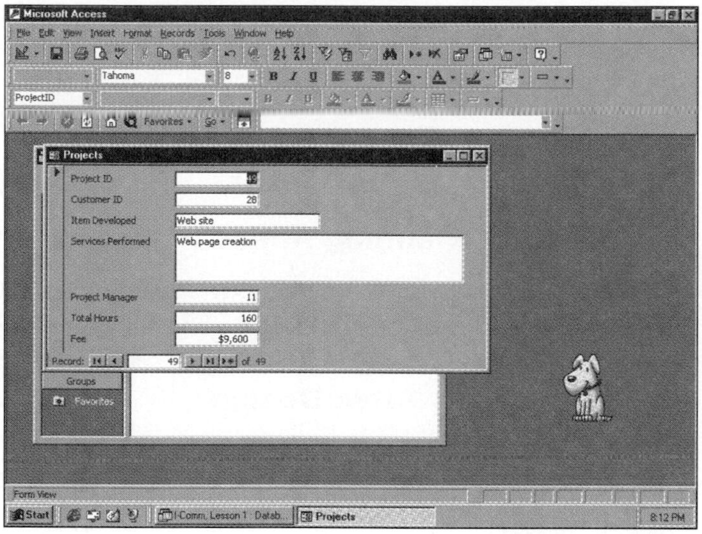

Figure 1.36

Project ID:	(AutoNumber)
Customer ID:	28
Item Developed:	Web site
Services Performed:	Web page creation
Project Manager:	11
Total Hours:	160
Fee:	$9,600

Open and scroll through the Projects report. Close all objects. Click Tools on the menu bar and click Options, then click the General tab. Click Compact on Close if it is not already selected and then click OK. Close the Database window. Exit Access.

LESSON 2

Designing and Creating Databases

CONTENTS

OBJECTIVES

After you complete this lesson, you will be able to do the following:

- Plan your database.
- Determine appropriate data inputs for your database.
- Determine appropriate data outputs for your database.
- Create table structure.
- Establish table relationships.
- Create a database using a Wizard or Design view.
- Create tables by using the Table Wizard.
- Set primary keys.
- Modify field properties.
- Use multiple data types.
- Modify tables using Design view.
- Use the Favorites menu on the Web toolbar.

In Lesson 2, you will see the importance of planning and organization. You will learn how to determine what data items to store and the number of tables you'll need. You then learn how to create a database, as well as different ways to create tables. Next you will find out how to save tables to use them for future work. Last, you discover how to modify existing tables, an indispensable skill in this world of constant change.

PLANNING AHEAD

Creating a database requires careful thought. Although you can certainly make changes to a database, making those changes is a bit more complex than when using some programs, such as a word processor. Advanced planning alleviates the problems you can experience from quickly creating a database without preparation. After you design your database, creating an Access database and building a few tables will be remarkably easy.

Before beginning to build a database, you should answer several questions:

- What is the database for and what should the database do?
- What categories of information (or fields) do you need to create to achieve the desired results?
- How should these fields be divided into separate tables?
- How might these tables relate to each other to use information from two or more of them simultaneously?

Determining the Purpose of the Database

The first step in determining how to configure your database is to decide how you will use the database. If you have an existing manual database system, investigate that system; review any reports and forms that you'll need to duplicate and note the items of information they must include. Also be sure to talk to people who actually use the database; check to see what they use the system for and what they need.

If you're not working with an existing system, think very carefully about what you want the new system to do; jot down the items of information the system should track and sketch out any forms and reports you think you'll need. Throughout the planning process, remember that as you determine what you want your database to do, you are learning what data you must have in your database. For example, if you need to be able to print salary reports according to department, your database must list the department for each employee. Also, consider how you want to sort or extract data. For instance, if you'll want to sort customers by last name, you'll need to include separate fields for a first name and a last name, rather than a single field to contain both names. At this stage in planning, you can make just one large list of all the information you need. You'll then learn how to organize this information into more manageable chunks.

 In the planning stage, you can ask users of the current system to supply you with a wish list of things they'd like to be able to do. Remember that you aren't confined to duplicating a current manual system; often you can improve on the existing system while computerizing.

Determining the Categories of Information You Need

The second step in creating a database is to determine all of the categories of information you need. At this point, you do not need to list the categories in any particular order. For instance, the sample application in this tutorial is the database for a fruit-of-the-month club called Be Fruitful. Members of this club can choose whether to order the fruit offered for a particular month, and they can also decide how much fruit to order. Some of the information categories needed in this database include:

- The name, address, and phone number of each customer, as well as notes about shipping
- The date the customer joined the club
- The types of fruit, their prices, and the units offered (3 pints strawberries, 2 dozen kiwis, and so forth)
- The number of units of fruit each member orders in a month
- The date an order was placed and when and how the customer paid

Determining How Many Tables You Need

All but the simplest of databases will contain multiple tables so that Access can use your data more efficiently. In other words, your task is not only to determine what categories of information (or fields) your database should contain but also how that information should be broken down logically into several tables.

The first thing to consider is that each table should contain information on a single subject. In the database for Be Fruitful, for example, you will have one table that contains customer information, a second table that includes information about available fruits, and a third one with order information. You wouldn't include customer names and addresses in the orders table, because these fields describe the customer, not the order. This way of breaking down your database avoids duplication of data. You want to avoid entering the customer's name and address in each order, for example, because this wastes storage space, requires extra typing, and increases the likelihood of data-entry errors. In addition, if you store the customer name and address information in a single customer record rather than in multiple order records, you can more easily update your data later. At first, you may believe dividing the data among multiple tables in this way is inefficient—for example, you may want to use information about both customers and orders in an invoice form—but remember that Access enables you to combine data from many sources as you create forms and reports.

Tables also should avoid multiple instances of the same field or a similar set of fields. For example, suppose you had a mail-order business and your customers often ordered multiple items at once. To record all of those orders in the orders table, you could have one long record with fields for each item ordered. A better solution would be to have a separate line-items table where each item being ordered is in a separate record.

Finally, as a general rule, do not include fields in your table that will contain data that you can calculate from other fields. For instance, if you have one field for price and one for quantity, you can calculate the total by multiplying these two values together—you don't need to create a separate field for the total. Figure 2.1 shows a tentative list of fields for the three tables in Be Fruitful's database.

When tables contain redundant data, they will retrieve data and update more slowly than more efficiently designed tables. You can use the Table Analyzer Wizard to store your data more efficiently.

BE FRUITFUL FIELDS

BFCustomers	BFFruit	BFOrders
Customer ID	Fruit Type	Order Number
Contact Last Name	Price	Customer ID
Contact First Name	Descriptive Units	Order Date
Billing Address		Fruit Type
City		Quantity
State or Province		Price
ZIP Code		Shipping Amount
Phone Number		Payment Date
Date Joined		Payment Amount
Notes		Payment Type
Extra Catalogs		Reference

Figure 2.1
Lists of fields in each table

Determining How Tables Will Work Together

After you've decided how to divide the database information into multiple tables, you have a corresponding task—to determine how to set up those tables to combine the information they contain into single forms or reports. For instance, if you have separate tables for orders and customers, you clearly need a way to pull the data from both tables to create an invoice that includes corresponding customer and order information.

For you to be able to use two tables in combination, they must include a *common field.* For example, to ensure that you can relate the fruit-of-the-month club's customers and orders tables, you could include a Customer ID field in both tables. This field would enable Access to match the order with the customer who placed the order. When determining the *relationships* (how tables are related) among tables, you must also consider the concept of primary keys: A *primary key* is a field or set of fields that uniquely identifies each record in the table. Assigning a primary key is particularly important if you must link data in two tables. In the fruit-of-the-month club's database, for instance, you need a primary key in the customers table—some way to uniquely identify each customer so that you can tell which orders belong to which customers. A Customer ID field can serve this purpose. (You wouldn't want to use the name fields as the primary key, in case you had two customers with the same name.) When you set a primary key, Access sorts records in order according to the values in that key. Because the primary key must uniquely identify each record, Access won't permit you to enter duplicate values in the primary key field(s).

Although determining how to link your tables can be more complex, at this stage of the game you'll just include common fields in the tables you need to use together and set some primary keys. In Lesson 4, you'll learn how to create queries that pull data from multiple tables.

CREATING A DATABASE

As you may remember from the previous lesson, in Access the term database means not just a collection of data but, a set of related tables, forms, reports, queries, and more. Before you begin to create tables in which to store your data, you need to create a database.

Opening and Naming a New Database

In this activity, you will create a database to hold your tables, as well as all the related queries, forms, data access pages, and reports you'll create throughout this tutorial. Then you'll assign a name to identify the data.

1. Start Access.

The Microsoft Access dialog box appears.

2. Click the Blank Access database option and click OK.

You should see the File New Database dialog box, as shown in Figure 2.2. Notice that this dialog box is very similar to the Open dialog box you saw in Lesson 1.

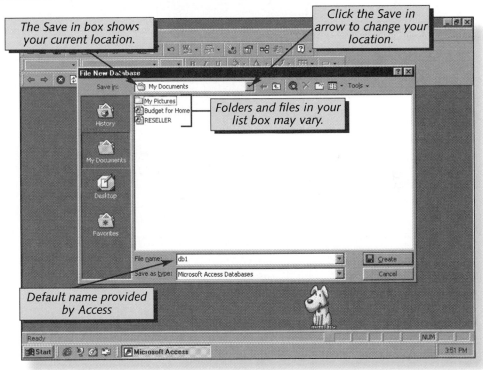

The Save in box shows your current location.

Click the Save in arrow to change your location.

Folders and files in your list box may vary.

Default name provided by Access

Figure 2.2
File New Database dialog box

3. Click the Save in arrow.

4. Select the location that contains your Student Data Disk files.

 Your instructor may direct you to save your files on a Zip disk, the hard drive of your computer, or a network folder. If you are not sure where to save your database, ask your instructor for direction.

Another Way

To create a database, you can click File on the menu bar and click New. Then, click the Database option on the General tab and click OK.

5. Click the *Tutorial* folder in the window below the Save in box; click the **Open button**.

The *Tutorial* folder opens and appears in the Save in box.

6. Double-click the file name in the File name text box.

7. Type Be Fruitful, Lesson 2 to replace the existing name.

Depending upon how your computer is set up, Access may automatically add an extension of *.mdb* to the file name. The extension identifies the file as an Access database.

8. Click the **Create button**.

After a pause, Access displays the Database window for the *Be Fruitful, Lesson 2* database, as shown in Figure 2.3.

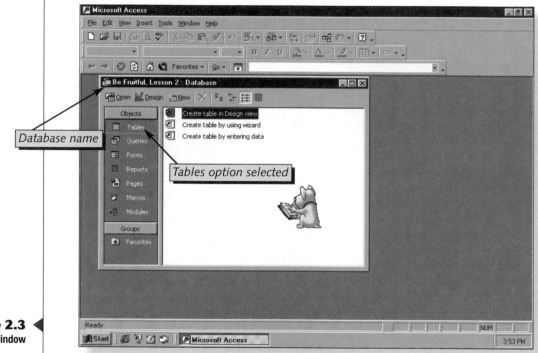

Figure 2.3
The Database window

When you create a new database, the fields are empty. Notice that the Tables option in the Objects bar is selected. Three options appear to help you create tables, but no actual tables exist yet. If you selected any of the other object options, you would see that they also contain no queries, forms, reports, or other objects—only options to create new objects.

CREATING TABLES

Now that you've created a database, the next step is to create some tables so that you can enter your data. You'll be creating the table structure—you'll spell out the fields that the table needs and select various properties for them. In the next lesson, you'll learn how to enter and edit data in the tables you've created. These are the first two essential steps for building a database.

Three ways exist to create tables in Access: First, you can use the Table Wizard, described next. Second, you can work in Table Design view, described later in this lesson. Lastly, you can create a table by entering data; using this method, you must later revise your table to create field names.

Creating a Table with the Table Wizard

During the following activities, you'll use the Table Wizard to design Be Fruitful's Customers table, which will include the names and addresses of the Be Fruitful customers. When you use a *wizard*, Access prompts you for the needed information each step of the way. The Table Wizard is a tool provided by Access used specifically to create tables. The Table Wizard gathers information through a series of dialog boxes. At any point in the table-creation process, you can click the Back button to move back one step. You'll use the wizard to select fields to be included in the database, deselect and rename fields, name the table, and select a primary key.

HANDS On

Selecting Fields

The first step in creating a table is to select the fields to be included. In this activity, you'll start the Table Wizard and select fields from the samples provided.

1. **With the Be Fruitful, Lesson 2 Database window still open, click the Tables option in the Objects bar if necessary.**

2. **Double-click the Create table by using wizard option in the Database window.**

The Table Wizard dialog box appears, as shown in Figure 2.4. Don't be overwhelmed by the number of options. This is simply a long selection of sample tables—and their accompanying fields—from which you can choose.

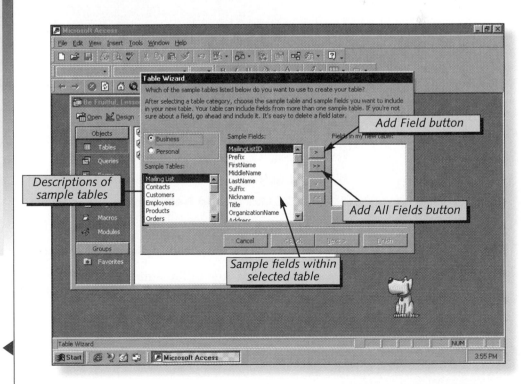

Figure 2.4
The Table Wizard dialog box

3. Click **Customers** in the Sample Tables list box.

Notice that the list of field names in the Sample Fields list box changes; this list box now includes sample fields appropriate for a table of customers. (If you want to see a list of sample tables that are targeted to personal use, click the Personal option button.)

4. Click the **CustomerID field name**, if it is not selected.

5. Click the **Add Field button** [>].

This button permits you to add one field at a time to your new table. As shown in Figure 2.5, Access lists the CustomerID field in the Fields in my new table list box on the right side of the Table Wizard dialog box. The CustomerID field will be used to link customers and orders.

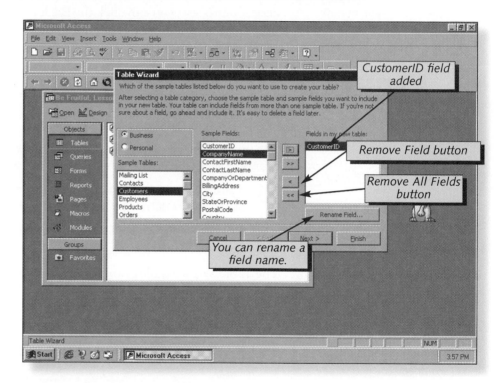

Figure 2.5
Adding a field

6. Click the **ContactFirstName sample field** and click the **Add Field button** [>].

The ContactFirstName field should appear directly under CustomerID in the Fields in my new table list box. Notice that Access places the added field below the CustomerID field. Note that the ContactLastName field in the Sample Fields list box is now selected.

7. Click the **Add Field button** [>].

Access adds the ContactLastName field to the Fields in my new table list box.

8. Double-click the **BillingAddress field** in the Sample Fields list box.

Access adds the BillingAddress field to the list on the right; double-clicking one of the sample fields is a shortcut for adding a field name to a table.

9. Add the fields City, StateOrProvince, PostalCode, PhoneNumber, FaxNumber, and Notes, in that order.

You may have to scroll down in the Sample Fields list box to find all of these fields. As shown in Figure 2.6, Access lists all the selected fields in the Fields in my new table list box.

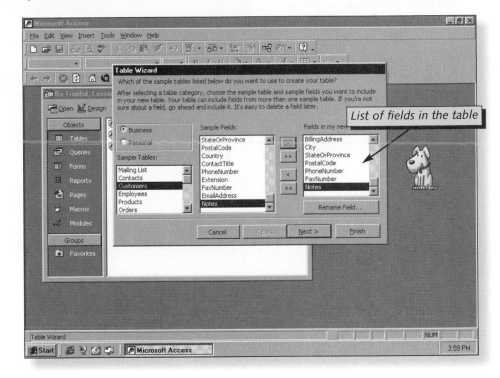

Figure 2.6
Fields to be included in the table

Removing and Renaming Fields

1. Click the field you wish to remove and click the Remove Fields button.

2. Click the field you wish to rename, click the Rename Field button, type the new name, and click OK.

Changing Fields in the Field List

At times you may decide against including a particular field in your table. Fortunately, this kind of change to the field list is relatively simple to make. In this activity, you will remove a field from the field list and rename another field.

1. Click **FaxNumber** in the Fields in my new table list box.

2. Click the **Remove Field button** ⬛.

Access promptly removes the FaxNumber field from the list. You can change field names with ease, too.

3. Click the **PostalCode field** in the Fields in my new table box.

4. Click the **Rename Field button**.

The Rename field dialog box appears with the current field name selected.

5. Type ZIPCode, **as shown in Figure 2.7.**

6. Click **OK**.

ZIPCode appears in the Fields in my new table box.

Hints & Tips

- You can click the Remove All Fields button or Add All Fields button to remove or add all of the fields at once.

- Typing new text will replace the selected text. Using keys such as `Delete`, `Backspace`, `Home`, and `End` work the same in text boxes as they do in word processing programs.

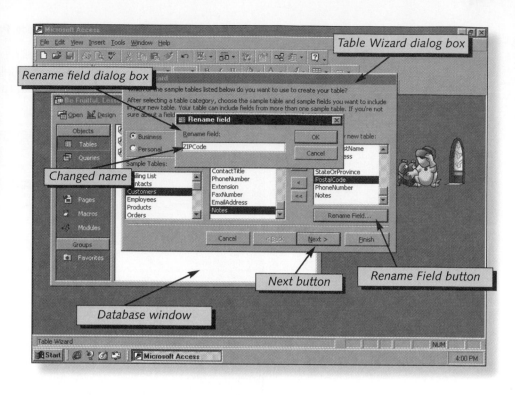

Figure 2.7 ◄
Rename field dialog box

Naming the Table and Selecting a Primary Key

1. Type a name for the table.

2. Click the *No, I'll set the primary key.* option and click Next.

3. Select the field to be used as the primary key and click Next.

Naming the Table and Selecting a Primary Key

You have now selected the desired fields for your table and are ready to choose a name for the table. In this activity, you provide a name when the Table Wizard prompts you to enter one. Then you will choose a field to act as the primary key.

1. Click the Next button near the lower-right corner of the Table Wizard dialog box.

You'll see the next Table Wizard dialog box shown in Figure 2.8, which lets you name your table and set the primary key.

Access suggests the name *Customers*—the name of the sample table you selected—for your new table. Object names such as table and field names can be up to 64 characters long. Access allows any combination of letters, numbers, spaces, and many punctuation characters. Access does not permit any of the following: period, exclamation mark, accent grave

, square brackets, or double quotation marks. Also, object names cannot begin with a space or an equal sign.

2. Click to the left of the letter *C*. (The table name will be deselected and the insertion point will move to the left of the letter *C*.) Then type BF before the word *Customers*.

The entire table name should read *BFCustomers*, indicating that this table will contain information about the customers of the Be Fruitful fruit-of-the-month club.

Omitting spaces from your object names will allow easier reference later. Also, limiting the length of the name of the object will be easier for you to remember and type more quickly. Don't worry about how the object name appears on the screen or report; you can change these later to more familiar terms.

Figure 2.8 ◄
Naming the table

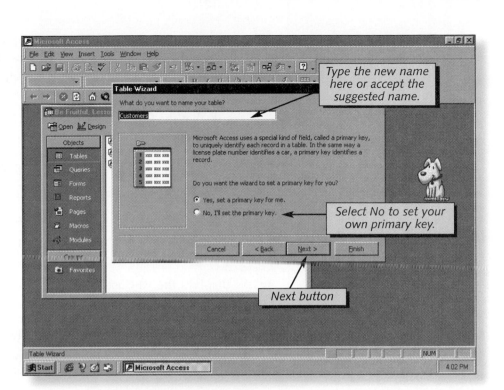

3. **Click the No, I'll set the primary key. option** and then click **Next**.

Access displays the next Table Wizard dialog box shown in Figure 2.9.

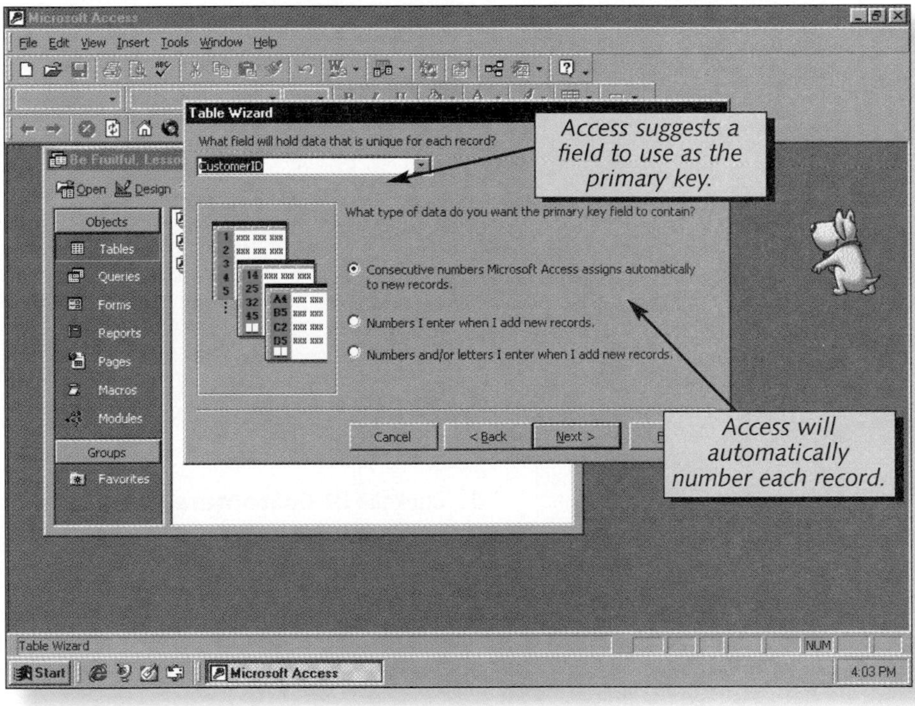

Figure 2.9 ◄
Selecting a primary key

Notice that Access suggests the CustomerID field as the primary key field. You could change this by selecting another field from the drop-down list; however, since each customer will have a unique ID number, this field is an appropriate one to set as the primary key.

Also notice that the *Consecutive numbers Microsoft Access assigns automatically to new records.* button is selected. When you choose this option, Access automatically provides the CustomerID numbers, ensuring that you don't enter duplicate values in any CustomerID field.

4. Click the **Next button** to accept the selections.

Access displays the final Table Wizard dialog box.

5. Choose the **Modify the table design. option button** and click the **Finish button**.

Access displays the BFCustomers table in Table Design view, as shown in Figure 2.10.

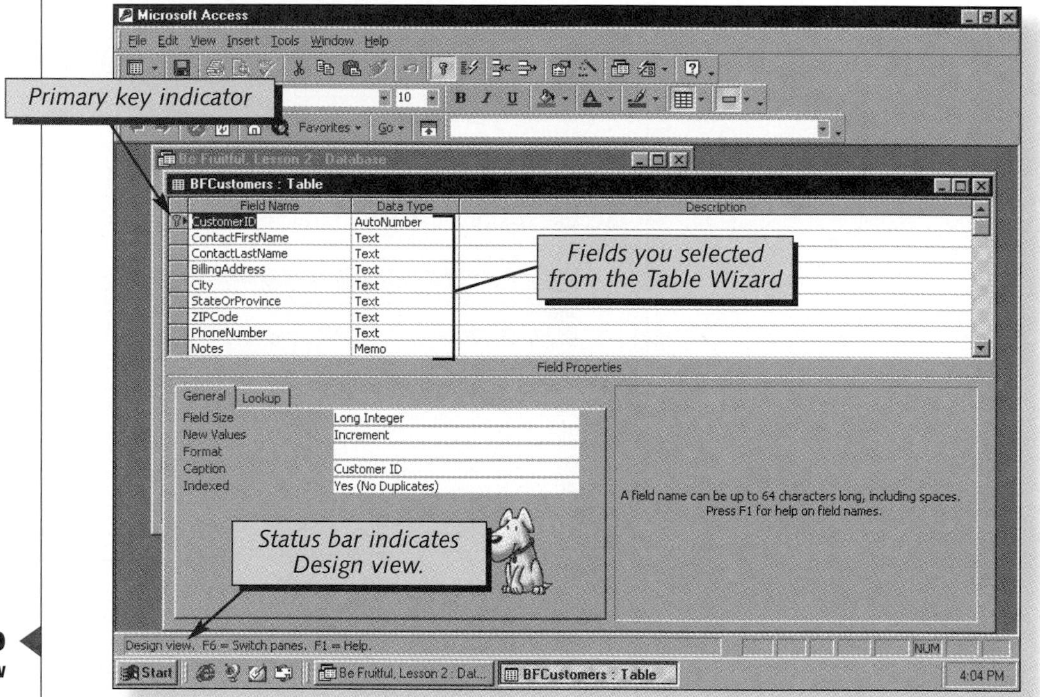

Figure 2.10
Table Design view

6. Click the **BFCustomers Table Close button** ☒.

Access returns you to the Be Fruitful, Lesson 2 Database window, which now includes the BFCustomers table.

Creating Tables in Table Design View

The Table Wizard makes creating a table a straightforward process, but allows you little flexibility. Fortunately, you can also create tables in Table Design view, which gives you much more control over field characteristics, including their size and the type of data they'll contain. You can use Table Design view both to create new tables and to modify existing tables—whether you created them in Table Design view or with the Table Wizard.

Creating a Table in Design View

1. Double-click the Create table in Design view option.

2. Type the first field name and press `Tab`.

3. Click the desired data type and press `Tab`.

4. If desired, type a description for the field and press `Tab`.

5. Repeat steps 2-4 for each field.

Touring the Table Design View

In this activity, you'll create a new table in Table Design view, which is slightly more involved than the Table Wizard. You'll create two fields in the orders table for Be Fruitful's database to get a feel for the process. After that, you'll learn more about the various aspects of fields before you complete the table.

1. **Click the Tables option in the Be Fruitful, Lesson 2 Database window, if it is not already selected.**

2. **Double-click the Create table in Design view option.**

Access opens an empty table in Table Design view, as shown in Figure 2.11.

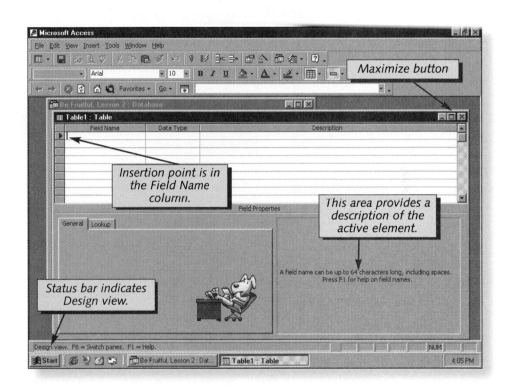

Figure 2.11
Blank Table Design view

Notice that the ***insertion point***—the flashing vertical line—is in the Field Name column. Read the information in the lower-right corner of the window, which describes field names.

3. **Click the Maximize button** ☐.

The screen fills with the Design view of the table you are creating.

4. **Enter the field name** OrderNumber **in the Field Name column.**

5. **Press** `Tab` **to move to the Data Type column.**

Access activates the Data Type column, displaying the default data type (Text) as well as a drop-down list arrow that provides you with access to other choices. Notice that the information in the lower-right corner of the window now describes data types.

Calculations can be performed more easily if your field names don't include spaces.

6. Click the **Data Type drop-down list arrow**.

Access reveals a drop-down list box displaying the available data types, as shown in Figure 2.12.

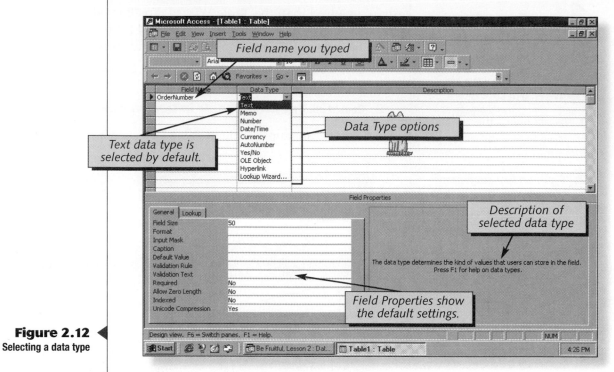

Figure 2.12
Selecting a data type

7. Click the **AutoNumber data type**. Then, press [Tab].

Your insertion point moves to the Description field. You can enter a description of up to 255 characters for each field. Access displays some information about field descriptions in the lower-right corner of the Table Design window.

8. Press [Tab] again to move to the second row in the Field Name column.

9. Type CustomerID and press [Tab].

The insertion point moves to the Data Type column.

10. Click the **Data Type drop-down arrow** and click the **Number data type**. Then, press [Tab].

11. Type the text Enter same Customer ID used in the BFCustomers table, **as shown in Figure 2.13.**

The Field Properties pane in the lower half of the Table Design view window lists the field size and other characteristics of the current field. You'll learn more about several of these characteristics later in this lesson.

12. Press [F6] to move to the Field Properties pane of the window; then press [F6] again.

Note that pressing [F6] a second time moves your insertion point back to the upper pane of the Table Design view window.

13. Press [Tab].

Access moves the insertion point down to the next row; now you can enter the specifications for another field. You'll enter additional fields later, after you learn more of the details about some of the field characteristics you've just encountered.

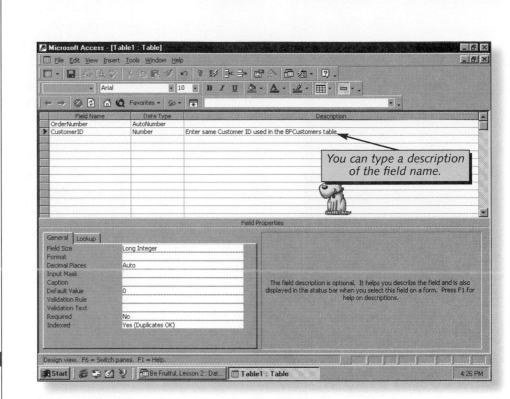

Figure 2.13
Typing a description

Selecting Data Types

When you work in Table Design view, you need to decide what data type to use. A ***data type*** controls the kind of data that can be entered into a field. For example, if you assign the Number data type to a field, you can't enter letters into that field. Most of the choices are fairly intuitive, and only ten data types exist, so you'll learn them quickly. Note that when you choose fields in the Table Wizard, Access automatically assigns them data types. The data type is just one of the properties that fields can have. ***Properties*** is the term used to describe the characteristics of fields, tables, databases, and so on. Field properties include the field's size and format, as well as limitations on how data can be entered into the field, as described in Table 2.1.

TABLE 2.1	DATA TYPES
Data Type - Field	**Description**
Text	Holds up to 255 characters, including letters, numbers, and punctuation marks. Use this data type for fields with (1) numbers that won't be used to perform calculations and (2) both numbers and some type of punctuation characters (such as phone numbers or Social Security numbers).
Memo	Holds up to 65,535 letters, numbers, and punctuation marks. Use this data type for fields with longer amounts of text (such as free-form comments or fairly lengthy descriptions).

TABLE 2.1	DATA TYPES—cont.
Data Type - Field	**Description**
Number	Holds only digits, the decimal point, and the minus (negative) sign. Use this data type (7 options) for fields with numbers only and for numbers to be used to perform calculations—for example, quantity or discount fields.
Date/Time	Holds dates and times. When you use this data type for dates and times, Access prevents you from entering invalid dates or times (such as 2/31/98 or 34:35). Access provides different display formats for dates and times and lets you sort dates and times into chronological order. You can also perform date arithmetic—subtracting one date from another to determine the number of days between them or adding or subtracting a specified number of days to or from a date to calculate a later or an earlier date.
Currency	Holds numeric values (such as salaries or prices) that you want to display with a currency symbol, a decimal point, and separators (usually commas) for every three digits.
AutoNumber	Holds numbers that Access increments by 1 automatically as each new record is added to the table. You cannot edit the values in these fields. AutoNumber fields can be used as primary keys because a unique value for each record will be created automatically.
Yes/No	Can accept only one of two logical values. Usually the responses are shown as either Yes or No, but they can also be displayed as True or False or as On or Off.
OLE Object*	Holds objects—such as Microsoft Word documents, pictures, graphs, and sounds—that have been created in other programs using the OLE protocol.
Hyperlink	Allows you to store text or graphics that links to a file or an Internet site.
Lookup Wizard	Lets you choose values from another table or create a list of values to be used. Choosing this option starts the Lookup Wizard.

The use of OLE object fields is beyond the scope of this tutorial. If you want to learn more about OLE objects, ask the Office Assistant for help.

Adding Fields in Design View

1. Click below the last field name.

2. Type the new field name and press `Tab`.

3. Click the desired data type and press `Tab`.

4. Type a description for the field, if desired. Press `Tab`.

5. Repeat steps 2-4 for each new field.

To select the data type more quickly, type the first letter while the insertion point is in the Data Type column; for example, type n to choose number, c to choose currency, and so on.

Adding Field Names and Types

In this activity, you will add more field names and types to the table you are creating.

1. **Click in the row below the CustomerID field name.**

The insertion point moves to the third row in the Field Name column.

2. **Type OrderDate and press** `Tab`**.**

Access moves you to the Data Type column, automatically selecting Text as the data type.

3. **Click the Data Type arrow and click Date/Time.**

4. **Click directly below the OrderDate field.**

5. **Type FruitType as the field name and press** `Tab`**. Accept Text as the data type and press** `Tab` **twice to move to the next row.**

6. **Enter the remaining field names and types as shown in Table 2.2.**

TABLE 2.2	FIELDS AND DATA TYPE INFORMATION
Field Name	**Data Type**
Quantity	Number
Price	Currency
ShippingAmount	Currency
PaymentDate	Date/Time
PaymentAmount	Currency
PaymentType	Text
Reference	Text

After you have entered the field names and data types, your screen should look like Figure 2.14.

Setting Field Sizes

For many data types, Access automatically sets the field size. For Text and Number fields, however, you may want to change the size of the field. As you learned earlier, Text fields can be anywhere from 0 to 255 characters long; you determine the size simply by clicking the Field Size text box in the Field Properties area and entering the desired value. The number you enter determines the maximum number of characters that will fit in the field.

When you create tables with the Table Wizard or in Table Design view, the default (preset) sizes for Text fields are usually rather high. You'll usually want to decrease the sizes of such fields, using only as many characters as you need.

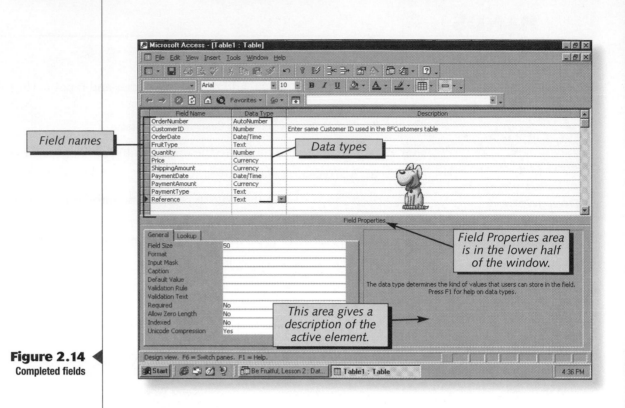

Figure 2.14
Completed fields

Among other reasons, decreasing field sizes helps ensure that correct values are entered. As an example, you would set the field size of a field to hold state abbreviations to two characters. Limiting this field size will prevent users from unintentionally entering three-digit state codes. For Number fields, in contrast, you can choose one of the seven number types described in Table 2.3.

TABLE 2.3	NUMBER TYPES
Type	**Lets you . . .**
Byte	Store whole numbers from 0 to 255; you can't enter fractional values in this field type.
Integer	Store whole numbers from -32,768 to 32,767; you can't enter fractional values in this field type.
Long Integer	Store whole numbers from roughly -2.1 billion to 2.1 billion; you can't enter fractional values in this field type. (Note that AutoNumber fields actually have the Long Integer number type.)
Single	Store real numbers (fractional values allowed) with 7 decimal digits of precision.
Double	Store real numbers (fractional values allowed) with 15 decimal digits of precision.
Replication ID	Establish a unique identifier for replication used to identify tables, records, and other objects.
Decimal	Store numbers and set the exact decimal digits of precision.

![Access Basics logo]

Changing the Size of Fields

1. Click the name of the field that you wish to change.

2. Press F6.

3. Type the new field size in the Field Size box.

Editing Field Sizes

In this activity, you will change some of the default field sizes for the table you are creating.

1. **Click the FruitType field name.**

2. **Press F6.**

Access moves to the Field Size text box under Field Properties. Note the default size for the FruitType field is 50.

3. **Type 20 in the Field Size text box.**

The value you type replaces the default as shown in Figure 2.15.

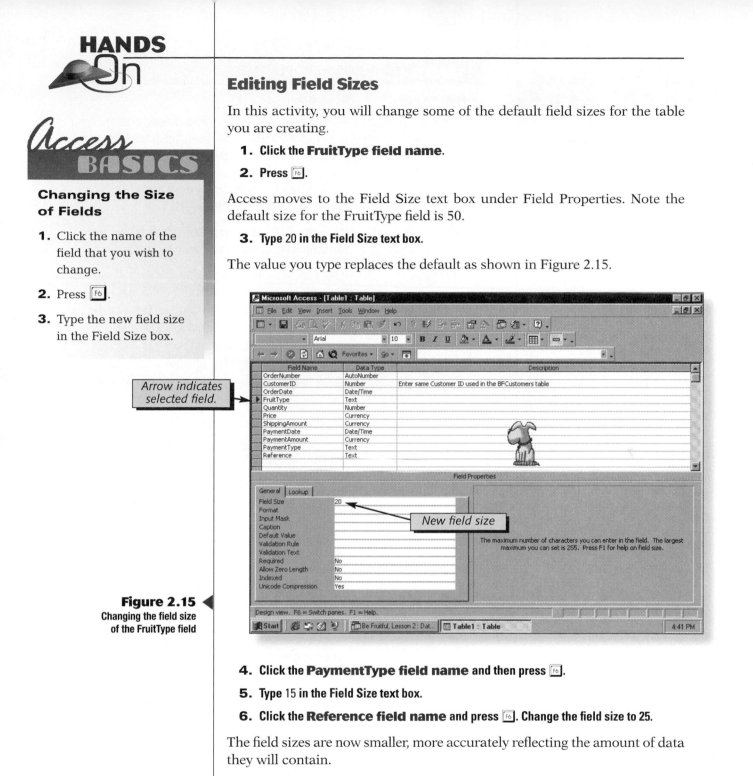

Figure 2.15 ◄
Changing the field size
of the FruitType field

4. **Click the PaymentType field name and then press F6.**

5. **Type 15 in the Field Size text box.**

6. **Click the Reference field name and press F6. Change the field size to 25.**

The field sizes are now smaller, more accurately reflecting the amount of data they will contain.

Setting Other Field Properties

In the Field Properties area at the bottom of the Table Design view window, Access presents various text boxes. The text boxes displayed vary depending on the data type of the selected field. These text boxes enable you to change a range of properties associated with the current field. *Field properties* control the way the field looks and behaves. One such property is field size, as discussed earlier. You can also change other field properties, as described in Table 2.4.

If you're curious about some of the field properties not discussed in Table 2.4, select the field property and read the descriptions.

TABLE 2.4	FIELD PROPERTIES
Field Property	**Description**
Format	For Number and Date/Time fields (among others), you can choose from a number of predefined formats. For example, you can choose the Percent format to display numbers as percentages or the Medium Date format to display dates in the *dd-mm-yy* format (as in 19-Jun-99).
Decimal places	If you choose the Number or Currency data type, you can control the number of decimal places displayed.
Input mask	If you choose the Text, Number, Date/Time, or Currency data type, you can create an input mask to ensure that a particular format is applied to the data in that field. For example, you could create an input mask to guarantee that all Social Security numbers would match the format *###-##-####* or that all phone numbers would be in the form *(###) ###-####*.
Caption	If you have long field names, you can enter captions for certain fields. These captions are used as column headings in tables and as field labels in forms. (You can enter two-word captions such as *First Name* when you have single-word field names such as *ContactFirstName*.) If you leave the caption property blank, the field names themselves are used as labels.
Default value	Typing a value in the Default Value text box instructs Access to automatically enter that value in this field for new records. For instance, if you have a Yes/No field in which 90 percent of your records contain a Yes response, you can save time by giving the field a default value of Yes. Other examples are default state codes if most of your employees live in a certain state and default quantities if the majority of your customers order the same number of items.
Required	No is the default for this property. A setting of Yes means that the field must be filled in when you enter a record; that is, Access will not allow you to continue entering data for the next record if you leave the field blank.

HANDS On

Modifying Field Properties

Now that you have additional knowledge of some of the basic field properties, you're ready to complete Be Fruitful's orders table in Table Design view. In this activity, you'll change properties of some of the fields.

1. Click the CustomerID field name, and press F6.

The Field Size text box says *Long Integer.*

Modifying Field Properties

1. Click the name of the field you wish to change.

2. Press F6.

3. Click the property box that you wish to change.

4. Type or click a new property.

Note *If Long Integer does not appear in the Field Size box, display the drop-down list by clicking the Field Size drop-down list arrow and click Long Integer.*

Now this field will match the CustomerID field in the BFCustomers table, which is an AutoNumber field.

2. Click the Quantity field name and press F6.

The Field Size is displayed as Long Integer. You can save storage space by making this field smaller.

3. Click the Field Size arrow.

The list of size options appears, as shown in Figure 2.16.

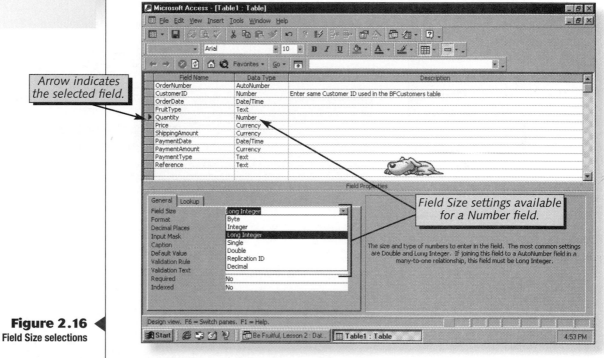

Arrow indicates the selected field.

Field Size settings available for a Number field.

Figure 2.16
Field Size selections

4. Click Integer.

5. With the Quantity field still selected, double-click the Default Value text box.

The 0 in the box is highlighted.

6. Type 1 in the Default Value text box.

Now when an order is completed, Access will assume the quantity ordered is one.

7. Type Enter check or credit card number **in the Description column of the Reference field.**

The default settings set by Access have been modified now to meet your needs.

Hints & Tips

To find out which field is active, look at the top part of the Table Design view window. An arrow to the left of the field name points to the active field.

Choosing a Primary Key

When creating a table with the Table Wizard, you set the primary key in the Table Wizard dialog box or you allow Access to set one. When you create a table in Design view, you must set the primary key yourself. To set the primary key, you first select a field with the row selector. The *row selector* is the small box to the left of a field.

Setting the Primary Key

In this activity, you will designate the OrderNumber field as the primary key.

1. Click the row selector to the left of the OrderNumber field.

The entire OrderNumber row is highlighted.

2. Click the Primary Key button 🔑 **on the Database toolbar.**

Access places a small key-shaped icon in the row selector for the OrderNumber field, as shown in Figure 2.17.

Key icon indicates that this field is set as the primary key.

Row selectors

Figure 2.17
Setting the primary key

Some tables require you to set a combination of two or more fields as the primary key. For instance, if the orders table didn't contain the OrderNumber field, no other single field could be used as a primary key since none uniquely identify each record. For instance, if you picked the CustomerID field as the primary key, you would not be able to distinguish between different orders made by the same customer. In this case, you could select the CustomerID, OrderDate, and FruitType fields and then issue the Primary Key command. The combination of these three fields would be considered the primary key.

You've completed the structure for the orders table, but you need to complete one more step; you need to save this table design for future use.

SAVING THE TABLE DESIGN

As you may know, to *save* is the process of taking information from your computer's memory and storing it on a more permanent medium—usually a hard drive or a removable disk. When you create tables with the Table Wizard, Access automatically saves them, using the table name you supply. When you create or modify tables in Table Design view, in contrast, you need to tell Access to save the table, much as you need to save documents you create with a word processing program. You'll want to save frequently as you work in case of a power outage or other event that can cause you to lose data that hasn't been saved.

When you use the Save command to save a table for the first time, Access requests a table name. When you update your table design and save again, the modified table is simply saved under the same name, so Access has no need to prompt you for a new file name. If for some reason you want to save a copy of the table under a new name, however, you can do so by clicking Save As on the File menu.

HANDS
On

Saving the Orders Table

In this activity, you'll save Be Fruitful's orders table so you can change the design later if necessary, and, equally important, so you can enter data in the next lesson.

1. Click the **Save button** 🖫 on the Database toolbar.

Access displays the Save As dialog box, as shown in Figure 2.18; you will enter a name for your table in this dialog box.

Figure 2.18
Save As dialog box

Another Way

To save a file, click File on the menu bar and click Save.

2. **Type** BFOrders **in the Table Name text box and click OK.**

Access returns you to Table Design view, with your table design still visible. Note, however, that the table name BFOrders now shows in the title bar. This indicates that the file has been saved.

3. **Click the Close button** ☒ **at the right end of the menu bar.**

Access closes the BFOrders table and returns you to the Database window for the *Be Fruitful, Lesson 2* database.

If you attempt to close a table design that includes unsaved changes, Access displays a dialog box asking whether you want to save your changes. You would choose *Yes* if you want to save the changes, *No* to discard them, or *Cancel* to cancel the operation and return to Table Design view.

Using HELP

Understanding Relationships Among Tables

Now that you've created two tables, use Help to learn more about how the tables can be related to each other.

1. **Click the Office Assistant.**

2. **Type** relationships among tables **in the *What would you like to do?* box.**

3. **Click the Search button.**

4. **Click the Create or modify relationships option** to open the associated Help window.

Figure 2.19
The Access Database Help window

5. **Click the Learn about relationships in a database link** (Figure 2.19).

6. **Scroll and read all of the information in the Help window to learn about the different types of relationships that you can assign to fields in tables.**

7. **Find and click the glossary term *relationships* to view the definition.**

8. **Click the button or link that leads you to more information on how to define a relationship.**

9. **Read the new text and explore other links.**

10. **When you are finished exploring, click the Close button ☒ to close the Help window.**

MODIFYING TABLES USING DESIGN VIEW

Whether you've created a table with the Table Wizard or in Table Design view, at some point you may need to make changes to the structure of your table. You might need to change field names or data types, to add a field you left out, to eliminate a field you no longer need, or to reorder your fields to better suit your needs or your sense of order. All of these changes can be made in the Table Design view.

You may also want to consider an input mask. An input mask is a specific field or control property that you use to ensure data is entered in a specific format, such as (555) 555-5555 for a phone number. Using an input mask allows you to enter just the numbers; the other characters are automatically placed, because of the input mask. To use the Input Mask Wizard, select the appropriate field in Design view, click the Build button next to the Input Mask property box and follow the instructions to complete the field formatting. Formatting applied by an input mask is overridden by anything in the Format property field.

 Warning *You can change the table structure after you've entered data into the table, but proceed with caution if you do. You run the risk of losing or unintentionally modifying your data.*

HANDS On

Access BASICS

Adding Captions

1. In Design view, click the field to which you want to add a caption.

2. Type a caption in the Caption box in the Field Properties pane of the window.

Adding Captions to Fields

As you learned earlier, *captions* are the words and phrases you type to abbreviate or clarify field names. Captions are used as labels in forms, reports, tables, and other objects. In this activity, you will add a field to the end of the table and create captions for fields. The captions you create will clarify field names that you will later use in reports and other objects. For example, rather than a report heading of *ExtraCatalogs* (one word), you can change the caption so the heading will appear as *Extra Catalogs* (two words).

1. In the Be Fruitful, Lesson 2 Database window, click the **BFCustomers table** and then click the **Design button** 📐 Design.

You'll see the BFCustomers table in Table Design view.

2. Click directly below the field name Notes.

3. Type ExtraCatalogs and press ⎇Tab to move to the Data Type column.

To add a new field at the end of the table structure, you go to the bottom of the display and enter the information for the new field.

4. Type y to select the Yes/No data type and press ⎇Tab.

5. Type Offers for holiday specials, exotic fruits, and more in the Description field.

Your new field should look like Figure 2.20.

6. Type Extra Catalogs in the Captions text box in the Field Properties area.

7. Click the **BillingAddress field** in the top portion of the window.

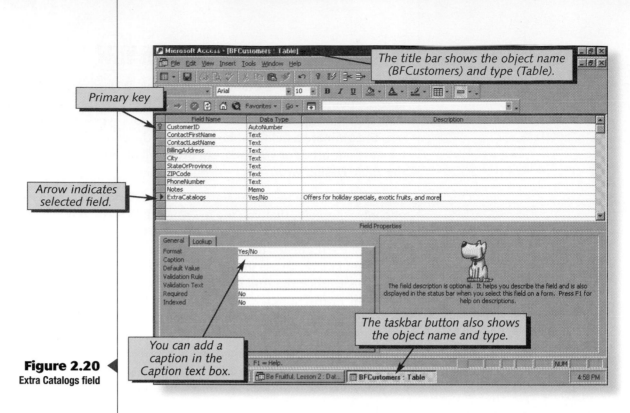

Figure 2.20
Extra Catalogs field

Callouts in figure:
- Primary key
- Arrow indicates selected field.
- You can add a caption in the Caption text box.
- The title bar shows the object name (BFCustomers) and type (Table).
- The taskbar button also shows the object name and type.

Notice that the Caption box contains the text *Billing Address*. When a field name is selected from the Table Wizard—as this one was—a caption is automatically assigned to a field name that contains two or more words. However, when you create fields in Design view, captions are not automatically created. For consistent spacing within labels (which will appear on reports and forms), add captions to those field names that you create in Design view.

8. Click the **ZIPCode field** in the top portion of the window.

9. Type ZIP Code **in the Caption text box.**

During data entry and the display of the table, your fields will now appear with easier-to-read labels.

Adding and Removing Fields

Although you should always plan ahead regarding fields to be included in your database, sometimes you'll discover that you need to make changes. Access allows you to add and remove fields within Design view. You can add a field to the end of a table, as you previously learned, but you can also insert field names between other fields. You can also delete fields that become unnecessary. There are several ways to insert a row: click Rows on the Insert menu; right-click the field and click Insert Rows on the shortcut menu; or click the Insert Rows button. There are also several ways to delete a field: click Delete Rows on the Edit menu; right-click the field and click Delete Rows on the shortcut menu; or click the Delete Rows button.

Access also provides an Undo feature that lets you reverse the last action you completed. You'll learn how to add and remove fields and use the Undo feature in the following activity.

Clicking the row selector highlights the entire field. You can select multiple adjacent fields by dragging over their row selectors. You can select nonadjacent fields by pressing Ctrl and clicking the row selector of each field to be selected.

Inserting and Deleting Categories

In this activity, you will add a new field between existing fields. Then you'll learn how to remove a field. Lastly, you'll undo a change.

1. Click anywhere within the Notes row in the top pane of the Design view window.

2. Click the Insert Rows button ▐ᶳ.

As shown in Figure 2.21, Access adds a blank row above the Notes field and places the insertion point within this row. You use this technique to insert new rows between existing ones rather than after the last row.

Figure 2.21 ◀
Inserting a row

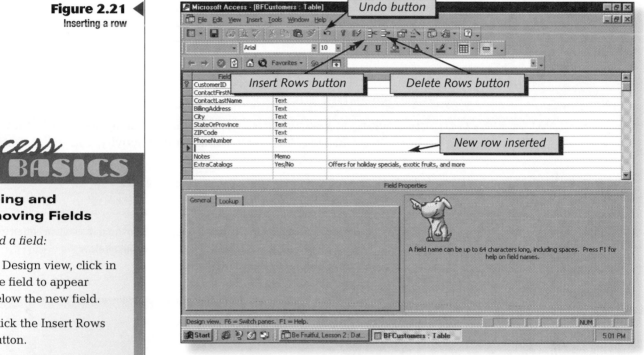

Access
BASICS

Adding and Removing Fields

To add a field:

1. In Design view, click in the field to appear below the new field.

2. Click the Insert Rows button.

3. Type the field name, data type, and description in the new row.

To delete a field:

1. Click the field that you wish to delete.

2. Click the Delete Rows button.

To undo a change:

Click the Undo button.

3. Type DateJoined **in the Field Name column and press** ⎄Tab⎄.

4. Choose the Date/Time data type.

5. Type the caption Date Joined **in the Caption box.**

6. Click anywhere within the Notes field.

7. Click the Delete Rows button ▐ᶳ.

Access deletes the active row—in this case, the Notes field. Now you realize that you actually need to retain the Notes field.

8. Click the Undo Delete button ↶.

Access restores the Notes field.

Another Way

To undo a change, click the Undo command on the Edit menu.

Warning

You can take advantage of the Undo command only if you act quickly enough. Choosing Undo generally undoes your most recent action only, whether you deleted a row, moved a row, typed some text, or chose a new data type. If you've done something else in the interim, however, such as deleting another field or typing some text, you won't be able to undo your earlier action with this command.

Moving a Field

At times, you'll include all of the correct fields in your database but later notice that the order in which they appear could be improved. Instead of using the methods to add and delete fields, Access allows you to change the order of fields by dragging them to their new locations in Design view.

Reorganizing the Fields

After looking at your database, you decide to display each customer's last name before the customer's first name. In this activity, you will switch the order of these two fields.

1. **Click the row selector for the ContactFirstName field.**

Access highlights the entire row.

2. **Point to the row selector for the selected row, click and hold the mouse button to drag downward until the dark horizontal line appears just below the ContactLastName field, as shown in Figure 2.22.**

Moving a Field

1. Click the row selector of the field you wish to move.

2. Drag the row selector to its new position.

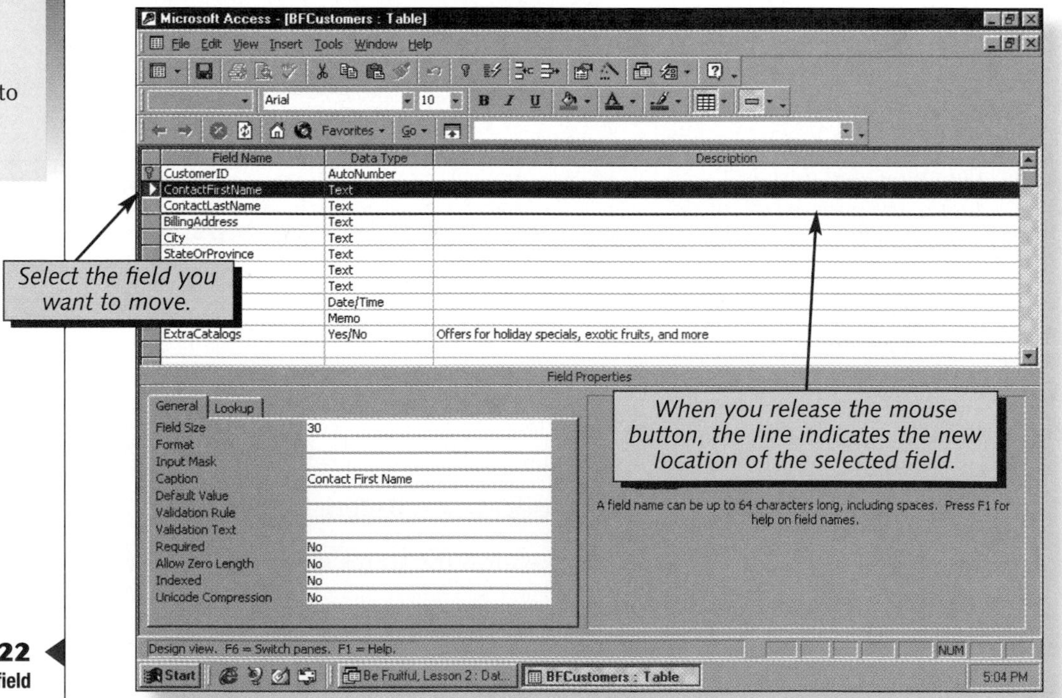

Select the field you want to move.

When you release the mouse button, the line indicates the new location of the selected field.

Figure 2.22
Moving a field

Access attaches a small grayed rectangle to the bottom of the pointer and also displays a dark horizontal line; the selected field will move to just below the horizontal line when you release the mouse button. Access moves the field to the new location in the table, below the last name field. You even can move several adjacent fields at once by using this method.

HANDS On

Improving the Tables

You can improve the appearance and efficiency of the tables in your database by adding descriptions, modifying field sizes, and making other changes. In this activity, you'll practice the skills you've learned in this lesson by making some modifications to the two tables you created.

1. **With the BFCustomers Table Design view still open, change the field size of the ContactLastName field to** 30.

2. **Change the size of the BillingAddress field to** 50.

3. **Change the size of the City field to** 30.

4. **Change the size of the StateOrProvince field to** 2.

5. **Type** List preferences, allergies, and shipping notes **in the Description for the Notes field.**

Your Design view window should resemble the one in Figure 2.23. Now that you're through modifying the BFCustomers table, you need to save again to preserve your changes.

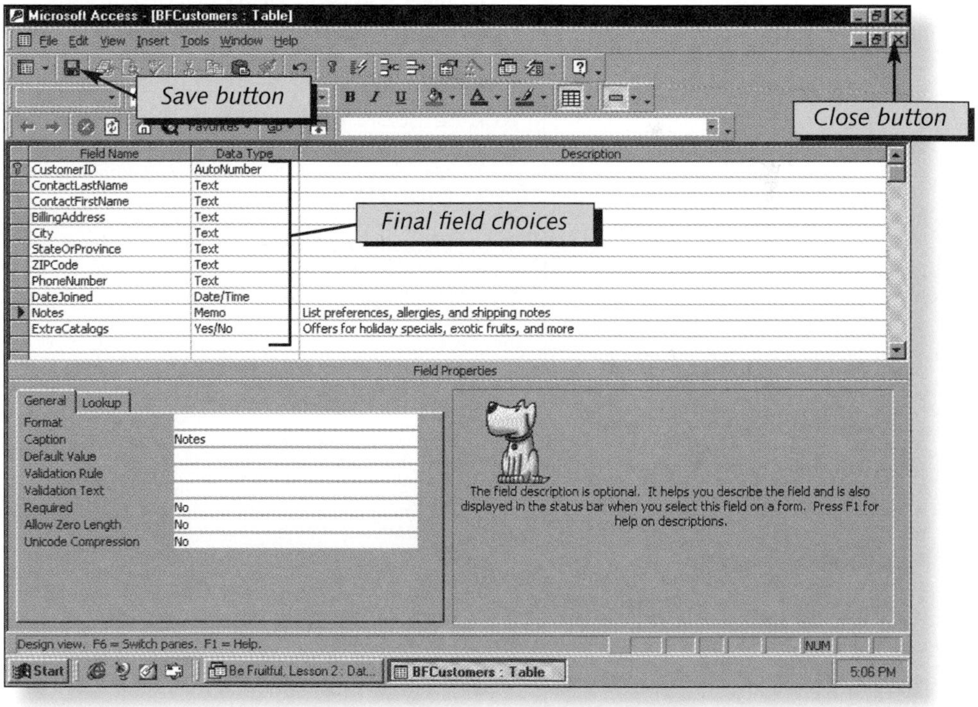

Figure 2.23
BFCustomers table in Design view

6. Click the **Save button** 🖫.

Since you named and saved this table earlier, Access saves the updated table without first prompting you for a table name.

7. Close the BFCustomers table.

8. Select the BFOrders table in the Database window and click the **Design button** 🗗 Design .

9. Create captions for each of the fields shown in Table 2.5.

TABLE 2.5	CAPTIONS FOR YOUR TABLE
Field	**Caption**
OrderNumber	Order No.
CustomerID	Customer ID
OrderDate	Order Date
FruitType	Fruit Type
ShippingAmount	Shipping Amt.
PaymentDate	Payment Date
PaymentAmount	Payment Amt.
PaymentType	Payment Type

10. Save and close the BFOrders table.

11. Click **Options** on the Tools menu, click the **General tab**, and select the **Compact on Close option**, if necessary.

As shown in Figure 2.24, a check mark appears in the Compact on Close box. Remember, choosing this option minimizes the size of a database and improves performance, if neccessary.

12. Click **OK**.

13. Close the *Be Fruitful, Lesson 2* database.

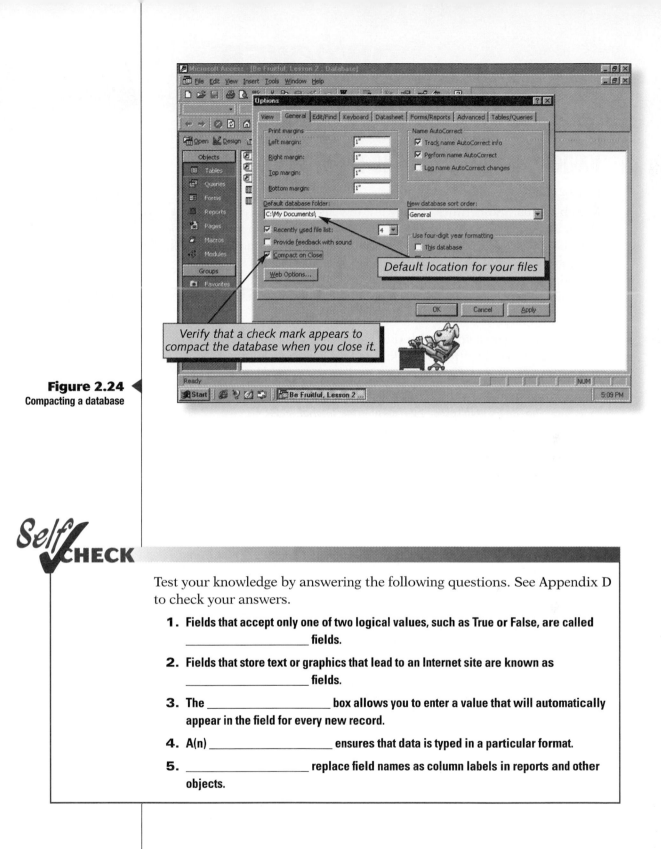

Figure 2.24
Compacting a database

Self CHECK

Test your knowledge by answering the following questions. See Appendix D to check your answers.

1. Fields that accept only one of two logical values, such as True or False, are called _____ fields.

2. Fields that store text or graphics that lead to an Internet site are known as _____ fields.

3. The _____ box allows you to enter a value that will automatically appear in the field for every new record.

4. A(n) _____ ensures that data is typed in a particular format.

5. _____ replace field names as column labels in reports and other objects.

ON*the*WEB

NAVIGATING AND RETURNING TO FAVORITE SITES

In Lesson 1, you learned that you can navigate to Web pages using the Web toolbar. Sometimes you'll want to visit a Web site just once while you are working in Access. Other times, you'll find Web sites that you will visit often, so you'll want to be able to return to them. Regardless, these sites may not be directly related to a specific database. For that reason, Access allows you to access any Web site directly. You can even add the Web sites to a list of personal favorites so that you can return to them quickly and easily.

In this activity, you'll visit a Web site that provides information about a credit card. Be Fruitful is thinking about starting to accept this credit card as payment from customers, but you would like to learn more first.

1. Open the *Be Fruitful, Lesson 2* database in the *Tutorial* folder.

2. Click the **Go button** ⌷ on the Web toolbar and click **Open**.

The Open Internet Address dialog box appears.

3. In the Address box, type www.novusnet.com and click **OK**.

If your connection to the Internet is already active, Access will jump directly to the Novus Web site. If your connection is not active, sign in or connect to your Internet service provider to continue.

The Novus credit card Web page appears. Novus offers several popular credit cards including the Discover Card. Be Fruitful currently accepts Visa and MasterCard as payment and is trying to learn more about the benefits of accepting the Discover Card as well. You'll use this Web page to explore those benefits.

4. Explore the links on the Novus Web page to learn about the services Novus offers and about becoming a Novus merchant.

If a connection to a Web site is taking too long or if you need to cancel for any other reason, click the Stop Current Jump button ⊗ on the Web toolbar.

5. Close the browser window and return to Access by clicking the taskbar button.

As you may realize, hundreds of thousands of Web sites are available at the click of a mouse button. With so many sites available, you may have difficulty keeping track of the ones that you'll use most often. Access provides an easy way to do just that. You can keep a list of favorites or bookmarks to which you can return quickly.

6. Type www.fedex.com in the Address box of the Web toolbar and press ⌷Enter⌷.

In a moment, the Federal Express home page will appear on your screen. Be Fruitful sometimes uses this delivery service for rush deliveries.

7. Explore the links on this page. See if you can find out what the cost would be to mail a 10-pound package valued at $50.00 from the city in which you live to ZIP Code 44117. Assume that you would use a FedEx box and schedule a FedEx courier to pick up the package.

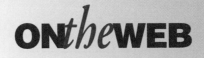
8. Return to the Federal Express home page.

You can return to a home page by using the Back button ⬅ or by typing its address in the Address box. Some Web pages offer a hyperlink that you can click to return to the home page.

9. Add this site to your list of favorite places.

The steps you take to add an Internet site to your list of favorites will vary depending on the browser software you are using. Most browsers show a Favorites or Bookmarks menu from which you can select an option such as Add to Favorites or Add Bookmark. If you are unsure how to add this site to your list of favorite places, access the Help menu on your browser software.

10. Close the browser window.

11. Click the *Be Fruitful, Lesson 2* database taskbar button.

Access allows you to add databases and other documents to your list of favorites. You can use this feature to open documents quickly that you frequently use.

12. Click the **Favorites button** [Favorites ▾] on the Web toolbar and choose **Add to Favorites**.

13. When the Add To Favorites dialog box appears, make sure that *Be Fruitful, Lesson 2* appears in the File name box and click the **Add button**.

14. Close the Be Fruitful, Lesson 2 Database window.

Now you can return easily to the sites that you've designated as favorites or bookmarks.

15. Click the **Favorites button** [Favorites ▾] and click *Be Fruitful, Lesson 2* in the list of favorites that appears.

Access remembers where the database is stored and automatically retrieves the file. The Database window appears on the screen.

16. Click the **Favorites button** [Favorites ▾] and choose **FedEx** (or Welcome to FedEx) from the list of favorites that appears.

The Federal Express home page appears on the screen. Notice that you did not type the address to return to this Web page.

17. Close all browser windows, disconnect from the Internet, and return to Access.

18. Close the open database and exit Access.

Warning

You may proceed directly to the exercises for this lesson. If, however, you are finished with your computer session, "shut down" the computer you are using following the procedures for your lab or school environment.

Lesson Summary & Exercises

SUMMARY

Lesson 2 taught you the importance of planning and organizing. You learned how to determine the fields required in your tables and how to separate information for easy access later. You also learned to modify existing tables including changing the field properties. These skills will increase your efficiency in the workplace. You learned how easy it is to add favorites to your Web browser and in Access.

Now that you have completed this lesson, you should be able to do the following:

- Determine the purpose of your database. (Access-58)
- Determine the categories of information needed in a database. (Access-58)
- Determine how many tables are needed in a database. (Access-59)
- Determine which fields should go in each table and how the tables will work together. (Access-60)
- Create a new database. (Access-61)
- Create a table using the Table Wizard. (Access-63)
- Select fields using the Table Wizard. (Access-63)
- Remove and rename fields with the Table Wizard. (Access-65)
- Select a primary key and name the table in the Table Wizard. (Access-66)
- Create a table using Design view. (Access-69)
- Select data types. (Access-71)
- Add field names and types. (Access-73)
- Edit field sizes. (Access-75)
- Modify and set other field properties. (Access-76)
- Choose a primary key in Design view. (Access-78)
- Save the table design. (Access-79)
- Understand relationships among tables. (Access-80)
- Modify tables using Design view. (Access-81)
- Add captions to fields. (Access-81)
- Add and remove fields. (Access-82)
- Move fields. (Access-84)
- Navigate the Web, set favorite sites, and return to them. (Access-88)

CONCEPTS REVIEW

1 TRUE/FALSE

Circle T if the statement is true and F if the statement is false.

T F **1.** Creating a table in Design view allows you more flexibility than when you create one with the Table Wizard.

T F **2.** The Objects bar in the Database window allows you to view existing tables, forms, and other objects quickly.

T F **3.** To relate two tables to each other, they must share a common field.

T F **4.** When you use the Undo command, only your last action is reversed.

T F **5.** Text, Number, and Currency are examples of data types.

T F **6.** Object names can contain up to 104 characters.

T F **7.** You should always create at least two tables that contain redundant data to help you check for data-entry errors.

T F **8.** In Design view, the small box to the left of each field is called the row selector.

T F **9.** The extension of *.sdb* is used to identify Access database files.

T F **10.** Captions are automatically created when you type field names in Design view.

2 MATCHING

Match each of the terms on the left with the definitions on the right.

TERMS

1. primary key
2. input mask
3. row selector
4. AutoNumber
5. Date/Time
6. default value
7. Undo
8. common field
9. Number
10. insertion point

DEFINITIONS

a. Data type for numbers that will be used to perform calculations

b. Value that Access enters into fields automatically

c. Feature that enables you to reverse your previous action

d. Field of same name in two tables that enables you to link those tables

e. Flashing vertical line that appears in text boxes

f. Data type that enables you to perform date arithmetic

g. Field property that forces your data into a particular format

h. Box that you click to highlight an entire field in Design view

i. Field or fields that uniquely identify each record in a table

j. Field that Access increments by 1 for each new record

Lesson Summary & Exercises

3 COMPLETION

Fill in the missing word or phrase for each of the following statements.

1. The _____ guides you through each step of creating a table, prompting you for the needed information.

2. When a field name is long or difficult to identify, you can use a(n) _____ to abbreviate or clarify.

3. In the top pane of the Table Design view window, you may specify the _____, _____, and _____ for each field.

4. To specify that a field must be filled in, set the _____ property to Yes.

5. The purpose of a(n) _____ is to format your data in a particular way.

6. To make sure your table is not lost due to a power outage, you should _____ your work frequently.

7. To navigate to a site, click the _____, on the Web toolbar.

8. Text fields can hold up to _____ characters.

9. To reverse your previous action, click the _____ button.

10. A(n) _____ is an option that controls the kind of information that can be entered into a field.

4 SHORT ANSWER

Write a brief answer to each of the following questions.

1. What must two tables share for you to be able to link them together?

2. List at least two reasons to divide your data into multiple tables instead of placing all the information in one large table.

3. Identify one advantage and one disadvantage of creating tables using the Table Wizard.

4. List two reasons why you should use a Date/Time field rather than a Text field for dates.

5. Which data type would you use for Social Security numbers and why?

6. Explain why you can't enter duplicate values in primary key fields.

7. Under what circumstances would you use a Memo data type rather than a Text data type?

8. List the steps you would perform to add a new field between the DatePurchased and Amount fields in a table.

9. List the steps you would perform to remove the Amount field from a table.

10. How would you make a field called AccountNumber the primary key in a table when in the Design view?

5 IDENTIFICATION

Provide a brief description of each element of the Table Wizard dialog box shown in Figure 2.25.

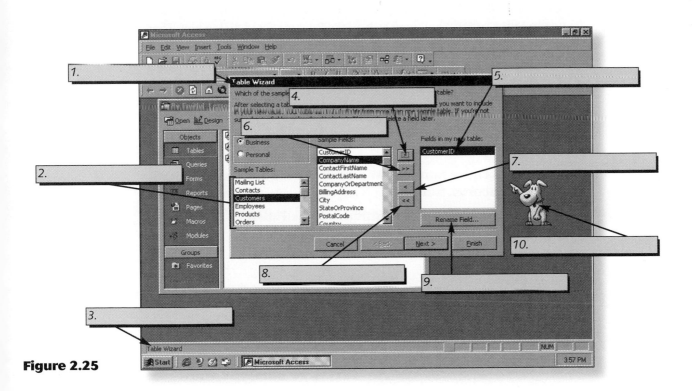

Figure 2.25

SKILLS REVIEW

Complete each of the Skills Review problems in sequential order to review your Access skills to create a database and add and modify tables.

1 Create a New Database

1. Start Access. When the Microsoft Access dialog box appears, click the **Blank Access database option** and click **OK**.

2. In the Save in box, navigate to the ***Skills Review*** folder on your Student Data Disk.

3. Type Smyth Business College, Lesson 2 in the File name box. Click the **Create button**.

4. In the Database window, double-click the **Create table by using wizard option**.

5. In the Sample Tables box, click **Students**.

6. Click the **StudentID field name** and click the **Add Field button** [>].

7. Double-click the **FirstName field** to add it to the Fields in my new table box.

8. Add the following fields to the Fields in my new table box: MiddleName, LastName, ParentsNames, Address, City, StateOrProvince, PostalCode, PhoneNumber, and Major.

2 Work with Tables

1. Click the **ParentsNames field** in the Fields in my new table box and click the **Remove Field button** [<].

2. Click the **StateOrProvince field** in the Fields in my new table box. Click the **Rename Field button** and type State in the Rename Field dialog box. Then click **OK**.

3. Click **Next** in the Table Wizard dialog box.

4. Edit the suggested name *Students* to be Student Information.

5. Click the **No, I'll set the primary key. option** and click **Next**.

6. Select the **StudentID field** from the drop-down list, if it is not already selected.

7. Click the **Consecutive numbers Microsoft Access assigns automatically to new records. button**, if it is not already selected. Then, click **Next**.

8. Click **Modify the table design. option** and click **Finish**.

9. Close the table by clicking the **Close button** [X].

3 Create a Table in Design View

1. Double-click the **Create table in Design view option**. Type StudentID in the first row of the Field Name column; then press [Tab].

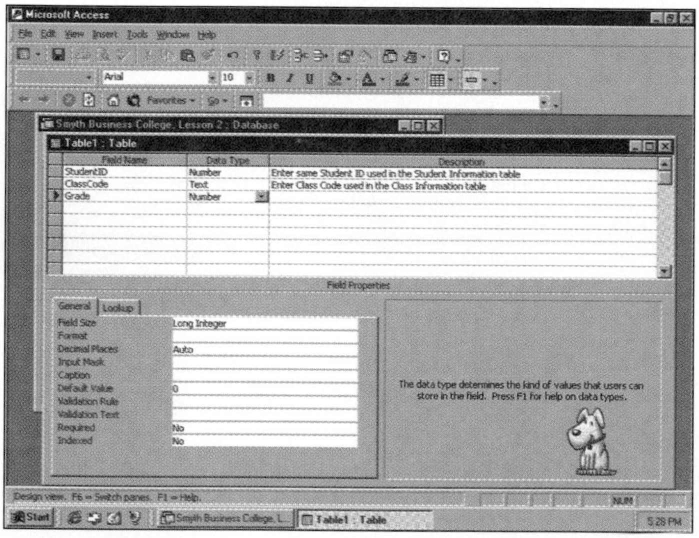

Figure 2.26

2. Click the **Data type arrow**, click **Number**, and press [Tab].

3. Type Enter same Student ID used in the Student Information table in the Description column and press [Tab].

4. Type ClassCode as the second field name. Press [Tab] twice to accept Text as the data type and to move to the Description column.

5. Type Enter Class Code used in the Class Information table in the Description column and press [Tab].

6. Type Grade as the third field name and press [Tab].

7. Click the **Data type arrow** and click **Number** (Figure 2.26).

4 Change Field Properties and Save Tables

1. Click the **ClassCode field**, press ⌗, and type 7 in the Field Size text box.

2. Click the **Grade field** and press ⌗. In the Field Size box, click **Byte**.

3. Click the **ClassCode field**, press ⌗, and click the **Input Mask text box**. Type LLL000 (three Ls and three zeros). This input mask will require three letters and three numbers to be typed when you add data to this field.

4. Click the **row selector** to the left of the StudentID field to select the entire field.

5. Drag to include the ClassCode field and both rows will be highlighted.

6. Click the **Primary Key button** ⌗.

7. Click **Save** ⌗, type Grades for Accounting Classes in the Table Name box, and click **OK**.

8. Close the Table Design window by clicking the **Close button** ⌧.

5 Add Captions

1. In the Database window, click the **Student Information table** and click the **Design button** ⌗.

2. Click the **PostalCode field**, press ⌗, click the **Caption box**, double-click the word **Postal**, and type ZIP.

3. In the next blank row, type FullTime in the Field Name column and press ⌗.

4. Click **Yes/No** in the Data Type column.

5. Type Full Time in the Caption text box.

6 Add a Field

1. Click anywhere within the Major field in the top pane of the Design window.

2. Click the **Insert Rows button** ⌗.

3. Type GradePointAverage in the Field name column and press ⌗.

4. Type n to select the Number data type and press ⌗.

5. Type the caption GPA in the Caption text box.

7 Remove Fields, Undo a Change, and Move a Field

1. Click anywhere in the FirstName field.

2. Click the **Delete Rows button** ⌗.

Lesson Summary & Exercises

3. Since you realize you meant to delete the MiddleName field instead, click the **Undo Delete button** 🔄.

4. Click the **MiddleName field** and click the **Delete Rows button** ⊟.

5. Click the **row selector** in front of the FirstName field.

6. Drag the row selector down so that the dark horizontal line appears directly below the LastName field and release.

8 Finalize the Tables

1. In the Student Information table, change the field size of the LastName field to 30, the FirstName field to 30, the Address field to 50, the City field to 30, the State field to 2, and the Major field to 20.

2. Click **Save** 💾 and then close the Student Information table.

3. Click the **Grades for Accounting Classes table** and click the **Design button** 🔧 Design.

4. Create these captions: Student ID for the StudentID field and Class Code for the ClassCode field.

5. Click **Save** 💾 and then close the Grades for Accounting Classes table.

6. Click **Options** on the Tools menu. On the General tab, click the **Compact on Close option** and click **OK**.

7. Close the *Smyth Business College, Lesson 2* database.

LESSON APPLICATIONS

1 Create a Database and Use the Table Wizard

Create a new database and use the Table Wizard to create a table, add fields, remove and rename fields, name the table, and assign a primary key.

1. Start Access and create a new database. Name the database Payton Properties, Lesson 2 and save it in the *Lesson Applications* folder.

2. Create a table using the Table Wizard. Use the Employees sample table to add the following fields: DepartmentName, EmployeeID, FirstName, LastName, Address, City, StateOrProvince, PostalCode, HomePhone, Birthdate, and DateHired.

3. While using the Wizard, remove the Birthdate field from the Fields in my new table box.

4. Rename the EmployeeID field to AgentID.

5. Name the table Employees and select the AgentID field as the primary key. Close the table.

2 Create a Table in Design View

Create a table in Design view and add field names, data types, and descriptions.

1. Open the **Payton Properties, Lesson 2** database in the **Lesson Applications** folder on your Student Data Disk. In the Database window, create a new table in Design view.

2. Enter the field names, data types, and descriptions found in Table 2.6.

TABLE 2.6	INFORMATION TO ADD	
Field Name	**Data Type**	**Description**
Address	Text	Enter street address of home for sale
Bedrooms	Number	
Baths	Number	
Rooms	Number	
YearBuilt	Number	
Price	Currency	
SellingPrice	Currency	
AgentID	Number	Enter Agent ID from Employees table

3. Assign the Address field as the primary key.

4. Save the table as Homes for Sale.

3 Change Field Properties and Add Captions

Change field sizes and other properties in the Homes for Sale table. Then add captions to a few of the fields.

1. In the **Payton Properties Lesson 2** database in the **Lesson Applications** folder on your Student Data Disk, open the Homes for Sale table in Design view.

2. Change the field size of the Address field to 40.

3. Click the Price field and change the Decimal Places box in the lower pane to 0 (zero).

4. Click the SellingPrice field and change the Decimal Places box in the lower pane to 0 (zero).

5. Click the Baths field. Change the Field Size to Decimal, change the Format to General Number, change the Precision to 4, and change the Scale to 1.

6. Add appropriate captions to the YearBuilt, SellingPrice, and AgentID fields.

7. Save the table design.

Lesson Summary & Exercises

4 Insert and Remove Fields

Add and delete fields by using the Insert Rows and Delete Rows buttons.

1. Open the **Payton Properties, Lesson 2** database in the **Lesson Applications** folder on your Student Data Disk. Use the Insert Rows button to add a field between the Baths and Rooms fields. In the new field, type SquareFeet as the field name and assign Number as the data type.

2. In the lower pane for the SquareFeet field, type Sq. Feet as the caption, assign a format of Standard, and enter 0 (zero) in the Decimal Places box.

3. Insert another field between the Rooms and YearBuilt fields.

4. Since you decide that you don't want to add another field, use the Undo command to reverse the change.

5. Delete the SellingPrice field, since this table will only list homes currently for sale.

6. Save the table design and close the table.

5 Move Fields and Change Field Properties

Edit the Employees table to change field sizes and modify the order of fields.

1. Open the **Payton Properties, Lesson 2** database in the **Lesson Applications** folder on your Student Data Disk. Open the Employees table in Design view.

2. Create a caption for the AgentID field.

3. Change the field size of the DepartmentName field to 20 and type Sales in the Default Value box.

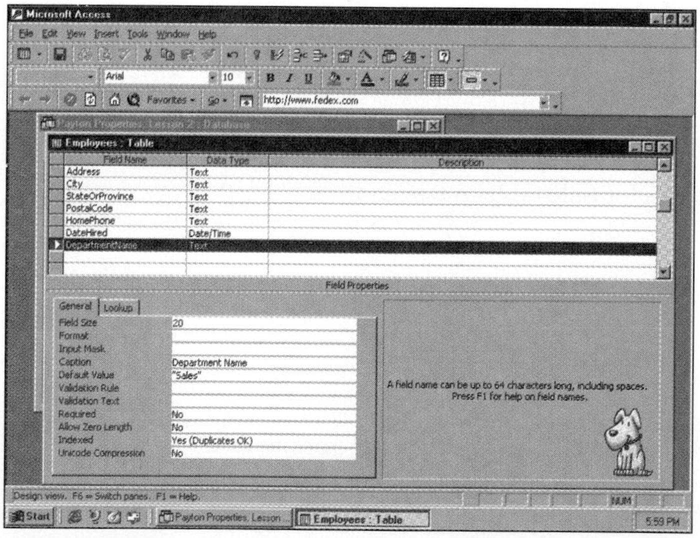

Figure 2.27

4. Change the field size of the FirstName field to 20, the LastName field to 30, the Address field to 50, the City field to 30, and the StateOrProvince field to 2.

5. Click the PostalCode, HomePhone, and DateHired fields, one at a time, and notice the input masks that the Wizard entered.

6. Reverse the order of the FirstName and LastName fields.

7. Move the DepartmentName field to appear as the last field (Figure 2.27).

8. Save the table design and close the table.

9. Open the Options dialog box on the Tools menu. On the General tab, select the Compact on Close command.

10. Close the **Payton Properties, Lesson 2** database and exit Access.

PROJECTS

1 Calling All Be Fruitful Employees

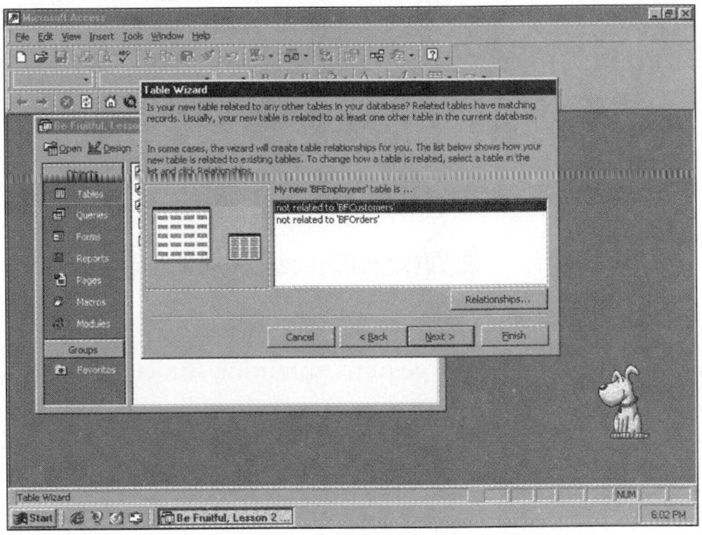

As an employee of the Be Fruitful fruit-of-the-month club, you've already created tables to hold customer information and order information. Your supervisor has requested that you develop a third table to hold employee data. Open the **Be Fruitful, Lesson 2** database in the **Tutorial** folder. Create a table with the Table Wizard. Base your new table on the Employees sample table. Add the following fields: EmployeeID, SocialSecurityNumber, LastName, FirstName, MiddleName, Address, City, StateOrProvince, PostalCode, and Salary. Rename the Postal Code field to ZIPCode and the StateOrProvince field to State. Remove the MiddleName and Salary fields. Name the table BFEmployees and let Access create the primary key for you. Since other tables exist, the wizard will ask if the new table is related to any of the existing tables in the **Be Fruitful, Lesson 2** database (Figure 2.28). Click Next to indicate that this new table is not related.

Figure 2.28

In the final Table Wizard dialog box, choose the *Modify the table design.* option and click Finish to view the newly created table in Table Design view. Notice the primary key. On a separate sheet of paper, state the field that was selected as the primary key and explain why you think Access chose this field as the primary key. When you are finished, close the table.

2 Improving the BFEmployees Table

To improve the efficiency of your database, you decide to reduce the size of some of your fields and add some captions. Open the BFEmployees table in the **Be Fruitful, Lesson 2** database in Design view and make the changes described in Table 2.7. Then, save and close the table. Make sure the Compact on Close option is selected and close the **Be Fruitful, Lesson 2** database.

Lesson Summary & Exercises

TABLE 2.7	CHANGES TO BFEMPLOYEES TABLE	
Field Name	**Property**	**Change to**
SocialSecurityNumber	Caption	SS#
ZIPCode	Caption	ZIP Code
LastName	Field Size	30
FirstName	Field Size	20
Address	Field Size	50
City	Field Size	30
State	Field Size	2

3 When Does that Class Start?

You work in the Administration building at Smyth Business College and are in charge of maintaining student records and class schedules. In the Skills Review activities, you created tables to hold student information and grades. Now you need to create a table to hold class-scheduling information. Open the **Smyth Business College, Lesson 2** database in the **Skills Review** folder. Create a table in Design view called Class Schedules. Include the fields and assign the properties found in Table 2.8. Assign the ClassCode field as the primary key and save and close the table.

TABLE 2.8	INFORMATION FOR CLASS SCHEDULES TABLE			
Field	**Data Type**	**Field Size**	**Caption**	**Input Mask**
ClassCode	Text	6	Class Code	LLL000 (three zeros)
ClassName	Text	30	Class Name	
Time	Text	20		
Days	Text	5		

4 Improving the Class Schedule

You decide that the Class Schedules table could be improved by adding a field so that students know which instructor teaches each course. You also decide to change some other elements of the table. Open the Class Schedules table of the **Smyth Business College, Lesson 2** database in the **Skills Review** folder in Design view. Add a field between the ClassName and Time fields called Instructor. Assign a data type of Text and a field size of 30. Switch the order of the Time and Days fields. Save and close the table. Make sure the Compact on Close option is selected and close the **Smyth Business College, Lesson 2** database.

5 Tracking Your Agents

At Payton Properties, you have been tracking the homes sold. Your manager has asked you to provide a table in the existing database that tracks the number of homes sold, the number of new listings, and the commissions earned by each sales agent. Open the **Payton Properties, Lesson 2** database in the **Lesson Applications** folder. Create a table in Design view called Agent Statistics. Include the fields and assign the properties found in Table 2.9. Assign the AgentID field as the primary key and save and close the table.

TABLE 2.9	INFORMATION FOR AGENT STATISTICS TABLE		
Field	**Data Type**	**Field Size**	**Caption**
AgentID	Number	Long Integer	Agent ID
AgentLastName	Text	30	Last Name
Y-T-DHomesSold	Number		Homes Sold
Y-T-DateListings	Number		Listings
Y-T-DateCommissions	Currency		Commissions

6 Deleting Redundant Information

Since each sales agent's name is provided in the Employees table, you realize that repeating this information in the table you created in Project 5 could cause potential problems. Open the Agent Statistics table of the **Payton Properties, Lesson 2** database in the **Lesson Applications** folder in Design view. Delete the AgentLastName field. Change the data type of the Y-T-DListings to Text. Then, since you realize this change was made in error, undo the change. Save and close the table. Make sure the Compact on Close option is selected and close the **Payton Properties, Lesson 2** database.

7 Making Sense Out of a Lot of Data

Electro Shop, a retail store that sells televisions, stereos, and other electronics has asked you to set up a database for them. After interviewing several employees who will use the database, you've discovered that they want to include the following information in the database:

- Employee names and ID numbers
- Employee's Social Security numbers
- The hourly rate earned by each employee

- The employee's working status (full time or part time)
- A product number that identifies each product they carry
- The general category (TV, stereo, VCR, etc.) for each product they carry
- The brand of each product
- The price of each product
- Notes about each product
- A sale number for each sale made in December and which salesperson made the sale
- The product ID for each item sold in December and the quantity sold in each individual sale
- The date of each sale

On paper, sketch how you would set up tables to contain the information to be included in the database. Provide a name for each table. (Hint: Use at least two or three tables of logical categories.) Under each table name, list the fields to be included and the data type of each field.

8 Setting Up the Electro Shop Tables

Create and name a new database *Electro Shop, Lesson 2* in the *Projects* folder. Use the wizard or Design view to create two or three new tables that contain the fields that you listed in Project 7. If you did not complete Project 7, ask your instructor to provide the list of tables and fields. Assign appropriate data types, field sizes, captions, and other field properties to each field. Set a primary key for each table. After saving and closing each table, choose the Compact on Close option and close the *Electro Shop, Lesson 2* database.

9 Getting Product Information Online

Reopen the *Electro Shop, Lesson 2* database in the *Projects* folder and connect to the Internet. A friend told you that the *Consumer Reports* magazine publishes a Web site with information about electronics that might be useful to you during your work at Electro Shop. Navigate to the site at www.consumerreports.com and click the Electronics link. *Do not subscribe to the site,* but look only at those sections that you can view without a subscription. Find and read the article featured in the Electronics section. Return to the Consumer Reports home page and designate the page as a favorite place. Return to the *Electro Shop, Lesson 2* database and then use the Favorites menu to return to the Consumer Reports site. Close the browser and the *Electro Shop, Lesson 2* database. Disconnect from the Internet unless your instructor tells you to remain connected.

Lesson Summary & Exercises

Project in Progress

10 Setting Up the I-Comm Tables

Create and name a new database *I-Comm* in the **Projects** folder. Use the Table Wizard to create a table called Customers and use Design view to create a table called Projects. Create and modify the two tables so that they contain the fields and field properties listed in Table 2.10. After saving and closing each table, choose the Compact on Close option and close the *I-Comm* database.

TABLE 2.10	INFORMATION FOR TABLES			
Field Name	**Data Type**	**Field Size**	**Caption**	**Other**
Table Name: Customers				
*CustomerID	AutoNumber	Long Integer	Customer ID	
CompanyName	Text	50	Company Name	
ContactLastName	Text	30	Contact Last Name	
ContactFirstName	Text	20	Contact First Name	
ContactTitle	Text	30	Contact Title	
BillingAddress	Text	50	Billing Address	
City	Text	30		
State	Text	2		
ZIPCode	Text	20	ZIP Code	
PhoneNumber	Text	30	Phone Number	
Table Name: Projects				
*ProjectID	AutoNumber	Long Integer	Project ID	
CustomerID	Number	Long Integer	Customer ID	
ItemDeveloped	Text	30	Item Developed	
ServicesPerformed	Memo		Services Performed	
I-CommProjectManager	Number	Long Integer	I-Comm Project Mgr.	
TotalHours	Number	Long Integer	Total Hours	
Fee	Currency	Currency		zero decimal places

* Set as primary key.

Adding and Maintaining Data in Tables

CONTENTS

OBJECTIVES

After you complete this lesson, you will be able to do the following:

- Add data to your tables in Datasheet view.
- Copy and paste data from another database.
- Import data from another application.
- Navigate the datasheet.
- Select fields, columns, and records.
- Edit records.
- Delete records.
- Undo changes.
- Search for and replace particular strings of characters.
- Change column widths and row heights in the datasheet.
- Rearrange datasheet columns.
- Hide and freeze datasheet columns.
- Understand the types of relationships that can exist between two tables.
- Create a relationship between two tables.
- Open and close a subdatasheet.
- Use a search engine.

This lesson develops the skills you need to create, use, and navigate the database. You will learn all the basics about entering data in the tables. As soon as you enter data, you must know how to edit to correct errors and then how to update records. In addition to correcting errors, editing also means verifying that your data is correct and that you have established the correct relationships between your tables. Some of the most beneficial editing skills you learn are how to erase data and how to undo your changes.

Creating new databases
and editing the existing
information are essential
skills in the workplace.
Entering data in a table
gives you the power to
organize information in a
clear format. Then, as you
learn to edit data, you can
correct errors, update
records, modify table
design, and establish table
relationships.

HANDS
On

Access
BASICS

Opening a Table

1. Open the database that
contains the table.

2. Click the table name.

3. Click the Open button
in the Database
window.

Another Way

To open a table, double-
click the table name in the
Database window.

ENTERING RECORDS USING A DATASHEET

In Lesson 2, you learned how to create tables. You built table structures—
choosing the fields that your tables would include and their properties. Now
that these structures are in place, you're ready to actually enter data into
them. You can add data to your tables by using custom forms, which you'll
learn more about in Lesson 5. However, Access also provides the ***datasheet,***
a layout of rows and columns that permits you to add, edit, and view your
data immediately. The column-and-row format of your datasheet will
remind you of a spreadsheet or worksheet if you've ever used one. Even if
you devise custom forms for data entry, the datasheet remains useful for
browsing a large number of records at once and making minor additions
and modifications as you go along.

Opening a Table

Before you can add data, you must open the table. An open table displays in
Datasheet view by default.

Opening the BFCustomers Table

In this activity, you'll open a table.

> **1.** If necessary, turn on your computer. Then start Access.
>
> **2.** When the initial Microsoft Access dialog box appears, double-click **More Files**
> in the list box at the bottom of the dialog box. Navigate to the *Tutorial* folder on your
> Student Data Disk and double-click *Be Fruitful, Lesson 3.*

Access displays the Be Fruitful, Lesson 3 Database window.

> **3.** Click the **Tables option** in the Database window, and click the
> **BFCustomers table**.
>
> **4.** Click the **Open button** 📂Open in the Database window.

Access opens the BFCustomers table in Datasheet view, as shown in Figure
3.1. You can see some of the field names (or captions) at the top of each column, but the table is empty; that is, it contains no data. A single blank row
appears, waiting for your input.

The triangle to the left of the record indicates the ***current record,*** sometimes called the record with the focus. The box to the left of each record in
Datasheet view is called the ***record selector.***

Adding Records

After you open a table, the data displays in Datasheet view—that is, in column and row format. In the case of the BFCustomers table, you'll see no
data, since you have not yet entered any. You can use the mouse or keyboard
commands to move from field to field so that you can type new data in the
record.

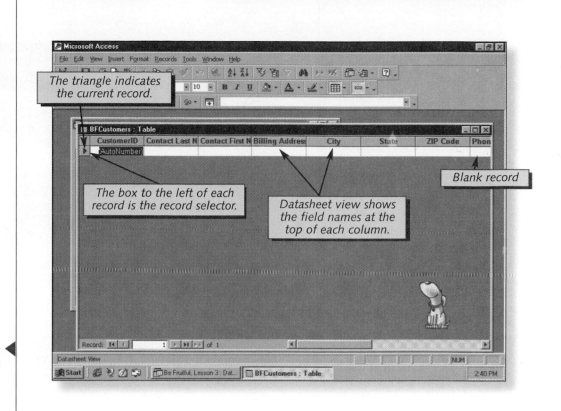

The triangle indicates the current record.

The box to the left of each record is the record selector.

Datasheet view shows the field names at the top of each column.

Blank record

Figure 3.1
BFCustomers table

Adding Data to the BFCustomers Table

In this activity, you'll type the information for several records in the table.

1. Press `Tab` or click the blank box under the Contact Last Name field.

Access moves the insertion point into the Contact Last Name field.

2. Type Kenber in the Contact Last Name field and press `Tab`.

As soon as you start typing, Access automatically enters a value into the Customer ID field for this first customer. When you press `Tab`, the insertion point moves into the Contact First Name field. Note that Access has created a second blank record with an asterisk (*) in the record selector. An asterisk indicates a new record in which you can type data. The record in which you are typing has a pencil icon in the record selector, as shown in Figure 3.2. The pencil icon indicates that you are currently editing the record and the edits have not yet been saved.

3. Type Franklin in the Contact First Name field and press `Tab`.

Access moves the insertion point into the Billing Address field.

4. Type 1777 Lois Ln. in the Billing Address field and press `Tab`.

5. Type Rock Creek in the City field and press `Tab`.

6. Type NC in the State field and press `Tab`.

7. In the ZIP Code field, type 28333 and then type 1234.

Note that you don't have to enter the hyphen; because of the input mask, Access automatically formats the ZIP Code as 28333-1234.

8. Press `Tab` to move to the Phone Number field, type 919, type 555, and finally type 9999 and press `Tab`.

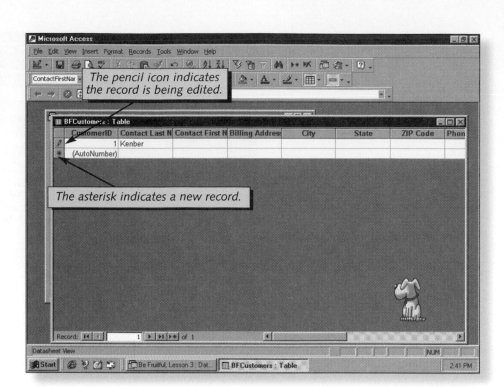

Figure 3.2
Typing data for a record

Notice that Access once again enters the punctuation because of the input mask associated with the Phone Number field. Access scrolls the display so you can see the Date Joined field in full. Only some of the fields of a large table show in Datasheet view at once. Pressing ⌷Tab⌷ automatically scrolls the display to bring any additional fields into view.

9. Type 4/15/94 in the Date Joined field and press ⌷Tab⌷.

 If you enter an invalid date, such as 13/15/92, you will see a warning box about your error. If you enter 13/5/92, Access will assume that you intend to enter the 13th day of the 5th month and will translate the date to 5/13/1992.

A description of the Notes field appears on the status bar as shown in Figure 3.3.

10. Press ⌷Tab⌷ to leave the Notes field blank.

You should now see a box in the Extra Catalogs field. Clicking this box adds a check mark to the box, meaning Yes. Leaving the box blank means No. Also, since you entered a description for this field, the description appears in the status bar.

11. Press ⌷Tab⌷ to accept the default value of *No.*

12. Press ⌷Tab⌷ and type Reid in the Contact Last Name field. Then press ⌷Tab⌷ again.

As before, Access automatically increments the value in the Customer ID field and creates a new blank record at the end of the table.

13. Type Alice in the Contact First Name field and press ⌷Tab⌷ .

14. Type 7374 Backwoods Rd. in the Billing Address field and press ⌷Tab⌷ .

If you want to move back to
a previous field, you can
click the field or press ⌷←⌷ .

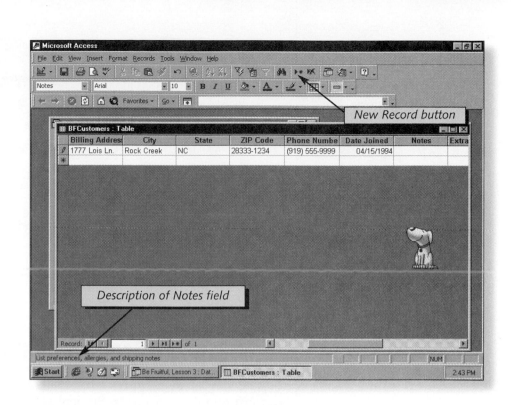

Figure 3.3 ◀
Scrolling the records

As you typed, some of the address scrolled out of view. When you pressed
⌨Tab to move to the next field, only the beginning of the address appeared.
The information is still there, even though you cannot see everything in the
datasheet display. Later in this lesson, you'll change column widths and row
heights so you can see more of your data on the screen.

15. Type Sebastopol **in the City field and press** ⌨Tab **.**

16. Type CA **in the State field and press** ⌨Tab **.**

17. Type 97777-1111 **in the ZIP Code field, press** ⌨Tab **, and type** (415) 555-5432 **in the
Phone Number field. (Remember, you do not need to type the punctuation.)**

18. **Press** ⌨Tab **and type** 11/21/94 **in the Date Joined field.**

You have now entered all of the data for the second record. The remaining
fields will be left blank or take on their default value.

19. **Click the New Record button** ▶* **on the Database toolbar.**

Access moves down to the next row (the new blank record) into which you
can enter data.

20. **Enter the names and addresses listed in Table 3.1. Leave all Notes fields blank and
retain the default setting of *No* for all the Extra Catalog fields.**

If you're used to word processing and spreadsheet programs, you may be
wondering when to save your data. Access automatically saves your data
when you move to a new record. If you want to save before that point, however—perhaps you're entering a long memo field—click Records on the
menu bar and then click Save Record or press ⌨Shift + ⌨Enter .

The New Record button
creates a new record at the
bottom of the table. You can
use this button to complete
your entry of a record. As
you saw with the entry of
the first record, pressing
⌨Tab in the last field also
moves you to a new blank
record.

Field	Record 3	Record 4	Record 5
TABLE 3.1	**NAMES AND ADDRESSES TO ENTER**		
Contact Last Name	Turlow	Zheng	O'Hara
Contact First Name	Will	Anne	Joan
Billing Address	1 Oak Pl.	25 Forest Knoll	2234 Hanley Pl.
City	Providence	Santa Rosa	Baltimore
State	RI	CA	MD
ZIP Code	02900-2338	99887-2355	21122-5634
Phone Number	(401) 555-9972	(707) 555-9876	(301) 555-4567
Date Joined	1/5/95	7/15/95	2/5/96

RETRIEVING DATA FROM ANOTHER TABLE

So that you can work with a more realistic amount of material, you'll now retrieve some data from the Student Data Disk. Because you want to add data from another database, you can't just open the other database. Instead, you'll learn a simple way to do so with standard Windows techniques for cutting and pasting. Remember, however, that this technique enables you to retrieve data only from Access, not from other programs; also, for this technique to work smoothly, you must be gathering data from a table with the same structure as the one into which you're placing the data.

Copying Data from Another Table

To retrieve data from another table, first open the table, select the data, and then issue the Copy command. The data is pasted to the Windows *Clipboard*—a temporary storage space in the memory of your computer. You can then paste the data to another location in the same database or to another database.

Copying Records from the Fruitful, Lesson 1 Database

In this activity, you will retrieve data from your Student Data Disk. To copy the data, you first have to open the table that contains the records you want to add.

1. Click **File** on the menu bar and click **Open**. Navigate to your Student Data Disk files.

2. Double-click the *Fruitful, Lesson 1* database.

Access BASICS

Copying Records from Another Table

1. Open the table from which you wish to copy records.

2. Select the records to copy.

3. Click the Copy button.

4. Close the table, answering Yes when the warning box asks if you want to save the data on the Clipboard.

You should see the Fruitful, Lesson 1 Database window. The BFCustomers, BFFruit, and BFOrders tables appear within the Tables box.

3. **Open the BFCustomers table in Datasheet view.**

4. **Click the field selector in front of record 6 and drag down to select records 6 through 35.**

Access highlights records 6 through 35 in the table, as shown in Figure 3.4.

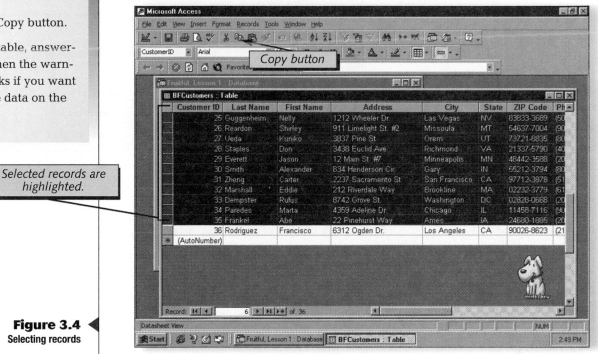

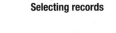
Selected records are highlighted.

Figure 3.4
Selecting records

Another Way

To copy, click Edit on the menu bar and click Copy.

5. Click the **Copy button** 📋 on the Database toolbar.

Although you can't see any change to the screen, Access has copied all of these records to the Clipboard.

6. Click the **Close button** ❌ to close the BFCustomers table.

Access displays a warning box about the data on the Clipboard, as shown in Figure 3.5.

7. Read the text in the warning box, and click **Yes** to save the data on the Clipboard.

Access closes the BFCustomers table and returns you to the Fruitful, Lesson 1 Database window.

Pasting Data into a Table

After you copy data to the Clipboard, you can paste the data into another table in the same database or in another database. Remember, for the pasting function to work well, the two tables must have very similar structures.

Figure 3.5
Clipboard warning

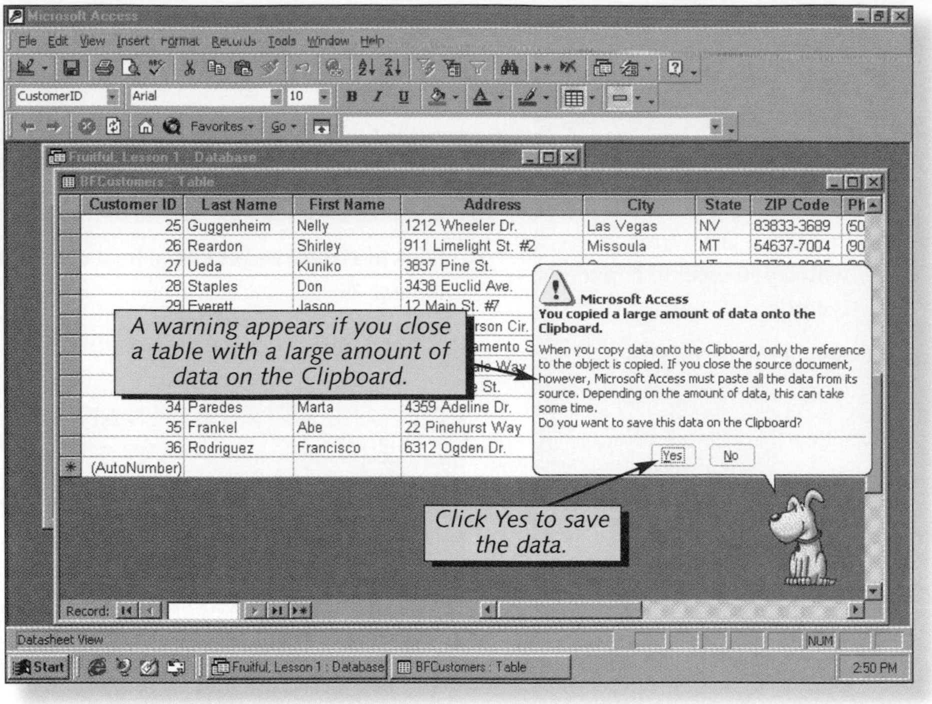

Pasting Data to the Be Fruitful, Lesson 3 Database

In this activity, you will reopen the **Be Fruitful, Lesson 3** database and copy the data on the Clipboard into the BFCustomers table.

1. Click the **Open button** 📄 on the Database toolbar. Navigate to and open the **Be Fruitful, Lesson 3** database in the *Tutorial* folder on your Student Data Disk.

2. Double-click the **BFCustomers table**.

You will see the BFCustomers table with the records that you entered earlier.

3. Click **Edit** on the menu bar and click **Paste Append**.

Note — If the Paste Append command doesn't appear, click the double arrow at the bottom of the Edit menu to display the expanded menu.

The Paste Append option lets you add records to the end of your table. Before the option adds the records, however, Access displays the message shown in Figure 3.6. In this box, you can click *Yes* to add the records or *No* to cancel the operation.

Warning — You can't use the normal Paste button 📋 on the Database toolbar to paste these records from the Clipboard; you must use the Paste Append command on the Edit menu.

4. Read the text in the dialog box and click **Yes** to add the records from the Clipboard to the BFCustomers table.

Access BASICS

Pasting Records to a Table

1. Open the table to which you want to paste records.

2. Click Edit on the menu bar and click Paste Append.

3. Click Yes when the message box asks if you want to paste the records.

Hints & Tips

Remember that you can copy and paste between tables with the same structure. If Access identifies a problem, Access creates a Paste Error table to hold the data that could not be pasted.

New records

Figure 3.6
Pasting records

5. Click anywhere within the table to remove the highlighting. Then click the Maximize button ☐.

The display at the bottom of the table window indicates that the table now contains 35 records.

6. Close the BFCustomers table.

HANDS On

Copying and Pasting Data to the BFOrders Table

Now that you've copied and pasted data from one table to another, you can reopen the first database and copy data from another table. In this activity, you will copy the records from a table on the Student Data Disk into your BFOrders table, using the same technique you used in the previous activity.

1. Open the *Fruitful, Lesson 1* database on your Student Data Disk. Open the BFOrders table in Datasheet view.

Note

*The names of the most recently used databases appear at the bottom of the File menu. You can click File on the menu bar and then click the **Fruitful, Lesson 1** file name to open the database.*

2. Press [Ctrl] + A to select all records.

All of the records in the BFOrders table are selected (or highlighted), as shown in Figure 3.7.

3. Click the Copy button 🖹 and then close the BFOrders table.

The warning box asks if you want to save the data you copied on the Clipboard.

Another Way

To highlight all records, click Edit on the menu bar and click Select All Records.

Figure 3.7
Selecting all records

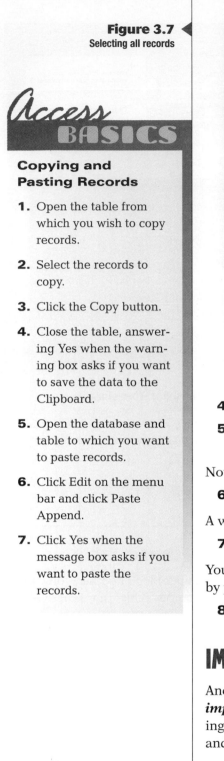

Copy button

Table name

You can press Ctrl + A to select all records at one time.

Copying and Pasting Records

1. Open the table from which you wish to copy records.

2. Select the records to copy.

3. Click the Copy button.

4. Close the table, answering Yes when the warning box asks if you want to save the data to the Clipboard.

5. Open the database and table to which you want to paste records.

6. Click Edit on the menu bar and click Paste Append.

7. Click Yes when the message box asks if you want to paste the records.

4. Click **Yes**.

5. Open the *Be Fruitful, Lesson 3* database in the *Tutorial* folder on your Student Data Disk. Open the BFOrders table.

Notice that no data has been entered into the table yet.

6. Click **Edit** on the menu bar and click **Paste Append**.

A warning box asks if you want to paste 187 records into the table.

7. Click **Yes**.

You now have a table with 187 records. Imagine how much time you saved by pasting the data rather than entering each record one at a time!

8. Close the BFOrders table.

IMPORTING DATA

Another method you can use to add data from another database is to *import*—the process of bringing data from one file into another. In importing, however, you copy an entire table into your database. The new records and the structure of the table you'll import are on your Student Data Disk.

HANDS On

Importing a Table from Another Database

In this activity, you will use Access's Import feature to bring all of the records from a table into your *Be Fruitful, Lesson 3* database.

1. With the Be Fruitful, Lesson 3 Database window on the screen, click **File** on the menu bar, point to **Get External Data** on the expanded menu, and then click **Import** on the submenu.

Importing a Table

1. Click File on the menu bar, point to Get External Data, and click Import.

2. Double-click the database name in the Import dialog box.

3. Click the table name you wish to import in the Import Objects dialog box and click OK.

The Import dialog box appears.

2. **Navigate to and double-click the** *Fruitful, Lesson 1* **database on your Student Data Disk.**

The Import Objects dialog box appears, as shown in Figure 3.8. This dialog box lets you select the objects that you want to copy from the *Fruitful, Lesson 1* database into the *Be Fruitful, Lesson 3* database.

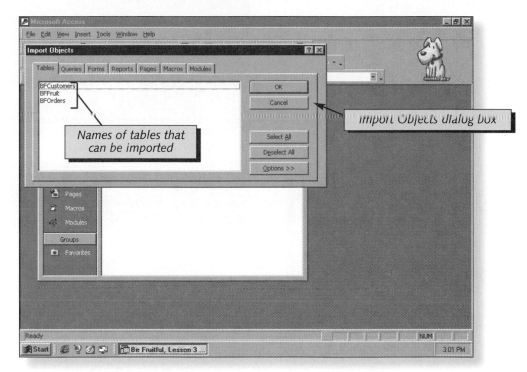

Figure 3.8
The Import Objects dialog box

3. **Click the Tables tab, if necessary, and click BFFruit. Then, click OK.**

After a short pause, the BFFruit table—and all of the records in the table—are copied into the *Be Fruitful, Lesson 3* database. You should see the BFFruit table in the Be Fruitful, Lesson 3 Database window.

You can convert an Access table to a Microsoft Excel or Word document by clicking the table name, clicking the arrow next to the OfficeLinks button, and selecting the Analyze It with MS Excel or Publish It with MS Word option.

Importing from an Excel Worksheet

In this activity, you will import an Excel worksheet into an Access database.

1. **Open the** *Best of the Orchard* **database on your Student Data Disk. Click the Tables option, if necessary.**

2. **Click the File menu, point to Get External Data, and click Import.**

The Import dialog box appears.

3. **In the Files of type list box, click Microsoft Excel.**

4. **Navigate to your Student Data Disk files and double-click the Excel file,** *BFCustomers*.

The Import Spreadsheet Wizard dialog box appears, as shown in Figure 3.9.

5. **Click Show Worksheets and click Next.**

6. **Verify that a check mark appears before First Row Contains Column Headings and click Next.**

Figure 3.9
Import Spreadsheet Wizard
dialog box

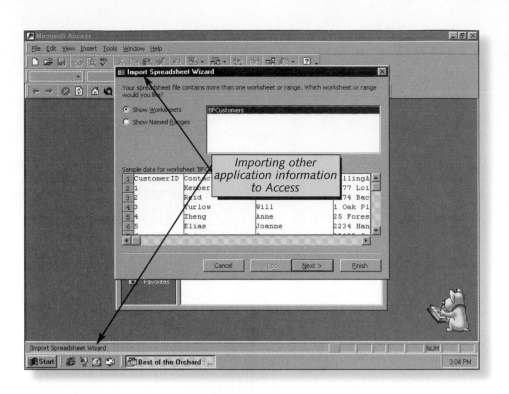

Importing Data from Another Application

1. Click File on the menu bar, point to Get External Data, and click Import.

2. Change File type and double-click the desired file.

3. Follow the Wizard directions for importing.

The Import Spreadsheet Wizard dialog box now asks where you want to store your data.

7. Click **In a New Table**, if necessary, and click **Next**.

8. In the Field Options section, click the **Indexed drop-down arrow** and click **Yes (No Duplicates)**. Then, click **Next**.

9. Click **Choose my own primary key**. In the drop-down box, click **Customer ID**. Then, click **Next**.

The wizard now requests the name of the table. The wizard suggested name appears in the Import to Table box.

10. Change the name to Customers and click **Finish**.

After importing, the Import Spreadsheet Wizard gives a message listing the file that was imported and the name of the new data.

11. Click **OK**.

Access returns you to the Database window and you should see your new Customers table.

12. Open the Customers table and review the data you imported. Then, close the table and the database.

EDITING AND VIEWING RECORDS IN THE DATASHEET

After you've entered a substantial amount of data into your table, you need to know how to move around in the datasheet. When you have only a few records, you can always move the focus to another record just by clicking. When you have larger amounts of data, you need a few additional strategies to find the records you want and select the fields you want to work on. You'll learn both keyboard and mouse techniques for navigating the datasheet while you move through the records that you just entered into the

BFCustomers table. Remember, the record with the focus is simply the one you're editing at the moment. This record usually has a triangle in the record selector, but will have a pencil if you've made any changes that you haven't yet saved.

Navigating Records and Fields

As you've learned, each record is displayed in a unique row in Datasheet view. To read and edit data in a table, you need to move from one row to another. To navigate records, you can use the buttons at the bottom of the Datasheet view, or you can use various keys on the keyboard. To navigate fields, you can use these keys: [Tab], [⇧ Shift] + [Tab], [End], [Home], [Ctrl] + [Home], and [Ctrl] + [End], as well as the arrow keys. If your table includes more records than will fit on the screen at one time, you can also use the vertical or horizontal scroll bars to scroll up and down or to the left or right in your table. However, when you use the scroll bars, the display moves but the focus doesn't change. To switch the focus to a record that you've scrolled into view, click anywhere within the record.

Moving Among Records and Fields

In this activity, you will navigate records and fields in a table.

1. **Open the *Be Fruitful, Lesson 3* database in the *Tutorial* folder and double-click the BFCustomers table. Click the Maximize button .**

Notice the navigation buttons at the bottom of the window, as shown in Figure 3.10. You use these buttons to move from record to record. Note that the text box reads "1" and the gray area to the right reads "of 35." This tells you that the table has 35 records and the focus is on the first record.

Figure 3.10
Navigation buttons

CustomerID	Contact Last N	Contact First N	Billing Addres:	City	State	ZIP Code	Phone Numbe
1	Kenber	Franklin	1777 Lois Ln.	Rock Creek	NC	28333-1234	(919) 555-9999
2	Reid	Alice	7374 Backwood	Sebastopol	CA	97777-1111	(415) 555-5432
3	Turlow	Will	1 Oak Pl.	Providence	RI	02900-2338	(401) 555-9972
4	Zheng	Anne	25 Froest Knoll	Santa Rosa	CA	99887-2355	(707) 555-9876
5	O'Hara	Joan	2234 Hanley Pl.	Baltimore	MD	21122-5634	(301) 555-4567
6	Quinonez	James	32123 Overlook	Portland	OR	99876-2389	(503) 555-1499
7	Bechdel	Mason	75 Grizzly Peak	Orinda	CA	94700-5412	(510) 555-3337
8	Isherwood	Emma	1314 23rd Ave.	Biddeford	ME	57432-6034	(207) 555-3445
9	Smith	Christine	5457 Park Pl.	New York	NY	10001-8763	(212) 555-8881
10	Jackson	Jacqueline	6633 Dallas Wa	Houston	TX	47532-7843	(502) 555-2256
11	Everett	Richard	1310 Arch St.	Berkeley	CA	98765-3368	(510) 555-9932
12	Wintergreen	Shelly	21 Barbary Ln.	Omaha	NE	66332-9004	(303) 555-9753
			303 Hollywood	Los Angeles	CA	99887-3489	(213) 555-3344
			32 B St.	Ashland	OR	97998-5098	(503) 555-1577
15	Ng	Patrick	1112 Spruce St	Shaker Heights	OH	45678-7842	(219) 555-1112
16	Apfelbaum	B		Santa Fe	NM	55554-3449	(801) 555-0864
	Hatfield	James		Ashland	OR	97998-6907	(503) 555-1928
	Marais	Jean-Luc	1379 Montgome	Boston	MA	02101-3930	(617) 555-4321
19	Savallis	Jordi		York	NY	10025-8035	(212) 555-4322
20	Yates	Lily		land	CA	94602-8532	(510) 555-8881
21	Criton	Molly	71 Panoramic V	Seattle	WA	99981-9532	(205) 555-3349
22	Xia	Gong	853 Gateway St	Venice	CA	92231-0045	(213) 555-2736

Current record number

Last Record

Previous Record

New Record

First Record

Next Record

Total number of records

Navigating a Table

To navigate records:

- Use the navigation buttons to move to the first, last, previous, or next record.

- To move to a specific record, type the number of the record to which you want to move in the text box at the bottom of the datasheet, and press `Enter←`.

- Press `↓` or `↑` to move to an adjacent record.

To navigate fields:

- Press `Tab` to move one field to the right.

- Press `⇧ Shift` + `Tab` to move one field to the left.

- Press `End` to move to the last field of a record.

- Press `Home` to move to the first field of a record.

- Press `Ctrl` + `Home` to move to the first field of the first record.

- Press `Ctrl` + `End` to move to the last field of the last record.

2. Click the **Last Record button** ▐►|.

Access moves the focus to the last record in the table, placing a triangle in the record selector and highlighting the data in the Customer ID field. The current record is now listed as record 35.

 When you use any of the navigation buttons, Access moves the focus to a new record but leaves the same field highlighted. For instance, if the Contact First Name field is selected, clicking the Last Record button ▐►| moves the focus to the last record in the table and highlights that record's Contact First Name field.

3. Click the **First Record button** |◄▐.

Access moves the focus to the first record in the table—the record for Franklin Kenber. Once again, the data in the Customer ID field is selected.

4. Double-click the **Next Record button** ►|.

Access moves the focus to the record for Will Turlow, the third record.

5. Click the **Previous Record button** |◄.

The focus moves to the record for Alice Reid, the second record.

6. Double-click the current record number in the text box at the bottom of the screen.

7. Type 25 and press `Enter←`.

As shown in Figure 3.11, the focus moves to record 25—that of Nelly Guggenheim. Easy keyboard techniques also exist for moving from record to record.

8. Press `↓` twice.

Figure 3.11
Using the Go To command

Another Way

To use the shortcut key for the Go To command, press ⎡F5⎤ and type the number of the record you want to go to.

Warning *If you are using the ⎡↓⎤ and ⎡↑⎤ keys in the numeric keypad, deactivate ⎡Num Lock⎤.*

The focus moves down two rows, to the record for Kuniko Ueda.

9. Press ⎡↑⎤ three times.

The focus moves up three rows, to the Customer ID field in Madhu Vargas' record.

10. Press ⎡Tab⎤.

The highlighting moves over to the Contact Last Name field within the same record. Pressing ⎡Tab⎤ moves you to the next field or to the first field of the next record if you're in the last field of the record.

11. Press ⎡⇧ Shift⎤ + ⎡Tab⎤.

The highlighting moves back to the Customer ID field. Pressing ⎡⇧ Shift⎤ + ⎡Tab⎤ moves you to the previous field or to the last field of the previous record if you're in the first field of the record.

12. Press ⎡End⎤ to move to the last field in the current record.

Access selects the Extra Catalogs field in Madhu Vargas' record.

13. Press ⎡Home⎤ to move to the first field in the current record.

Access selects the Customer ID field in Madhu Vargas' record.

Warning *If you are using the ⎡End⎤ and ⎡Home⎤ keys in the numeric keypad, deactivate ⎡Num Lock⎤.*

14. Press ⎡Ctrl⎤ + ⎡End⎤ to move to the last field of the last record.

15. Press ⎡Ctrl⎤ + ⎡Home⎤ to move to the first field of the first record.

Editing Records

After you've tracked down the records in which you're interested, you're ready to begin editing. You can delete or replace the contents of a particular field, and you can add to or change the contents of a field easily. You can delete one or more entire records as well. The Undo feature is useful when you need to reverse your previous action.

If ⎡Home⎤, ⎡End⎤, ⎡Ctrl⎤ + ⎡Home⎤, and ⎡Ctrl⎤ + ⎡End⎤ aren't working as anticipated, first press ⎡F2⎤ to highlight the current field and then try again. The ⎡F2⎤ key lets you switch between editing and navigating your data.

Editing the BFCustomers Table

In this activity, you'll edit the BFCustomers table.

1. If any records or columns are selected in the BFCustomers table, click anywhere within the table to remove the highlighting.

2. Press ⎡F5⎤, type 5, and press ⎡Enter⎤ to move to the record for Joan O'Hara.

3. Press ⎡Tab⎤ or ⎡⇧ Shift⎤ + ⎡Tab⎤ until you get to the Contact First Name field for Joan O'Hara.

Access selects the first name *Joan.* Note that the entire field is highlighted. ***Select*** means to choose an item to indicate to Access that you want to operate on that particular item. You now see the field in ***reverse video,*** with white text against a dark background.

 If you press [Delete] *when any field is selected, you will delete the contents of the field, and anything you type will replace that content.*

4. Click after the *n* in Joan or press [F2].

Notice that the highlighting disappears and is replaced by a blinking insertion point immediately after the *n* in Joan. As you probably know, the insertion point indicates where the text you type will appear, as well as where any deletions will occur.

5. Type ne to change the name to *Joanne.*

6. Press [←].

This action does not move you to the previous field but instead moves the insertion point one character to the left, as shown in Figure 3.12.

Figure 3.12 ◄
Insertion point within a word

Contact Last N	Contact First N	Billing Addres:	City	State	ZIP Code	Phone Numbe	Date Joined
Kenber	Franklin			NC	28333-1234	(919) 555-9999	04/15/1994
Reid	Alice			CA	97777-1111	(415) 555-5432	11/21/1994
Turlow	Will			RI	02900-2338	(401) 555-9972	01/05/1995
Zheng	Anne	25 Froest Knoll	Santa Rosa	CA	99887-2355	(707) 555-9876	07/15/1995
O'Hara	Joanne	2234 Hanley Pl.	Baltimore	MD	21122-5634	(301) 555-4567	02/05/1996
Quinonez	James	32123 Overlook	Portland	OR	99876-2389	(503) 555-1499	04/27/1996
Bachdel	Mason	75 Grizzly Peak	Orinda	CA	94700-5412	(510) 555-3337	06/14/1996
Isherwood	Emma	1314 23rd Ave.	Biddeford	ME	57432-6034	(207) 555-3445	09/04/1996
	Christina	5457 Park Pl.	New York	NY	10001-8763	(212) 555-8881	11/11/1996
		6633 Dallas Wa	Houston	TX	47532-7843	(502) 555-2256	03/17/1997
Everett	Richard	1310 Arch St.	Berkeley	CA	98765-3368	(510) 555-9932	05/24/1997
Wintergreen	Shelly	21 Barbary Ln.	Omaha	NE	66332-9004	(303) 555-9753	06/04/1997
Menendez	Erica	303 Hollywood §	Los Angeles	CA	99887-3489	(213) 555-3344	08/22/1997
Zheng	Alicia	32 B St.	Ashland	OR	97998-5098	(503) 555-1577	11/01/1997
Ng	Patrick	1112 Spruce St	Shaker Heights	OH	45678-7842	(219) 555-1112	03/29/1998
Apfelbaum	Bob	81 Hacienda Bl\	Santa Fe	NM	55554-3449	(801) 555-0864	08/29/1998
Hatfield	James	15A Vine St.	Ashland	OR	97998-6907	(503) 555-1928	09/05/1998
Marais	Jean-Luc	1379 Montgome	Boston	MA	02101-3930	(617) 555-1444	11/25/1998
Savallis	Jordi	100 Riverside D	New York	NY	10025-8035	(212) 555-1122	12/19/1998
Yates	Lily	999 35th Ave.	Oakland	CA	94602-8532	(510) 555-1281	03/22/1999
Criton	Molly	71 Panoramic V	Seattle	WA	99981-9532	(205) 555-1449	04/03/1999
Xiao	SongGong	853 Gateway St	Venice	CA	92231-0045	(213) 555-1256	06/18/1999

Insertion point moves within word

Record being edited

Record: [◄][◄] 5 [►][►I][►*] of 35

Datasheet View

7. Press [F2] to select the contents of the Contact First Name field.

8. Press [←] again.

This time, pressing [←] selects the Contact Last Name field for Joanne O'Hara's record.

9. Type Elias

Access automatically deletes the last name *O'Hara,* replacing it with the name *Elias.*

Undoing Editing Mistakes

When you're making changes to a table, you can make changes to the wrong field or the wrong record. Fortunately, the Undo feature that you used in the previous lesson works here, too. In this activity, you will use the Undo feature to reverse changes.

1. **Click the arrow at the bottom of the scroll bar on the right side of the window until you can see record 28.**

As shown in Figure 3.13, the top records scroll out of view.

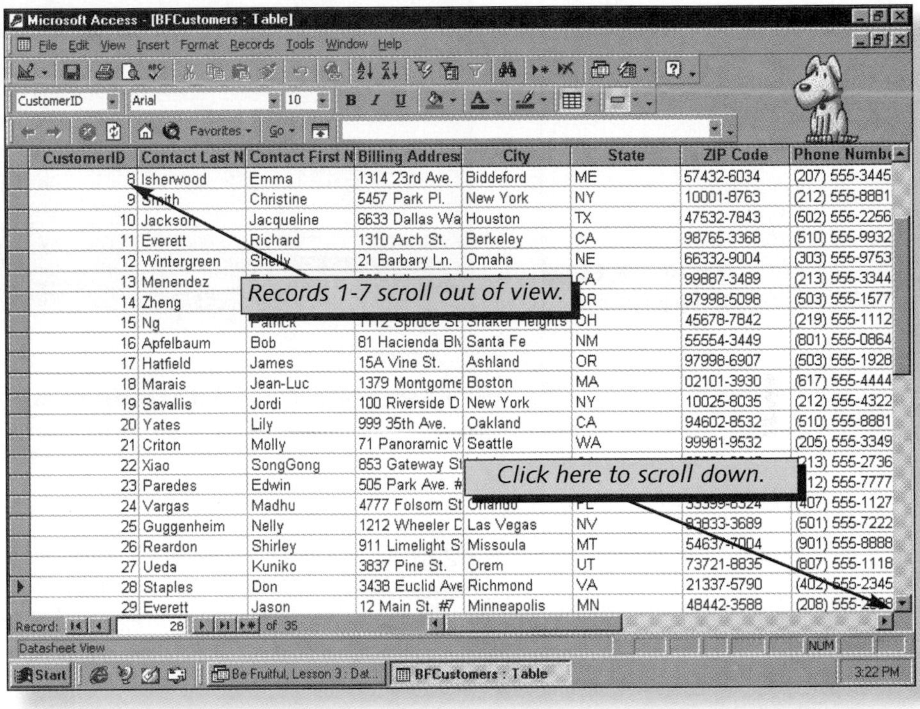

Figure 3.13
Scrolling records

2. **Double-click the last name** *Staples* **in record 28.**

3. **Press** `Delete` **to delete the entire name.**

4. **Click the Undo button** .

Access reverses the change, bringing back the last name you just deleted.

5. **Double-click the last name** *Isherwood* **in record 8.**

6. **Type** Hernandez **and press** `Tab` **to move to the Contact First Name field.**

Access replaces the old last name with the new one.

7. **Type** Rosa **and press** `Tab` **again.**

8. **Type** 204 Panoramic Way **in the Billing Address field.**

9. **Press** `Esc` **or click the Undo button** .

As shown in Figure 3.14, the address changes from *204 Panoramic Way* back to *1314 23rd Ave.*

Another Way

To undo an action before you press `Enter`, press `Esc`.

When you press Escape or click the Undo button, text in the Billing Address field changes back to the original text.

Figure 3.14 ◀
Undoing a change

10. Press ⌨️ again or click the **Undo button** 🔙 two more times.

Access reverses the rest of the changes to the current record all at once, restoring the name *Emma Isherwood*.

Note

Depending on the last action you performed, the Undo button's name changes. For instance, if you just typed text and want to undo it, the ToolTip for the Undo button reads Undo Typing. *If you want to undo a deletion you just made, the name changes to* Undo Delete.

HANDS
On

Access
BASICS

Undoing Changes to a Saved Record

1. Click Edit on the menu bar.

2. Click Undo Saved Record.

Undoing Changes to a Saved Record

Thus far, you have learned how to undo changes to the current field or undo multiple changes to the current record. When you complete the edits in a record and move to another record, your changes are saved automatically. You might think that the regular Undo keys will not reverse these changes. Fortunately, the Undo option will fix the changes if you catch them in time. In this activity, you will use the Undo option to reverse unwanted or accidental changes.

1. Move the insertion point to the Notes field for record number 4, Anne Zheng.

2. Type Loves kiwis and press ⎡Tab⎤ to move to the Extra Catalogs field.

3. Press ⎡Spacebar⎤.

Pressing ⎡Spacebar⎤ puts a check mark in this Yes/No field.

4. Press ⎡Tab⎤ .

Another Way

To select or deselect a check box, click it.

Access automatically saves the changes to Anne Zheng's record when you move to the next record.

5. Click Edit on the menu bar and click Undo Saved Record.

Access reverses the changes to the Zheng record, even though the record had been saved. This Undo command reverses only the most recent action; if you've done anything else since then, you can't undo the changes to a saved record in this way.

Deleting Records

You can delete entire records from the table. To do so, you must first select the record. In this activity, you'll remove one of the records from the table.

1. Click the record selector for Richard Everett's record (record number 11).

The entire record is selected.

2. Click the Delete Record button.

Access displays the warning box shown in Figure 3.15, warning you that you're about to delete a record and giving you a chance to stop the change.

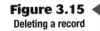

Deleting a Record

1. Click the record selector of the record you wish to delete.

2. Click the Delete Record button.

3. Click Yes when the warning box appears.

Figure 3.15
Deleting a record

3. Read the text in the box and click Yes.

Warning *When you delete one or more records, you cannot undo the operation with the Undo command. Your only way out is to click No to cancel the operation when Access displays the warning box.*

Another Way

To delete a record, press Delete.

Access deletes the selected record and moves the subsequent records up. Note, however, that the values in the Customer ID field have not changed. As you'd expect, customers retain the same ID numbers even if other customers are removed from the database.

You can also delete entire fields in Datasheet view by clicking Edit on the menu bar and clicking Delete Column. However, be extremely sure that you want to delete the field and all of the contents before issuing this command. This action cannot be reversed with the Undo command, so if you change your mind, you must add the field and retype all of the data in it.

Editing in the Zoom Window

When you have a lot of text in a field such as a large text or memo field, editing can be difficult. In this activity, you work with the fields more easily using the Zoom window.

1. **Press** `Tab` **repeatedly until you get to the Notes field for Shelly Wintergreen's record.**

2. **Press** `⇧ Shift` **+** `F2`.

Access opens the Zoom window shown in Figure 3.16; you can use this window to enter longer amounts of text or to edit fields that have a lot of text.

Editing in the Zoom Window

1. Move to the field you wish to edit.

2. Press `⇧ Shift` + `F2`.

3. Type the text and click OK.

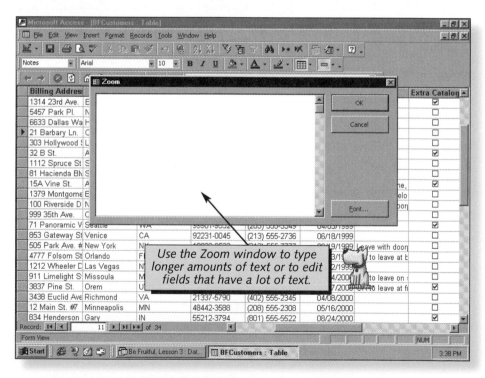

Figure 3.16
The Zoom window

3. **Type the following text:**

Mrs. Wintergreen is an elderly woman. If she is home and you have a moment, try to knock (loudly) on the door and chat for a minute. She is allergic to pomegranates but loves all other fruits we currently offer. OK to leave packages at the back door if she is not home.

4. Click OK.

You return to the Datasheet window, where you see only a tiny amount of the text you just typed.

5. Scroll the text in Mrs. Wintergreen's Notes field.

Notice how much more difficult this is than viewing the text in the Zoom window.

Adding Information with the Ditto Key

Earlier in this lesson, you added a new record to the table. In this activity, you duplicate information from the previous record with the ditto key. The key combination Ctrl + ' is known as the ***ditto key;*** it repeats the value from the same field in the previous record.

1. With the insertion point still in the Notes field for Shelly Wintergreen, press F2 so that the field is selected.

Pressing F2 takes you out of the edit mode of the memo field.

2. Press Ctrl + End.

You move to the end of the table. If you had not pressed F2 first, you would have been taken to the end of the text for the memo field you were editing.

3. Press Tab twice to move to the Contact Last Name field of the new blank record automatically generated by Access.

4. Press Ctrl + '.

Access inserts the name *Frankel* into the current field.

5. Press Tab and type Cassandra in the Contact First Name field of your new record.

6. Press Tab and then press Ctrl + ' again to duplicate the Billing Address field from the previous record. Continue in this manner, duplicating the City, State, ZIP Code, and Phone Number fields.

7. Type 4/22/01 in the Date Joined field.

The new record should look like similar to the previous record.

8. Press Tab three times to complete the new record.

SEARCHING FOR RECORDS BASED ON THEIR CONTENTS

When you move around in a small table, you usually can find the record you want either by scrolling or by using the navigation buttons and keyboard methods you learned earlier in this lesson. However, as your tables grow larger, it becomes more difficult to track down the records you need by these methods. Access provides the Find command, which lets you search for records based on their contents, and the Replace command, which lets you both search for and replace specific values.

Changing the Appearance of the Datasheet and Checking the Spelling

Now that you've added and edited text in your tables, you will use Help to learn how to modify the format properties (font, font size, and colors) in your datasheet and how to check the spelling of the text in your datasheet.

1. Click the **Office Assistant**. Type change font and size of text in a datasheet **in the** *What would you like to do?* **box. Click the Search button**.

2. Click the **Change the font size in Datasheet view option** (Figure 3.17). **Explore the Help information.**

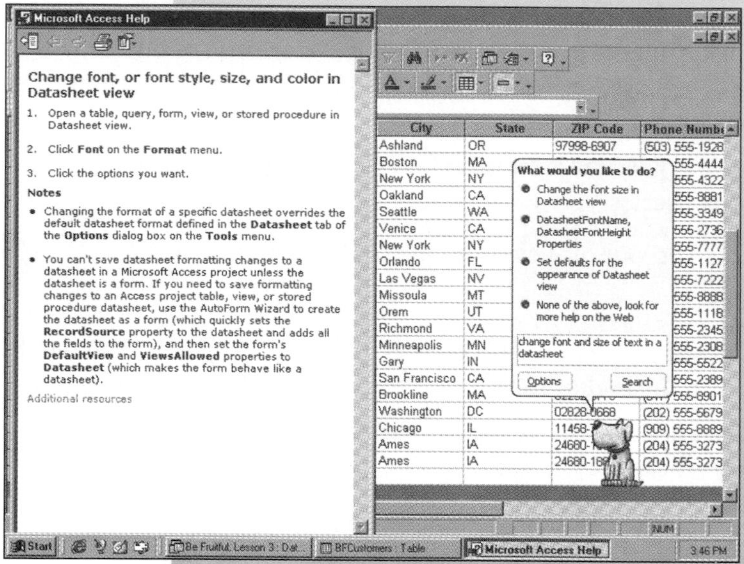

Figure 3.17
Formatting a datasheet

3. In the BFCustomers table of the *Be Fruitful, Lesson 3* database, click **Font** on the **Format menu**.

4. In the Font dialog box, click **Times New Roman** (Font), **Bold Italic** (Font Style), **12** (Size), and **Red** (Color). Then, click **OK**.

The appearance of the entire table is different. You can use buttons on the Formatting toolbar to change the font, size, and color and to add special effects.

5. Change the table back to **Arial** (Font), **Regular** (Font Style), **10** (Size), and **Black** (Color).

6. Type check spelling in a datasheet **in the** *What would you like to do?* **box, click the Search button, and click the Check the spelling of data option**.

7. Explore the Help information for Datasheet view.

8. Press Ctrl + A to select all of the BFCustomers table. Click the **Spelling button** ⚏.

9. In the Spelling dialog box, Access identifies the first word that is not in the dictionary. Click Ignore if the spelling is correct and to move to the next possible error, click Ignore All to ignore all instances of the word, click Change to edit the spelling, and click Change All to change all occurrences of the edited word. Continue checking the spelling of the entire table.

10. Close the Help window.

Finding Values in the Table

You can use the Find command with or without the Replace command. When you use it alone, it helps you to locate one or more occurrences of a value in a table. Using the Find dialog box, you can instruct Access to search for data in a specific field or you can tell it to search the entire table. The Find command allows you to find records that meet a specified criteria, but it shows these records one by one as you click the Find Next button. A filter, on the other hand, allows you to specify criteria and then generates a list displaying only those records that meet the criteria. You'll learn more about filters in Lesson 4.

HANDS On

Another Way

To issue the Find command, click Edit on the menu bar and click Find, or press `Ctrl` + F.

Figure 3.18
Find and Replace dialog box

Finding Data

1. If you wish to search a specific field, move to that field.

2. Click the Find button.

3. Type the desired text in the Find What box.

4. Change other settings as desired in the Find and Replace dialog box.

5. Click Find Next repeatedly to find all occurrences of the text.

Finding Customers with the Same Last Name

In this activity, you'll experiment with the Find command to see how you can find several occurrences of the name *Zheng*.

1. **Open the BFCustomers table in Datasheet view, if necessary, and move to the Contact Last Name field of the first record.**

2. **Click the Find button** 🔍.

Access displays the Find and Replace dialog box, as shown in Figure 3.18. Notice that the Look In box lists the current field, Contact Last Name. By default, Access looks for the specified value in the current field only.

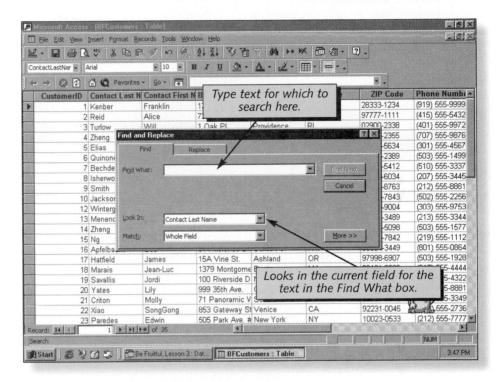

3. **In the Find What text box, type** Zheng **and click the Find Next button**.

The name *Zheng* is highlighted and the record for Anne Zheng now has the focus. Access leaves the dialog box open—in case you want to continue searching for other records.

4. **Click the Find Next button again.**

The record for the second customer with the last name of Zheng (Alicia Zheng) is selected.

5. **Click the Find Next button again.**

The record for Carter Zheng is selected.

6. **Click the Find Next button once more.**

The Office Assistant tells you that the search item was not found. This message means that no other customers with the last name of Zheng were found.

7. **Click OK to remove the message.**

Access returns to the Find and Replace dialog box.

8. Double-click the text in the Find What text box and then type Joanne. Then click the Find Next button.

Access alerts you that it has finished searching the records without finding the specified item. This message tells you that no customers with the last name of Joanne were found.

9. Click OK to clear the message.

10. Click the Look In drop-down arrow in the Find and Replace dialog box and click BFCustomers:Table.

11. Click Find Next.

This time, Access finds the record that contains the value *Joanne*—because the search is in all fields, not just the Contact Last Name field.

Replacing Values in the Table

If you repeatedly click Find Next, the focus moves to each subsequent record that contains the Find What value. But what if you want not only to find but also to change those values? As you'll discover, the Replace command is particularly valuable for changing multiple instances of the same characters. For example, suppose you abbreviated *Boulevard* incorrectly throughout your table—maybe you spelled it *Bvld*. You could correct every instance of the mistake with a few easy steps.

The Replace All option can be a great time saver, but remember that Replace is safer than Replace All. If you use Replace and Access stops on a record you don't want to change, you can click the Find Next button to go on to the next instance without changing the current one. If you use Replace All, you don't have the option to stop some occurrences. For instance, if you wanted to replace all occurrences of the word *red* with *blue*, Access will not only change occurrences of *red* but may also change words that contain *red*. Words such as *bred, predator,* and *poured* may be affected, depending on the match option you select.

Replacing Occurrences of a Specific Word

In this activity, you'll search for all occurrences of *Pl.* at the end of an address and replace them with the word *Place*. You'll replace one occurrence at a time and learn how to replace all occurrences at once.

1. Click outside of the Find and Replace dialog box. If the insertion point is blinking, press F2 to select any field.

2. Press Ctrl + Home to move to the top of the table.

3. Click the Replace tab within the Find and Replace dialog box.

Notice that the Find What text box shows the value from your previous Find operation. Also note that the Look In box indicates that the entire table will be searched; this, too, is a carry over from the previous Find operation. You want to change all of the abbreviations *Pl.* with the full word *Place*.

4. Click the **Match drop-down arrow** and click **Any Part of Field**.

This action is necessary because you're looking for characters *within* a field.

5. Click the text (*Joanne*) in the Find What box, type Pl. and then press `Tab`.

6. Type Place in the Replace With box and click **Find Next**.

As shown in Figure 3.19, Access moves the focus to Will Turlow's record, the first record containing the string of characters *Pl*.

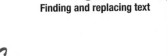

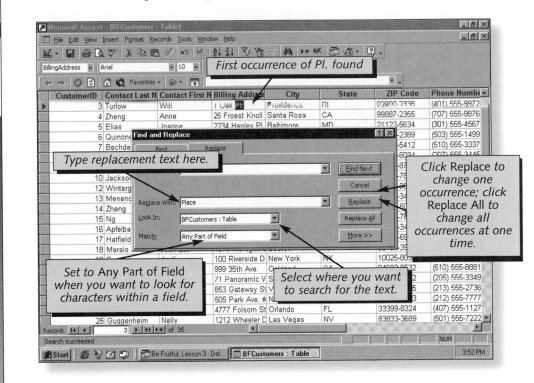

7. Click the **Replace button**.

Access replaces *Pl*. with *Place* in Will Turlow's record and also moves to the next record that contains the specified string, the record for Joanne Elias.

8. Click the **Replace All button**.

Access displays a warning box telling you that you will not be able to undo the changes made by this operation.

9. Click **Yes** to continue with this operation.

Access changes the records for both Joanne Elias and Christine Smith.

10. Close the Find and Replace dialog box.

CHANGING THE DATASHEET DISPLAY

In many cases, the default datasheet layout will adequately meet your needs. At times, however, you might like to customize the datasheet layout. Among other things, you can change column widths and row heights, move columns, hide columns, and freeze columns so that they're always visible on the screen. For example, you might want to reduce the widths of several

Hints & Tips

Although you can't undo column width changes with the Undo command, you can close the table and choose not to accept the changes to the layout of the table.

Access BASICS

Changing Column Widths and Row Heights

- Drag the border between the column selectors to resize a column.

- Drag the border between rows to resize rows.

columns so you can see more columns on the screen at once, or you might want to freeze the Contact Last Name column so you can always tell at a glance whose record you're working on, no matter which field you're in. Changes to the datasheet layout only affect the display of your data in the Datasheet view—they do not affect the table structure.

Changing Column Widths and Row Heights

You can change the size of columns and rows to view more (or less) data at a time. For instance, you can widen a column to see all of the data in a particular field. If you would rather that data for each record appear in two or more rows, you can expand the height of a row. Likewise, you can reduce the size of columns and rows to reduce white space between them and see more fields and records at one time.

Resizing Columns and Rows

In this activity, you will customize the datasheet by changing the widths of the columns and heights of the rows in the Datasheet display.

1. **With the BFCustomers table in Datasheet view, point to the border between the column selectors (the heading at the top of each column) for the Customer ID and Contact Last Name fields.**

The pointer will change into a vertical bar with a horizontal double-headed arrow attached. This pointer indicates that you drag to the left to narrow the column to the left of the pointer or drag to the right to widen the column to the left.

2. **Drag to the left to narrow the Customer ID field until the field is only two or three characters wide.**

Although the column heading won't be entirely visible, you'll still be able to see the complete Customer ID numbers.

3. **Point to the border between the column selectors for the State and ZIP Code fields and drag to the left to narrow the State field.**

At this point, your Datasheet window might look something like the one shown in Figure 3.20. Notice that you can now see more fields without scrolling to the right. Just as you changed the width of the columns, you can also change the height of the rows.

4. **Point to the border between any two record selectors.**

The pointer changes into a horizontal bar with a vertical double-headed arrow.

5. **Drag downward to the horizontal line indicating the next row and then release.**

Access increases the row height of all rows in the table to about twice their original size, as shown in Figure 3.21.

When you have long fields, increasing the row height lets you see more of the field contents at once. In the Billing Address field, for instance, notice that the longer addresses now wrap to the next line instead of disappearing from view.

Figure 3.20 ◄
Resizing columns

Change the column widths to an appropriate size for the data.

State column is narrower.

Customer ID field is narrower.

To automatically resize a column so you can see all of the data in the longest record (or the entire field name if it's longer than the data), double-click the right column selector border.

Figure 3.21 ◄
Resizing rows

All rows are resized.

Note — When you change a row height, Access changes the height of all rows in the table, not just one (in contrast to when you adjust column widths).

6. **Now return the rows to their original height by pointing to the border between any two record selectors, dragging upward until the black line is at the row's midpoint, and then releasing.**

HANDS On

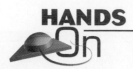

Changing the Order of Fields

When you rearrange the order of the fields in Datasheet view, only the datasheet is affected. The table design is not changed. You might change the order of the fields in Datasheet view if you reduce column widths and maximize the screen and you still can't see all the fields you want to view. Or, if you want to temporarily emphasize one or more specific fields, you can move those fields to the first columns. In this activity, you will move the Phone Number field to appear directly after the Contact First Name field.

1. Click the column selector for the Phone Number field.

Access highlights the column.

2. Still pointing to the column selector, drag the selected column to the left until the heavy vertical line is just to the right of the Contact First Name field and then release.

Notice that, as you drag, Access displays a heavy vertical line to indicate where the column will go when you release. Access places the Phone Number column immediately to the right of the Contact First Name column, as shown in Figure 3.22.

Access BASICS

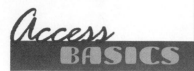

Changing Field Order

1. Click the column selector of the field you wish to move.
2. Drag the column selector to the new location.

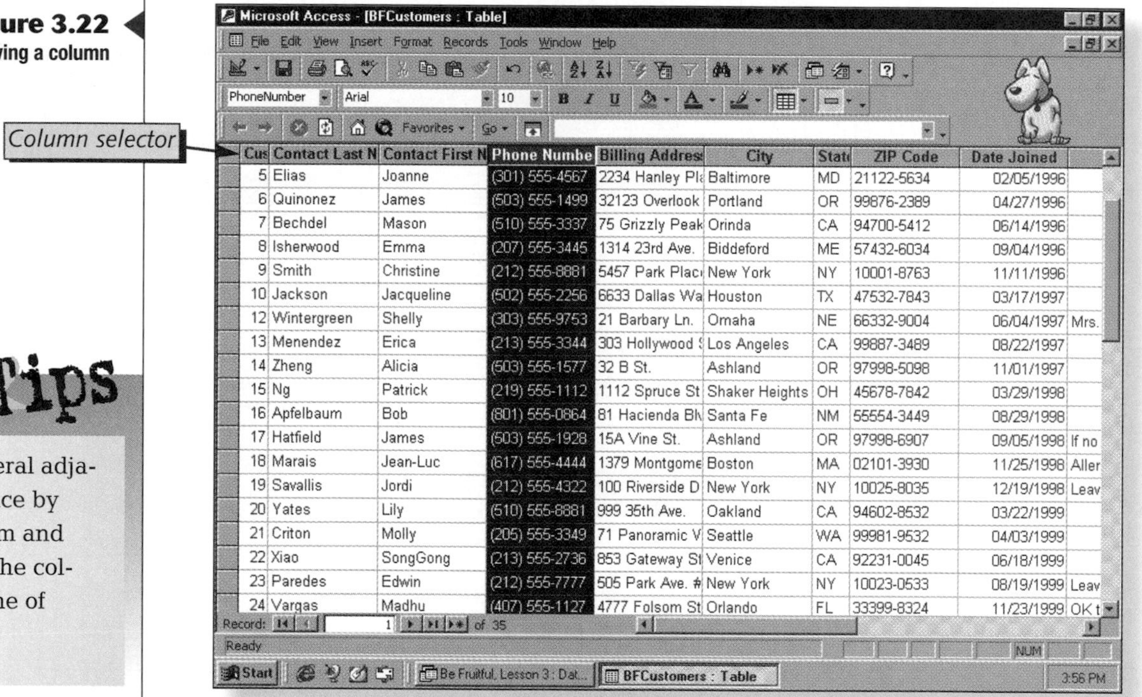

Figure 3.22
Moving a column

Hints & Tips

You can move several adjacent columns at once by selecting all of them and then dragging on the column selector for one of them.

HANDS On

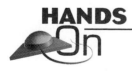

Hiding Columns

In some situations, hiding columns may be a better solution than moving them. If you wanted to view names, phone numbers, and date-joined information—but didn't need to see any other data in the table—you could hide all the other columns. In this activity, you'll hide a single field. Then you'll hide multiple columns and redisplay all columns.

Hiding and Unhiding Columns

- To hide one column, click the column selector, click Format on the menu bar, and click Hide Columns.

- To hide several columns, click Format on the menu bar, click Unhide Columns, deselect the check boxes next to the columns you wish to hide, and click the Close button.

- To unhide columns, click Format on the menu bar, click Unhide Columns, select the check boxes next to the columns you wish to unhide, and click the Close button.

Figure 3.23 ◀
The Unhide Columns dialog box

1. **Select the Customer ID field by clicking the column selector.**

2. **Click Format on the menu bar and click Hide Columns.**

Access removes the Customer ID column from view. You must use the Unhide command to redisplay one or more hidden columns.

3. **Click Format on the menu bar and click Unhide Columns.**

Access displays the Unhide Columns dialog box, as shown in Figure 3.23. In the Column box, check marks indicate which fields are displayed. You can hide or unhide columns in this dialog box by clicking in the check box.

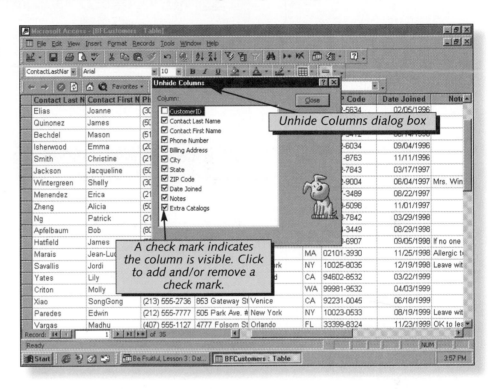

4. **Click the check box beside the Billing Address field.**

Access removes the check mark to the left of the field name and hides the Billing Address field in the Datasheet window.

5. **Click the check box beside the City field.**

Access removes the City field's check mark and hides the City field in the Datasheet window.

6. **Hide the Extra Catalogs, Notes, State, and ZIP Code fields.**

7. **Close the Unhide Columns dialog box.**

Access returns you to the datasheet, which should show only the Contact Last Name, Contact First Name, Phone Number, and Date Joined fields, as shown in Figure 3.24.

Figure 3.24 ◄
Hiding several columns

Microsoft Access - [BFCustomers : Table]

Contact Last N	Contact First N	Phone Numbe	Date Joined
▶ Kenber	Franklin	(919) 555-9999	04/15/1994
Reid	Alice	(415) 555-5432	11/21/1994
Turlow	Will	(401) 555-9972	01/05/1995
Zheng	Anne	(707) 555-9876	07/15/1995
Elias	Joanne	(301) 555-4567	02/05/1996
Quinonez	James	(503) 555-1499	04/27/1996
Bechdel	Mason	(510) 555-3337	06/14/1996
Isherwood	Emma	(207) 555-3445	09/04/1996
Smith	Christine	(212) 555-8881	11/11/1996
Jackson	Jacqueline	(502) 555-2256	03/17/1997
Wintergreen	Shelly	(303) 555-9753	06/04/1997
Menendez	Erica	(213) 555-3344	08/22/1997
Zheng	Alicia	(503) 555-1577	11/01/1997
Ng	Patrick	(219) 555-1112	03/29/1998
Apfelbaum	Bob	(801) 555-0864	08/29/1998
Hatfield	James	(503) 555-1928	09/05/1998
Marais	Jean-Luc	(617) 555-4444	11/25/1998
Savallis	Jordi	(212) 555-4322	12/19/1998
Yates	Lily	(510) 555-8881	03/22/1999

Only unhidden columns appear.

Record: 1 of 35

8. Click **Format** on the menu bar and click **Unhide Columns**.

9. Click all of the hidden columns so that check marks appear. Then, close the dialog box.

Access brings all of the columns back into view.

Freezing a Column

In some cases, you may want to *freeze* one or more columns. When you freeze a column, it remains in view on the screen even when you scroll past it. For instance, if you wanted to view one of the last fields, such as Date Joined, but always wanted to see the Customer ID associated with each record, you could freeze the Customer ID field so that it always remains in view. In this activity, you'll freeze the Contact Last Name column so that it remains on the screen when you scroll all of the fields.

1. Click the **Contact Last Name column selector**.

The entire column is selected.

2. Click **Freeze Columns** on the Format menu.

Access moves the Contact Last Name column to the left-most column in Datasheet view.

3. Scroll to the right, either by pressing [Tab] repeatedly or by using the horizontal scroll bar until you see the Extra Catalogs field.

The Contact Last Name field remains visible; it's frozen into place as the left-most column of Datasheet view, as you can see in Figure 3.25.

Figure 3.25
Freezing a column

4. Click Unfreeze All Columns on the Format menu.

Access unfreezes all columns. Any formerly frozen columns remain in the left-most position in the datasheet, until scrolling takes them out of view.

Canceling Changes to the Datasheet Layout

You can save or cancel any changes you make to the datasheet layout. If you like, you can move columns back to where they were by using the techniques you just learned for moving columns. Alternatively, you can close the table without saving the changes to the datasheet layout. At this point, you've finished experimenting with the datasheet layout and you've decided that you do not want to save the changes. In this activity, you'll close the datasheet and cancel the changes you made.

1. Close the BFCustomers table by clicking the Close button ☒.

Access displays a message asking whether you want to save the changes you've made to the datasheet layout for the BFCustomers table.

2. Click No to close the table without saving any of the changes to the datasheet layout.

Access returns you to the Be Fruitful, Lesson 3 Database window.

 *Even if you don't save the datasheet layout, Access still saves any edits or additions to your data. Remember, these changes are saved automatically when you move to the next record.*

ESTABLISHING AND DEFINING TABLE RELATIONSHIPS

Now that you've created several tables in your database, you can establish permanent relationships among them. This way, Access will always be certain which records match up and also will understand precisely the type of relationship the two tables have. Defining a relationship allows you to create reports and other objects that combine data from two or more tables. Defining formal relationships between tables involves only a few simple steps. First, however, you need to know more about the various types of relationships that can exist between tables.

Identifying Relationships Between Tables

Any two tables can have one of three types of relationships: one-to-one, one-to-many, and many-to-many. If two tables have a *one-to-one relationship,* every record in a table can have either no matching records or only a single matching record in the other table. This situation might arise, for example, if you want to keep track of mailing addresses as well as regular addresses. You could include the mailing addresses in a separate table; each person would have at most one mailing address in this table, and many people would have none, because their mailing addresses would be the same as their regular addresses.

When you have a *one-to-many relationship,* one of the tables is called the primary table, while the other is called the related table. The *primary table* holds a primary key that is unique. In your BFCustomers table, the Customer ID field is the primary key. You ensured that the Customer ID field would be unique by defining it as an AutoNumber field. In that way, no two customer records have the same Customer ID.

The second table in a one-to-many relationship is called the related table. The *related table* has a field that links it to the primary table. This field is called the *foreign key.* It need not be unique. In the BFOrders table, the foreign key is the Customer ID. This field was not defined as an AutoNumber field, because one customer can place many orders. Two tables have a one-to-many relationship when each record in the primary table can have no records, one record, or many matching records in the other table, but every record in the related table has exactly one associated record in the primary table—no more and no less.

In a *many-to-many relationship,* a record in either table can relate to many records in the other table. While you will not create such a relationship in the *Be Fruitful, Lesson 3* database, they are quite common.

Referential integrity refers to certain rules that Access enforces to safeguard your data, ensuring that it makes sense and does not violate the relationship that you have defined for the tables. In the *Be Fruitful, Lesson 3* database, every orders record must have an associated customer record but cannot have more than one related customer record. For instance, when referential integrity is enforced, Access won't let you delete a customer record if there are matching order records. After you have established the relationships, you can print this information for your reference while continuing to build and modify your database.

Bill Gates, founder of Microsoft Corporation, taught himself programming at the age of 13. As teenagers in Seattle, he and his friends rode their bikes to a local computer company to help the employees look for programming errors.

Creating One-to-Many Relationships

In this activity, you use the Relationships window to create the link between a primary and related table. Note that the primary table must have a unique primary key and the related table must have a foreign key that matches the field of the primary key.

1. Click the Relationships button 🔲.

The Show Table dialog box in Figure 3.26 appears, which lets you choose the tables you want to relate.

Figure 3.26 ◀
The Show Table dialog box

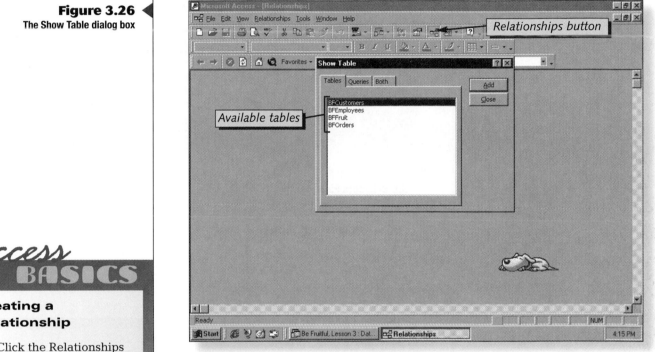

Access
BASICS

Creating a Relationship

1. Click the Relationships button.

2. Double-click the tables you wish to work with in the Show Table dialog box and then close the dialog box.

3. Drag a field name from one field list to the same field name on another field list.

4. If desired, click the Enforce Referential Integrity option and click the Create button.

5. Close the Relationships window.

2. Click BFCustomers and click Add.

A Field list appears for the BFCustomers table in the Relationships window.

3. Double-click BFOrders and then double-click BFFruit.

4. Click the Close button in the Show Table dialog box.

The BFCustomers, BFOrders, and BFFruit Field lists are displayed in the Relationships window.

5. Click the CustomerID field in the BFCustomers Field list.

6. Drag and drop the CustomerID field from the BFCustomers Field list onto the CustomerID field on the BFOrders Field list.

The Edit Relationships dialog box appears, as shown in Figure 3.27.

7. Click the Enforce Referential Integrity option so that a check mark appears in it and then click Create.

Access creates the relationship, the dialog box closes, and a line now appears between the CustomerID fields in the two tables.

Figure 3.27 ◄
The Edit Relationships dialog box

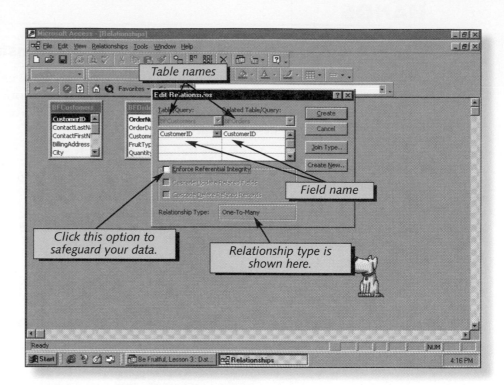

8. **Drag and drop the FruitType field from the BFFruit Field list to the FruitType field in the BFOrders Field list.**

9. **When the Edit Relationships dialog box appears, click the Enforce Referential Integrity box and click Create.**

Lines like the ones in Figure 3.28 join the related fields. The small 1 on the line indicates the one side of the relationship, while the ∞ on the line shows the many sides of the relationship.

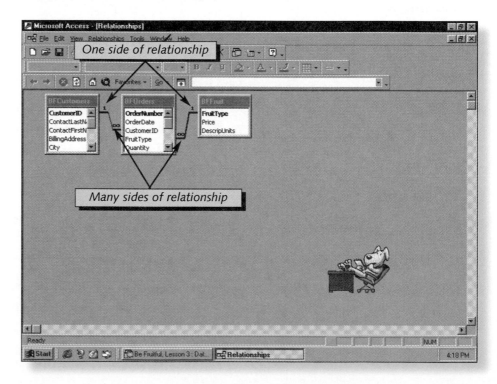

Figure 3.28 ◄
Assigning relationships

10. Click the **Close button** ☒ of the Relationships window.

A warning box asks if you want to save this relationship.

11. Click **Yes**.

The relationship is saved and you return to the Database window.

Printing the Database Relationships for the Be Fruitful Database

In this activity, you will print the database relationships you just created in the last activity.

1. With the *Be Fruitful, Lesson 3* database still open, click **Tools** on the menu bar, and click **Relationships**.

The Relationships window appears displaying the assigned relationships between the three tables, as shown in Figure 3.28.

2. Click **File** on the menu bar and click **Print Relationships**.

After a few moments, the database relationships report opens in Print Preview, as shown in Figure 3.29.

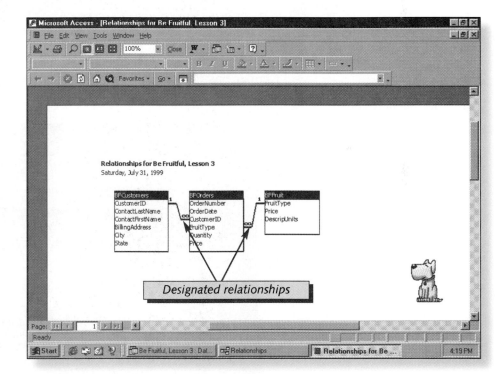

Figure 3.29
Print Preview of the
Relationships window

3. Click the **Print button** 🖨 to print the report.

4. Close the Print Preview.

A warning box appears and asks if you want to save changes to the design of the report.

5. Click **No** and then close the Relationships window.

Access closes the window and returns you to the Be Fruitful Database window.

Displaying Related Records in a Subdatasheet

When you create relationships between tables, Access automatically creates subdatasheets. *Subdatasheets* allow you to view and edit data in a related table, query, or form. For instance, since the BFCustomers table has a one-to-many relationship with the BFOrders table, you can view and edit the related rows of the BFOrders table in a subdatasheet. You can bring subdatasheets into view by clicking the plus sign in front of any record in a table.

Opening a Subdatasheet

In this activity, you'll open a subdatasheet for the first customer listed in the BFCustomers table.

1. Open the BFCustomers table.

A plus sign now appears before each record in the BFCustomers table.

2. Click the **plus sign** in front of the record for Franklin Kenber.

The subdatasheet for Franklin Kenber appears, as shown in Figure 3.30, showing the fields in the BFOrders table. All of the orders that Franklin Kenber has placed are listed in the subdatasheet. You can edit data in the subdatasheet here, if desired.

Opening and Closing a Subdatasheet

1. Click the plus sign in front of any record to open the subdatasheet.

2. Click the minus sign in front of any record to close the subdatasheet.

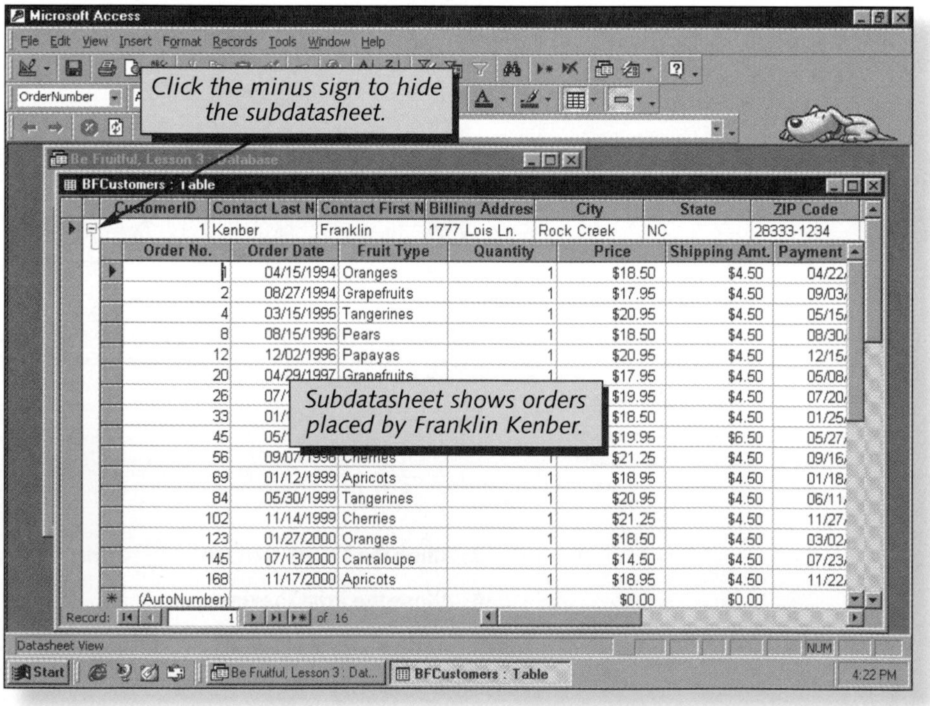

Figure 3.30 ◀
A subdatasheet

3. Click the **minus sign** in front of the record for Franklin Kenber.

Access hides the subdatasheet.

4. Close the BFCustomers table.

5. Click the **Tools menu** and click **Options**. On the General tab, click the **Compact on Close option**, if necessary.

6. Close the *Be Fruitful, Lesson 3* database.

Test your knowledge by completing the following statements. See Appendix D to check your answers.

1. The process of bringing data into one database from another is called _____.

2. Pressing _____ moves you to the previous field or to the last field of the previous record if you're in the first field of the record.

3. To delete an entire record, first click the _____ and then click the _____ button.

4. To view and edit text in a field that contains a long amount of text, you can open the _____ window.

5. To copy data from the previous record, press _____, known as the ditto key.

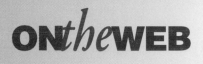

ON*the*WEB

ACCESSING THE SEARCH PAGE

In previous lessons, you've learned how to access Web pages by typing their addresses. However, often you'll want to use the Internet to find information on a specific topic, but you won't know the address of a specific site. In these cases, you can use the Search Page.

In this activity, you act as the marketing manager for Be Fruitful. Lately, you've been considering creating a Web site for the company in hopes of increasing sales. One link on the Web page would provide customers with recipes that contain fresh fruit. In this activity, you will use the Search the Web button 🔍 in Access to navigate to the Search page of your browser; then you'll search for Web sites that contain fruit recipes.

1. **Connect to the Internet.**
2. **Click the Microsoft Access taskbar button.**
3. **Click the Search the Web button 🔍 on the Web toolbar.**

Access launches your browser and the page that is specified as your Search page appears. A *Search page* allows you to type keywords that describe material for which you are looking and then searches the Web for documents that contain those keywords.

4. **If necessary, click a search engine option. (You may use the default if one is already selected or if you do not have a choice of search engines.)**

A *search engine* allows you to search for information on a particular topic. Some search engines search every word of every document they find on the Internet; others search only portions of documents they find.

5. **When your Search page appears, type** recipes **in the Search text box.**
6. **Click the button to process your search request.**

The button that processes your search request is often labeled *Search* or *Find*.

7. **When the results of your search appear, scroll down to see the numerous sites to which you can connect.**

The results of your search appear in the form of links that you can click to navigate to the page described. The results that you get from typing the keyword *recipes* will vary depending on the search engine you use. They will lead to a variety of topics including recipes of all sorts using many types of foods and for many different meals. The top of the page may tell you how many results were found. For a search as general as this one, you are likely to find thousands of recipes. Instead of muddling through thousands of results, many of which don't pertain to your situation, you can use several keywords to narrow your search. Most search engines display the results that contain more of your keywords at the top of the list.

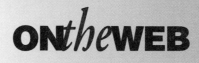

Many search engines allow you to use special symbols to narrow your results even further. For instance, most search engines allow you to use quotation marks around words that should always be found together. Some search engines, such as one called *Alta Vista,* allow the use of a plus symbol (+) to specify that the keyword must be found in the result and a minus sign (-) to indicate a word that should not be found in the resulting pages. For instance, the keywords + *fruit company "mail order" -balloons* will result in pages that contain the word *fruit,* may contain the word *company,* may contain the words *mail order* together but will exclude those pages that contain just the word *mail* and just the word *order,* and do not include the word *balloons.* To find out if your search engine allows the use of special symbols, look for a Help or an Advanced Search button that describes them.

8. **Return to the top of the Search Page (click the Back button on your browser toolbar if necessary) and type the keywords "fresh fruit" recipes in the Search text box.**

9. **Choose a search engine, if necessary, and click the button to process your search request.**

When the results appear, scroll down to see them. As you can see, the results using several keywords usually suggest sites that are more targeted to the information you are seeking.

10. **From your results, click one of the links that you think will lead you to a Web page that contains one or more fresh fruit recipes. Explore the site.**

11. **Using word processing software, describe what you do and do not like about the site and list any suggestions to improve the site. Then, click the Back button on your browser toolbar to return to the list of results.**

12. **Explore a link to another site. Using word processing software, describe your reactions to this site and list any suggestions to improve the site. If time allows, explore other related sites.**

13. **Close your browser, disconnect from the Internet (unless your instructor tells you to remain connected), and exit Access.**

Warning

You may proceed directly to the exercises for this lesson. If, however, you are finished with your computer session, follow the "shut down" procedures for your lab or school environment.

Lesson Summary & Exercises

SUMMARY

Working in Datasheet view is an important part of working with tables—the building blocks of databases. You learned in this lesson that you can add, edit, delete, find, replace, and manipulate data in Datasheet view. You can also reorganize the fields and records in Datasheet view to meet your needs. You learned how to assign relationships between tables and work with subdatasheets. Search the Internet for information involves displaying the Search page, choosing a search engine, entering keywords, and exploring the search results.

Now that you have completed this lesson, you should be able to do the following:

- Open a table in Access. (Access-106)
- Add new records and type data in Datasheet view. (Access-107)
- Use the Office Clipboard to copy data from another table. (Access-110)
- Use the Office Clipboard to paste the data. (Access-112)
- Import an entire table from another database. (Access-114)
- Import data from another application to a new table. (Access-115)
- Move among rows using keyboard commands, mouse commands, and the scroll bars. (Access-117)
- Move among columns using keyboard commands, mouse commands, and the scroll bars. (Access-117)
- Select fields and records. (Access-117)
- Edit data in records. (Access-119)
- Undo a change. (Access-121)
- Undo changes you have made to a saved record. (Access-122)
- Delete records. (Access-123)
- Open a Zoom window to look at and edit text. (Access-124)
- Add information with the ditto key. (Access-125)
- Search for and replace particular strings of characters. (Access-127)
- Change column widths and row heights in the datasheet. (Access-130)
- Move datasheet columns. (Access-132)
- Hide and freeze datasheet columns. (Access-132)
- Cancel changes to Datasheet view. (Access-135)
- Understand the types of relationships that can exist between two tables. (Access-136)
- Create a relationship between two tables. (Access-137)
- Print database relationships. (Access-139)
- Open and close a subdatasheet.(Access-140)
- Use a search engine to find information. (Access-142)

Lesson Summary & Exercises

CONCEPTS REVIEW

1 TRUE/FALSE

Circle T if the statement is true or F if the statement is false.

T   F   **1.** To copy selected records from one table to another, first select the desired records by clicking and dragging along their record selectors.

T   F   **2.** The record with the focus is the same thing as the current record.

T   F   **3.** You can press `Tab` or `⇧ Shift` + `Tab` to move among records.

T   F   **4.** The Replace command is useful for changing multiple instances of the same characters.

T   F   **5.** In a one-to-many relationship, the related table contains a foreign key which relates it to the primary table.

T   F   **6.** Although datasheets are very useful when making changes to a table, forms are usually more useful when browsing a large number of records.

T   F   **7.** A pencil icon in the row selector indicates a new record in which you can type.

T   F   **8.** The indicator under the datasheet shows the current record number and the total number of records in the table.

T   F   **9.** When you scroll records, the record with the focus is changed.

T   F   **10.** To view a table in Datasheet view, click the name in the Database window and then click the Open button.

2 MATCHING

Match each of the terms on the left with the definitions on the right.

TERMS	DEFINITIONS
1. ditto key	**a.** Temporary storage area in your computer's memory
2. record selector	**b.** The command used to copy data from Clipboard into current table
3. frozen	
4. datasheet	**c.** Column that has been removed from view on the datasheet
5. focus	**d.** Term describing the current record—record that will be affected by any actions
6. referential integrity	
7. reverse video	**e.** Repeats value from same field of previous record
8. Paste Append	**f.** Light text on dark background
9. hidden	**g.** Column-and-row layout you can use to enter, edit, and view data
10. Clipboard	**h.** Column that has been locked into place so that it is always visible on screen
	i. Box on which you can click to select a row
	j. Rules that Access enforces to safeguard data

Lesson Summary & Exercises

3 COMPLETION

Fill in the missing word or phrase for each of the following statements.

1. To move to the previous field in the current record, press _____.

2. To move to the last record in a database, press the _____ key combination or click the _____ navigation button.

3. A(n) _____ in the record selector indicates a new, blank record into which you may type data.

4. In a _____ relationship, every record in a table can have either no matching records or only a single matching record in the other table.

5. To copy an entire table into your database, you can _____ it.

6. Plus signs before the records in a datasheet indicate that a _____ exists for each record.

7. The _____ button lets you reverse your most recent changes.

8. The _____ command lets you substitute one set of characters for another throughout the table.

9. The _____ window makes editing large text or memo fields easier.

10. The Internet tool that allows you to search for information on a particular topic is called a _____.

4 SHORT ANSWER

Write a brief answer to each of the following questions.

1. Explain the differences between one-to-one, one-to-many, and many-to-many relationships.

2. Describe how data is saved in Access. When might you use the Save Record command?

3. Under what circumstances might you increase the height of rows in Datasheet view? When might you use the Zoom window instead?

4. What command do you use to reverse all changes you have made to the current record? What command would you use to reverse the changes to a record that has already been saved?

5. Briefly describe the advantages and disadvantages of using the Replace button rather than the Replace All button in the Replace dialog box.

6. If you know that someone lives on Riverside Drive but don't know the street number, which option would you pick from the Match drop-down list box in the Find dialog box?

7. How do you ensure that your changes to the datasheet layout will be retained?

8. Describe the steps you would take to copy some of the records from a table called Unpaid to a table called Payables.

9. Describe the steps you would take to copy a table from a database called Inventory into a database called Assets.

10. Describe the difference between hidden and frozen columns.

Lesson Summary & Exercises

5 IDENTIFICATION

Label each of the elements in the datasheet in Figure 3.31.

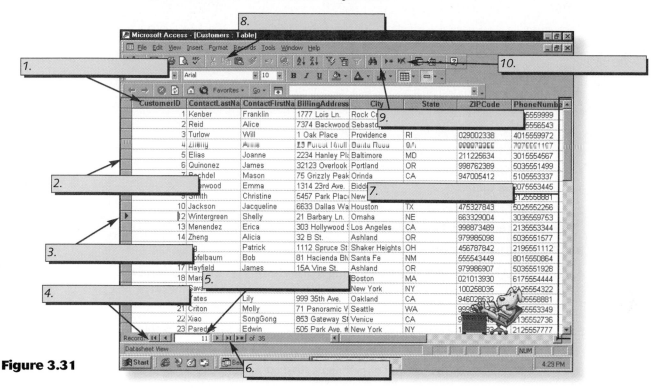

Figure 3.31

SKILLS REVIEW

Complete each of the Skills Review problems in sequential order to review your skills to add, copy and paste, import, edit, and find data in a table; change the datasheet display; and work with multiple tables.

1 Open a Table and Add Data

1. Start Access and open the *Smyth Business College, Lesson 3* database in the *Skills Review* folder on your Student Data Disk.

2. Click the **Class Schedules table** and click the **Open button** 🔲Open in the Database window.

3. Type **AC101** in the first row of the Class Code field and press ⟦Tab⟧.

4. Type **Accounting 1** in the Class Name field and press ⟦Tab⟧.

5. Type **Berbarg** in the Instructor Name field and press ⟦Tab⟧.

6. Type **MWF** in the Days field and press ⟦Tab⟧.

7. Type **8:00-8:50 am** in the Time field and press ⟦Tab⟧ to move to the second record.

8. Type the data in Table 3.2 into the table. Then, close the table.

Lesson Summary & Exercises

TABLE 3.2	CLASS SCHEDULES TABLE DATA			
Field	**Record 2**	**Record 3**	**Record 4**	**Record 5**
Class Code	AC102	AC201	AC202	AC203
Class Name	Accounting 2	Financial Accounting	Managerial Accounting	Cost Accounting
Instructor Name	Abner	Nieves	Way	Crawford
Days	MWF	TR	TR	MWF
Time	10:00-10:50 am	10:00-11:30 am	4:00-5:30 pm	12:00-12:50 pm

2 Copy and Paste Data from a Table

1. Open the *Smyth Business College, Lesson 1* database and open the Class Information table.

2. Click the **field selector** in front of the record for AC301 and drag down to select the records through MK202.

3. Click the **Copy button** 🖻 on the Database toolbar.

4. Close the table and click **Yes** if a warning box asks you if you want to save the data to the Clipboard. (Since you are copying only 18 records, the message may not appear.)

5. Reopen the *Smyth Business College, Lesson 3* database in the *Skills Review* folder and open the Class Schedules table.

6. Click **Edit** on the menu bar and click **Paste Append**.

7. When the message appears asking if you want to paste the records, click **Yes**.

8. Click anywhere in the table to remove the highlighting and click the **Maximize button** 🔲. Then, close the table.

9. Reopen the *Smyth Business College, Lesson 1* database and open the Student Information table.

10. Press Ctrl + A to select all of the records in the table, click the **Copy button** 🖻, and close the table. Click **Yes** to save the data to the Clipboard.

11. Reopen the *Smyth Business College, Lesson 3* database in the *Skills Review* folder.

12. Open the Student Information table, click **Edit** on the menu bar, and click **Paste Append**. Click **Yes** to paste the records. Then, close the table.

3 Import Data

1. Click File on the menu bar, point to Get External Data, and click Import on the submenu.

2. Navigate to your Student Data Disk files and open the *Smyth Business College, Lesson 1* database.

3. Click the **Tables tab**, and click **Grades for Accounting Classes**. Then, click **OK** to import the table.

4. Open the *Best of the Orchard* database on your Student Data Disk. Click **File** on the menu bar, point to **Get External Data**, click **Import**, and click **Microsoft Excel** as the Files of type.

5. Navigate to the *Fruit and Units* file on your Student Data Disk.

6. Double-click the file name and click **Next** to continue with the Wizard.

7. Click **Next** to accept First Row Contains Column Headings.

8. Click **Next** to accept In a New Table.

9. Click **Next** to accept the Field Options.

10. Click **Choose my own primary key**. Set Fruit Type as the primary key. Click **Next**.

11. Type Fruit and Units as the table name and click **Finish**.

12. Close the database.

4 Move Among Rows and Columns

1. Open the *Smyth Business College, Lesson 3* database in the *Skills Review* folder on your Student Data Disk. Open the Student Information table and maximize your view.

2. Click the **Next Record navigation button** ▶ five times. Note which record is current.

3. Click the **Last Record button** ▶|.

4. Double-click the **Previous Record button** ◀.

5. Click the **First Record button** |◀.

6. Double-click the current record number in the text box at the bottom of the datasheet.

7. Type **46** and press Enter↵. The focus moves to the record for Owen Shrimp.

8. Press ↑ four times. The focus moves to the record for Donald Brewer.

9. Press ↓ twice. The focus moves to the record for Glenn Comrey.

10. Press Tab four times.

11. Press ⇧Shift + Tab to move back one column.

12. Press Ctrl + End to move to the last field of the last record.

13. Press Ctrl + Home to move to the first field of the first record.

5 Edit Records and Undo Changes

1. Press F5, type **29**, and press Enter↵ to move to the record for Casey Bridges.

2. Press Tab to move to the Major field. Type **Accounting** and press Tab.

3. Press Tab three times to move to the Address field for Susan Ozinga. Click after the word *Spring* and type **Grove** so that the address reads *2475 Spring Grove Rd. SE.*

4. Press F2 to select the contents of the field.

5. Double-click the **City field** for Utamaro Isobe (record 12) and press Delete to delete the city name.

6. Click the **Undo button** ↺ to reverse the change.

7. Move to the first record (for George Robinson) and change the Phone Number field to **(770) 555-3536**. Press ⊞Tab and change the major to **Marketing**. Click the **Undo button** 🔄 to change the major back to Finance.

8. Double-click the **Undo button** 🔄 to change the phone number back to (770) 555-5180.

9. In record 9, change the text in the Last Name field to **Dorsey** and press ⊞Tab.

10. Change the text in the First Name field to **Mitchell** and press ⊞Tab.

11. Press ⬇ to move to record 10.

12. Click **Edit** on the menu bar and click **Undo Saved Record**.

13. Click the **record selector** for Stephen Carrington (record 23). Click the **Delete Record button** 📩. When the warning box appears asking if you want to delete the record, click **Yes**.

14. Move to the Address field for Marietta Jolly (record 2).

15. Press ⇧Shift + F2 to open the Zoom window. Change the apartment number to **#310**. Click **OK**.

6 Add Information with the Ditto Key

1. Press F2 to leave edit mode.

2. Press Ctrl + End and then press ⊞Tab to create a new record.

3. Press ⊞Tab to move to the Last Name field, press Ctrl + ' and press ⊞Tab to move to the First Name field.

4. Type **Mary** and press ⊞Tab.

5. Use the ditto key to copy the Address, City, State, ZIP Code, and Phone Number fields.

6. Type **Finance** in the Major field and press ⊞Tab to complete and save the record.

7 Find and Replace Data in the Table

1. Move to the City field of the first record and click the **Find button** 🔍.

2. Type **Marietta** in the Find What box. In the Look In box, click **City**. Click **Find Next** until all occurrences are found. When the message appears stating that the search item was not found, click **OK**.

3. Double-click the text in the Find What box, type **General Business** and then click the **Find Next button**. When the message appears saying the item was not found, click **OK**.

4. Click the **Look In drop-down arrow** in the Find and Replace box and click the **Student Information Table**.

5. Click **Find Next** to find each occurrence of *General Business*. When the message appears stating that the search item was not found, click **OK**.

6. Move to the top of the table and click the **Replace tab** in the Find and Replace dialog box.

7. Type **Mathematics** in the Find What box and type **Business Mathematics** in the Replace With box. Then click **Find Next**.

8. When the first occurrence of *Mathematics* is found, click **Replace**.

9. When the second occurrence of *Mathematics* is found, click **Replace All**. When the warning box tells you that you will not be able to undo changes, click **Yes**.

10. Close the Find and Replace dialog box.

8 Resize Columns and Rows

1. Point to the column border between the Address and City fields. Drag to the right to widen the Address column so that you can see the entire address in record 2.

2. Drag the column border between the Student ID and Last Name fields to the left to narrow the Student ID column so that it is about three or four characters wide.

3. Drag the border between any two rows down to double the size.

4. Narrow the Address field again so that the address for record 2 displays in full in two rows instead of one.

9 Change Field Order and Hide and Freeze Columns

1. Click the **column selector** for the Major field.

2. Drag the Major column to the left until the heavy vertical line is just to the right of the First Name column and release.

3. Click the **column selector** of the Address field.

4. Click **Format** on the menu bar and click **Hide Columns**.

5. Click **Format** on the menu bar and click **Unhide Columns**.

6. In the Unhide Columns dialog box, click the **check boxes** beside the City, State, and ZIP Code fields to remove the check marks in them.

7. Close the Unhide Columns dialog box.

8. Click **Format** on the menu bar and click **Unhide Columns**.

9. In the Unhide Columns dialog box, click the **check boxes** beside the Address, City, State, and ZIP Code fields to add check marks to them. Then close the Unhide Columns dialog box.

10. Click the **Last Name column selector**.

11. Click **Freeze Columns** on the Format menu.

12. Scroll to the Phone Number field. Notice that the Last Name field stays in view.

13. Click **Format** on the menu bar and click **Unfreeze All Columns**.

14. Click the **Close button** ☒.

15. When the message box appears asking if you want to save the changes, click **No**.

10 Create and Print Relationships

1. Click the **Relationships button** ⊞. When the Show Table dialog box appears, double-click the **Student Information table**, the **Class Schedules table**, and the **Grades for Accounting Classes table**. Close the Show Table dialog box.

2. Click the **Student ID field** in the Student Information Field list and drag it to the Student ID field in the Grades for Accounting Classes Field list.

3. When the Edit Relationships dialog box appears, click the **Create button**.

4. Click the **Class Code field** in the Class Schedules Field list and drag it to the Class Code field in the Grades for Accounting Classes Field list.

5. When the Edit Relationships dialog box appears, click the **Enforce Referential Integrity option** and click the **Create button**.

6. Close the Relationships window.

7. When the warning box asks if you want to save the relationship, click **Yes**.

8. Click **Tools** on the menu bar and click **Relationships**.

9. Click **File** on the menu bar and click **Print Relationships**. Then, click the **Print button** 🖨.

10. Close the Print Preview window, saving your changes with the default report name, and close the Relationships window.

11 Open a Subdatasheet

1. Open the Class Schedules table.

2. Click the **plus sign** in front of the record for AC203.

3. Look at the subdatasheet that appears listing the grades earned by students enrolled in this class.

4. Close the subdatasheet by clicking the **minus sign** in front of the record for AC203.

5. Close the Class Schedules table.

6. Select the **Compact on Close option** in the Options dialog box, if necessary.

7. Close the *Smyth Business College, Lesson 3* database and exit Access.

LESSON APPLICATIONS

1 Enter Record Data

As an employee of Payton Properties, Inc., you need to add data to the tables in the *Payton Properties, Lesson 3* database and add records to an existing table. You will also copy and paste records into the database.

1. Open the *Payton Properties, Lesson 3* database in the *Lesson Applications* folder of your Student Data Disk. Open the Homes for Sale table.

2. Type the data in Table 3.3 into records 1 through 4.

Lesson Summary & Exercises

TABLE 3.3		HOMES FOR SALE TABLE DATA		
Field	**Record 1**	**Record 2**	**Record 3**	**Record 4**
Address	1010 Springfield Pike	117 Pinehurst Dr.	121 Pleasant Ridge Ave.	1316 Morten Ct.
Bedrooms	4	2	4	3
Baths	2.5	2	1.5	1.5
Sq. Feet	2200	1560	1850	1250
Rooms	8	6	7	6
Year Built	1998	2001	1994	1967
Price	$176,000	$130,700	$104,000	$89,000
Agent ID	2	3	4	1

3. Click File on the menu bar, click Open, and open the **Payton Properties, Lesson 1** database on your Student Data Disk.

4. Open the Homes for Sale table and highlight records 5 through 16 (addresses from *1324 Alberta Way* through *861 Ridgedale Dr.*).

5. Click the Copy button. Then close the table.

6. Reopen the Homes for Sale table in the **Payton Properties, Lesson 3** database in the **Lesson Applications** folder on your Student Data Disk. Paste the records into the table using the Paste Append command. Close the table.

7. Open the **Payton Properties, Lesson 1** database, open the Employee Statistics table, and copy all of the records. Close the table.

8. Open **Payton Properties, Lesson 3** in the **Lesson Applications** folder on your Student Data Disk. Open the Agent Statistics table.

9. Paste the copied records into the table. Then, close the Agent Statistics table.

2 Import a Table and Edit the Data

Use the Import command to create a new table in the **Payton Properties, Lesson 3** database. Then edit some of the data in the new table.

1. Open **Payton Properties, Lesson 3** in the **Lesson Applications** folder on your Student Data Disk, if necessary.

2. Click File on the menu bar, point to Get External Data, and click Import.

3. Select **Payton Properties, Lesson 1** in the Import dialog box. Then, select the Employees table in the Import Objects dialog box. Click OK to import the Employees table.

4. Open the Employees table and read the data in it. Move to the field that contains the hire dates for each employee.

5. Move to the field that contains the address for Kelly Perez and change it to **1288 Gordon St.**

6. Click the View button to view the Employees table in Design view. Change the name of the first field to **AgentID** and change the caption to **Agent ID**.

7. Save and close the table.

Lesson Summary & Exercises

3 Edit a Table

Use the Homes for Sale table to edit data, undo a change, delete a record, and change the width of columns. Then close and save the table. Use the Find command to find all homes that were sold by a particular agent. Then use the Find and Replace command several times to make global changes to the table. Finally, change the format properties.

1. Open the Homes for Sale table in the **Payton Properties, Lesson 3** database in the **Lesson Applications** folder. Change the price of the house at 2600 Alexandria St. to $150,500.

2. You realize that you changed the price of the wrong home; reverse the change and then change the price of the house at 3237 Sugar Tree Rd. to $150,500.

3. The house at 1324 Alberta Way has just sold. Delete the record for this house.

4. Adjust the size of each column in the table to better fit the data contained in it.

5. Close the table. When the Office Assistant asks if you want to save the changes, click Yes.

6. Reopen the Homes for Sale table. Click Font on the Format menu.

7. Change the font to Times New Roman, size 11.

8. Click the Font button and change the font back to Arial.

9. Click the Font Size button and change the font back to 10.

10. Open the Homes Sold table. Use the Find command to find all of the houses in the table that were sold by Priscilla Mayer, agent ID 1.

11. Double the size of each row so that you can better see the address of each property.

12. To be consistent with the Homes for Sale table, you want to abbreviate the street descriptions. Use the Find and Replace command to change the following character strings in the Property Address field: change Drive to Dr., Avenue to Ave., Court to Ct., Street to St., Road to Rd., and Lane to Ln.

4 Zoom, Move, Hide, and Freeze Fields

First, use the Zoom feature to make editing of a field easier. Then use the skills you've learned in this lesson to move, freeze, hide, unfreeze, and unhide various columns. Close the database without saving the changes.

1. With the Homes Sold table still open (in the **Payton Properties, Lesson 3** database in the **Lesson Applications** folder), scroll to the Notes field for the home at 10 Anderson Pl.

2. Display the Zoom window for this field and edit the text to read as follows:

   Seller's company purchased home due to transfer. The company was going to switch to another real estate agency but Benji Eto convinced them to remain with Payton Properties. Benji sold the home one week later.

3. Move the Selling Price field so that it appears as the second field, immediately following the Property Address field.

4. Freeze the Property Address field and scroll until you can see the Notes field.

5. Hide the Buyer's Name and Percent of Listing Price fields.

6. Unfreeze and unhide all columns.

7. Close the table without saving the changes.

5 Create a New Record with the Ditto Key

Use the ditto key to help you enter data for a new record. Then when you discover the sellers have changed their minds, undo the changes to the saved record.

1. Open the Homes for Sale table in the *Payton Properties, Lesson 3* database in the *Lesson Applications* folder, and click the New Record button.

2. Type **804 Sycamore Dr.** in the Address field and press [Tab].

3. Use the ditto key to repeat the data in the Bedrooms and Baths fields of the previous record.

4. Type **1950** in the Sq. Feet field.

5. Use the ditto key to repeat the data in the Rooms, Year Built, Price, and Agent ID fields.

6. Press [Tab] to save the record.

7. You just found out that the sellers have decided to wait to sell their home. Use the Undo Saved Record command to remove the entire record you just created.

8. Close the table.

6 Define Relationships and View Subdatasheets

Join fields in all four tables in the *Payton Properties, Lesson 3* database to form relationships. Then, you will view two subdatasheets in two tables.

1. Open the *Payton Properties, Lesson 3* database in the *Lesson Applications* folder, if necessary.

2. Click the Relationships button [icon] to display the Relationships window. When the Show Tables dialog box appears, double-click each table to display it and then close the dialog box.

3. Create a relationship between the Agent Statistics and Employees tables by joining the AgentID fields. Do not choose the option to enforce referential integrity.

4. Create a relationship between the Employees and Homes for Sale tables by joining the AgentID fields. Choose the option to enforce referential integrity.

5. Create a relationship between the Employees and Homes Sold tables by joining the AgentID fields. Choose the option to enforce referential integrity.

6. Close the Relationships window, saving the relationships.

7. Open the Agent Statistics table and view the subdatasheet for the first record. Then, close the subdatasheet and then close the table.

8. Open the Employees table and click the plus sign in front of the record for Brian Matthews (record 3).

Lesson Summary & Exercises

9. Since the Employees table is related to more than one other table, the Insert Subdatasheet dialog box appears. Click Homes for Sale and then click OK. The list of homes for sale by this agent appears in the subdatasheet.

10. Close the table without saving the layout changes.

11. Select the Compact on Close option, if necessary, and close the database.

PROJECTS

1 'Tis the Shopping Season

You have recently created a database to track the products, employees, and sales for Electro Shop. Now that you have created the table designs, you are ready to enter data into them. Open the **Electro Shop, Lesson 3** database in the **Projects** folder, and open the December Sales table. Type the data for the first half of December found in Table 3.4 into the table. After you enter the data, close the table.

TABLE 3.4	DECEMBER SALES TABLE DATA			
Sale ID	**Employee ID**	**Product ID**	**Date Sold**	**Quantity Sold**
1	2	1	12/1/2001	1
2	8	3	12/1/2001	1
3	1	8	12/2/2001	1
4	6	16	12/2/2001	2
5	7	2	12/2/2001	1
6	2	6	12/2/2001	1
7	1	17	12/3/2001	1
8	3	12	12/3/2001	1
9	2	19	12/3/2001	1
10	6	8	12/3/2001	1
11	1	13	12/3/2001	1
12	2	16	12/3/2001	1
13	3	3	12/3/2001	1
14	6	9	12/4/2001	1
15	2	6	12/4/2001	1
16	3	16	12/4/2001	1
17	5	14	12/4/2001	1
18	7	19	12/4/2001	1

TABLE 3.4		DECEMBER SALES TABLE DATA—cont.		
Sale ID	**Employee ID**	**Product ID**	**Date Sold**	**Quantity Sold**
19	1	5	12/4/2001	3
20	9	1	12/5/2001	1
21	1	18	12/5/2001	1
22	4	9	12/5/2001	1
23	6	2	12/5/2001	1
24	8	7	12/5/2001	2
25	0	1	12/6/2001	1
26	5	10	12/6/2001	1
27	8	11	12/6/2001	1
28	2	1	12/6/2001	1
29	5	3	12/6/2001	1
30	4	13	12/6/2001	1
31	3	5	12/6/2001	1
32	5	10	12/7/2001	1
33	4	7	12/7/2001	1
34	8	17	12/7/2001	2
35	4	18	12/7/2001	1
36	8	11	12/7/2001	1
37	7	4	12/8/2001	1
38	7	17	12/8/2001	1
39	5	10	12/8/2001	1
40	4	15	12/8/2001	1
41	6	12	12/8/2001	2
42	3	4	12/8/2001	1
43	9	17	12/8/2001	1

2 In with the New, Out with the Old

Your next job is to add data to the table that contains descriptions and prices of
the products you carry in the **Electro Shop, Lesson 3** database in the **Projects** folder
on your Student Data Disk. You've just restocked your inventory with new television models, so you'll start by typing the televisions into the table. Open the
Products table and type the information in Table 3.5 as the first five records of
the table.

Lesson Summary & Exercises

TABLE 3.5		DATA TO ENTER			
Product ID	Product Type	Brand	Model	Price	Notes
1	TV	Keiko	KS250	$219.95	25" screen
2	TV	Keiko	KS450	$899.95	36" screen
3	TV	RML	1800	$548.95	32" screen
4	TV	RML	2000	$1299.95	52" screen
5	TV	ClearPict	CPX27	$396.95	27" screen

Now you need to add the other products. Since these haven't changed, you can copy them from another table. Open the **Electro Shop, Lesson 1** database and copy records 6 through 19 from the Products table. Then, reopen the Products table in the **Electro Shop, Lesson 3** database in the **Projects** folder and paste the records. Close the table.

3 Tell Us About Your Salespeople

The last table you need to add is a table that provides information about the Electro Shop employees. Since this table has been created previously, simply import the Employees table from the **Electro Shop, Lesson 1** database to the **Electro Shop, Lesson 3** database in the **Projects** folder on your Student Data Disk. After you import the table, open it to view the data. Then close the table.

4 More Product Changes

A few prices and features of some of your products have changed, so you need to edit the table that contains them. Open the Products table in the **Electro Shop, Lesson 3** database in the **Projects** folder on your Student Data Disk. Change the price of the RML 900 video camera (record 13) to $419.95 and change the price of the Keiko VCR (record 16) to $579.95. Reverse the last change (the price change to record 16) and change the price of the Wiley video camera to $579.95 instead. Open the Zoom window for the Notes field of the Keiko video camera (record 12) and type **Manufacturer is offering a $100 rebate on video cameras sold between 12/1/2001 and 12/15/2001.** Lastly, Wiley has just merged with another company and the new company name is Wiley/Markle. Find all occurrences of *Wiley* and replace them with *Wiley/Markle.* Close the table.

5 How Is Each Salesperson Doing?

Open the December Sales table in the **Electro Shop, Lesson 3** database in the **Projects** folder on your Student Data Disk. To record a few returns and exchanges, make the following changes:

- Delete record 22, since this item was returned.
- Delete record 12. Since this item was exchanged for a different VCR, add a new record at the end of the table. Include the same employee number (2), but change the product ID to 19 and the date to 12/9/2001. Leave the quantity as 1.

You'd like to know how each salesperson is doing so far this month. With the December Sales table still open, search for all occurrences of each employee number in the Employee ID field. Count the number of sales made by each employee and record them on a separate sheet of paper. For instance, first search for all sales made by employee 1, then for all sales made by employee 2, etc. Close the table when you are finished.

6 Connecting the Tables

Since you'd like to view subdatasheets, assign relationships among the tables in the *Electro Shop, Lesson 3* database in the *Projects* folder on your Student Data Disk. Create a one-to-many relationship, enforcing referential integrity, between the Employees and December Sales tables by joining the EmployeeID fields. Then create a one-to-many relationship, enforcing referential integrity, between the Products and December Sales tables by joining the ProductID fields. Then open the Products table. Open the subdatasheet for record 17 and see how many RML VCRs have been sold so far this month. Lastly, open the Employees table and use a subdatasheet to view the sales by David Trimble. Close all open tables.

7 How Do You Want to View That Data?

Open the Products table again in the *Electro Shop, Lesson 3* database in the *Projects* folder on your Student Data Disk. Maximize the window and adjust all of the column sizes so that you can easily view all data in them. Then freeze the Product ID field and scroll to see the Notes field. Unfreeze the column and hide the Product ID, Model, and Notes fields. Close the table without saving changes.

8 More Sales Coming In

Open the December Sales table in the *Electro Shop, Lesson 3* database in the *Projects* folder on your Student Data Disk. You've decided to rearrange this table so that you can see the Date Sold column sooner. Move the Date Sold column so that it appears immediately to the right of the Sale ID column. Adjust the sizes of all columns to best fit the labels and data in them.

Rosa Vazquez sold one ClearPict television on 12/9/2001. Add the record to the end of the table, using the ditto key to repeat some of the fields from the previous record. Then add another sale showing that Foster Nelson sold one ClearPict television on the same date. Move to the next record and then undo the change to the saved record, since the customer immediately returned the television.

Close the table, saving layout changes when prompted. Select the Compact on Close option, if necessary and close the *Payton Properties, Lesson 3* database.

Lesson Summary & Exercises

9 Higher Education on the Web

Assume you work at Smyth Business College as the assistant to the dean. Students often ask the dean about continuing their education after they graduate from Smyth. She would like you to use the Internet to research other schools in Georgia that offer graduate programs. Connect to the Internet and use a search engine to find information on graduate schools in Georgia. Click several links to results and generate a list of at least three schools that meet the dean's needs, listing their locations and the types of graduate degrees offered.

Project in Progress

10 Adding Data to the I-Comm Tables

Open the *I-Comm* database in the *Projects* folder that you created in Lesson 2. Open the Customers table and add the records listed in Table 3.6.

TABLE 3.6	RECORDS TO ADD TO CUSTOMERS TABLE		
Fields	**Record 1**	**Record 2**	**Record 3**
Customer ID	(AutoNumber)	(AutoNumber)	(AutoNumber)
Company Name	Liette Lawn Care	Eastwood Insurance Agency	Little Tots Daycare
Contact Last Name	Liette	Saini	Bess
Contact First Name	Alec	Reeta	Samuel
Contact Title	Owner	Human Resources Manager	Owner
Billing Address	34 Mitchell Ave.	1799 Northwest Blvd.	2020 Hopkins Rd.
City	Memphis	Bartlett	Memphis
State	TN	TN	TN
ZIP Code	38119-8324	38133-7444	38101-7233
Phone Number	(901) 555-2839	(901) 555-0034	(901) 555-7632

Copy records 4 through 32 from the Customers table of the *I-Comm, Lesson 1* database on your Student Data Disk to the new Customers table. Reopen the *I-Comm, Lesson 1* database and copy all of the records in the Projects table. Paste those records to your new, blank Projects table in the *I-Comm* database. Lastly, import the Employees table from the *I-Comm, Lesson 1* database to your new *I-Comm* database. Adjust the column sizes of each of the tables appropriately. With the *I-Comm* database open, make the following changes to your tables:

TABLE 3.7	REVISIONS TO TABLES
Table Name	**Revision**
Projects	Change the hours in record 11 to 26; change the fee for this record to $1,440.
Customers	Change the phone number in record 24 to (901) 555-7500.
Customers	Change the company name in record 29 to Kirsten Weinberg-Mertz, CPA and change the last name for this record to Weinberg-Mertz.

Open the Relationships window for the database and create a one-to-many relationship, enforcing referential integrity, between the Customers and Projects tables by joining the CustomerID fields. Then create a one-to-many relationship, enforcing referential integrity, between the Employees and Projects tables by joining the EmployeeID field to the I-CommProjectManager field. Print your database relationships. Compact and close the database.

LESSON 4

Retrieving Data

CONTENTS

_Sorting and Selecting Data

_Using the Sort Commands

_Filtering Your Data

_Designing Basic Queries

_Querying Multiple Tables

_On the Web: Creating
Hyperlinks

OBJECTIVES

After you complete this lesson, you will be able to do
the following:

■ Select an object using the Objects bar.

■ Sort records.

■ Apply and remove filters.

■ Specify criteria in a query.

■ Edit the data in the recordset of a query.

■ Save queries.

■ Create and modify a multi-table select
query.

■ Create a hyperlink to another object,
another database, and a Web site.

Raw data can supply lots of information, but often the best way to get your point across is to display only the necessary numbers. A well-conceived query, pulling data from multiple tables, can let you select just the records you need and put the data into the desired order.

Lesson 4 describes the tools Access has for manipulating data: sort commands and queries. Often you'll need to modify your initial query in some way. You'll learn several easy ways to fine-tune your queries—by changing the fields used and selecting data from multiple tables. You can also enhance your query results by only displaying the required results in the query's recordset. Finally, you'll save your queries for future use and modification.

SORTING AND SELECTING DATA

In the previous lessons, you devoted a considerable amount of energy to setting up tables and gathering data into them. But no matter how well you've thought out your table structures, this raw data may not prove to be all that useful, especially as your database accumulates more and more information. In this lesson, you'll begin to make sense of your data. You'll discover several ways to *sort* your data—rearranging records into alphabetical, numerical, or chronological order. You'll also find out how to select the data you need—extracting specified groups of data based on factors that you define. You might want to see all customers who live in California, for example, or all orders placed after some designated date.

For both sorting and selecting data, Access is immeasurably more useful than even the most well-organized manual system. In a manual system, you can sort in only one way unless you create duplicate sets of data; for instance, you might arrange your records in alphabetical order by customer last name. In Access, by contrast, you can sort the same set of data in any number of ways—you could sort by last name, by data joined, and by ZIP Code, and could then consult the sorted data that best fits the task at hand. The same applies to extracting data. In a manual system, pulling out just the records you need can be a laborious task. In Access, with a little knowledge you can select the precise data you need and can also extract many different groups from the same data.

This lesson first describes the Sort commands, which enable you to sort the data in a single table. Next you'll create filters to both sort and select the data from a single table. A *filter* is pretty much what its name implies: a way to filter, or sift, your data so you can see only a selected portion. Last, you'll learn about queries: Remember, queries allow you to ask questions about your data. You can use queries to both sort and select data, and you'll learn as well how to build queries that ask questions of multiple tables.

USING THE SORT COMMANDS

Access automatically arranges the data in your tables according to the value in the primary key. In the BFCustomers table, for instance, the customers are arranged by customer ID, with customer 1 appearing before customer 2, and so on. Undoubtedly, however, at times you'll want to view your data in some other sequence—maybe in order by last name or by ZIP Code.

You can sort data on any field except for Memo, Hyperlink, and OLE Object fields. Access sorts Text fields into alphabetical order, considers lower- and uppercase letters to be the same, and lists digits before letters. An *ascending sort* arranges data from A to Z, and a *descending sort* arranges data from Z to A. Access sorts Number or Currency fields into numerical order—from lower to higher values in an ascending sort and from higher to lower values in a descending sort. Finally, Access sorts Date/Time fields into chronological order. An ascending sort places the earliest dates first, while a descending sort places the most recent dates first.

HANDS On

Access
BASICS

Sorting a Table

1. Click within the field you wish to sort by

Or

Drag over the column selectors to choose more than one field.

2. Click the Sort Ascending or Sort Descending button.

Sorting a Table

In this activity, you'll experiment with the Sort command to rearrange the records in the BFCustomers table in a variety of ways.

1. Open the *Be Fruitful, Lesson 4* database in the *Tutorial* folder of your Student Data Disk. Then open the BFCustomers table. Maximize the table.

You'll see the BFCustomers table in Datasheet view.

2. Click anywhere within the Last Name field.

3. Click the Sort Ascending button ⬛.

Access rearranges the records in the table to display them in ascending order by last name, as shown in Figure 4.1. Notice, for instance, that the record for the customer named Jason Everett is placed after the record for Joanne Elias.

Figure 4.1
Records sorted in ascending order by last name

> *Note* When you close the table, the sort orders established by the Sort commands are only saved if you instruct Access to do so. So, you don't need to worry about returning your data to the original state.

4. Scroll down the records and notice that when there are duplicate last names, such as Smith and Zheng, the first names are not in any kind of order.

5. Select the Last Name and First Name column selectors so that both fields are high-lighted. Then click the Sort Ascending button ⬛.

Access sorts the records in order by last name, and then, where there are duplicate last names, sorts the records in order by first name. The Smiths and the Zhengs are now in alphabetical order by first as well as last names.

Another Way

To sort, click Records on the menu bar, point to Sort, and then click Sort Ascending on the submenu.

When you sort on more than one field, Access sorts first by the leftmost field, then by the field to the right, and so on.

6. Now click anywhere within the ZIP Code field and click the **Sort Descending button** .

Access rearranges the records in order by ZIP Code, with larger numbers first and smaller numbers last.

7. Click anywhere within the Date Joined field and click the **Sort Descending button** .

Access arranges the records in order by date joined. Notice that the most recent dates are displayed first. To see the earliest dates first, you would instead choose an ascending sort.

> *Note* — *Access interprets the dates 1/1/30 through 12/31/99 as 1/1/1930 through 12/31/1999. The dates 1/1/00 through 12/31/29 are interpreted by Access as 1/1/2000 through 12/31/2029. To override these interpretations, you can enter dates with four-digit years such as 5/12/2032.*

8. Click anywhere in the Customer ID field and click the **Sort Ascending button** .

Access returns the records to their original sort order—in ascending order by the primary key field, Customer ID. You can also return a table to its original state just by closing the table and not saving the changes.

FILTERING YOUR DATA

If you want to sort all of the data in a single table, the Sort commands work well. But if you want to do more—let's say you want to sort your records and view only those records for customers in California—a Sort command won't do the job. Instead, you could use a filter to sort your data into the desired order. Like the Sort commands, filters only work on the data in a single table; you usually use a filter to quickly and temporarily change the records you see. You can create a filter using one of four methods: Filter By Selection, Filter By Form, Filter For Input, and the Advanced Filter/Sort window. After you create a filter, you can print it by clicking the Print button on the Database toolbar.

Using the Filter By Selection Method

The simplest way to choose the records you wish to view is to use the Filter By Selection option, which allows you to select specific data in a particular field. Access will display only those records that contain the same data in the specified field. In this activity, you will use the Filter By Selection method to first filter those members who live in California. Then you'll use the same method to filter telephone numbers that contain the digits *901*.

1. In the BFCustomers table, double-click the first State field that contains the state code for California—CA.

1. Double-click the character string you wish to find.

2. Click the Filter By Selection button.

3. To remove the filter, click the Remove Filter button.

2. Click the Filter By Selection button 🔻 **on the Database toolbar.**

Within a few moments, only those records with the CA state code are displayed, as shown in Figure 4.2.

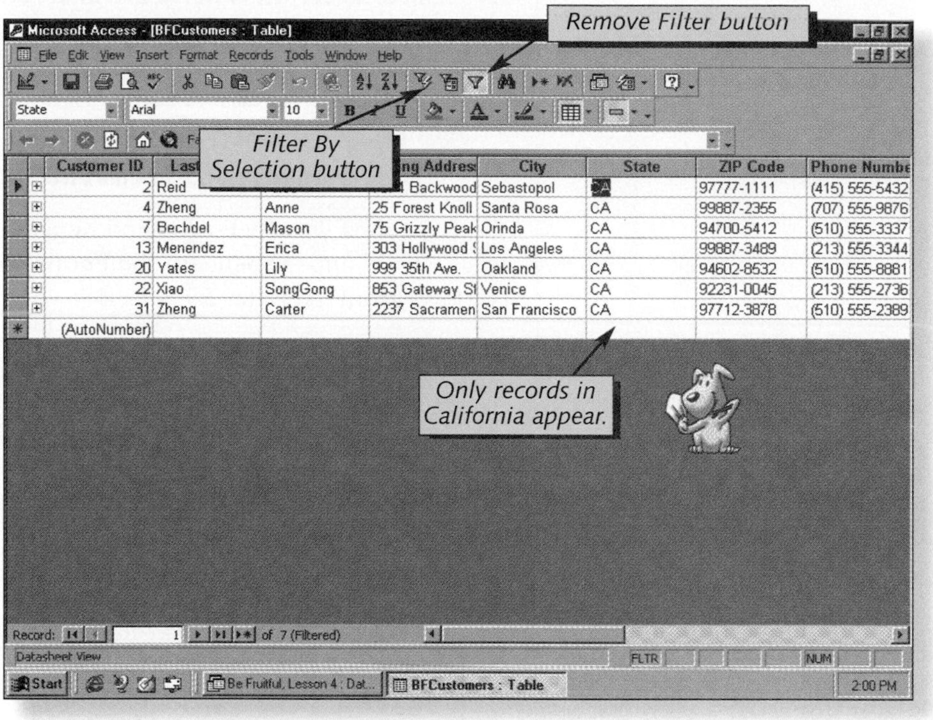

Figure 4.2
Results of a filter that shows only records in California

To display all the records on the datasheet, you must remove the filter.

3. Click the Remove Filter button 🔻 **on the Database toolbar.**

All of the records now reappear on the datasheet. The data you select does not have to be an entire field—you can select only part of a field, and then Access will filter out any records not containing those characters in that field.

4. Select the last two digits of the date from any Date Joined field ending in 98.

5. Click the Filter By Selection button 🔻.

Access displays only those records whose Date Joined field ends in 98.

6. Click the Remove Filter button 🔻.

7. Select a telephone area code that is 901. Only select the digits 901; do not highlight the parentheses surrounding the area code.

8. Click Records on the menu bar and point to Filter. From the submenu that appears, click Filter By Selection.

Two records appear. The first record does have an area code of 901, but the second record has an area code of 617. What happened? As you may have noticed, the second record in the display has 901 as the last three digits of the phone number. When you use Filter By Selection, Access will show records that contain the selection anywhere in the field.

9. Click Records on the menu bar and click Remove Filter/Sort.

Filter By Selection is a convenient locating method—as long as you can select the exact data in a field you want to match. For more flexibility, you need to use another filtering method.

You can also filter for records that do *not* contain a certain string of characters. Highlight the character string you wish to exclude, click Records on the menu bar, point to Filter, and click Filter Excluding Selection.

Using the Filter By Form Method

The Filter By Form method lets you choose more than one selection criteria at once. **Selection criteria** are instructions that tell Access exactly which records to gather from the database. Even when a filter is in effect, you can work in the datasheet much as before: You can add and edit data; hide, move, and resize datasheet columns; and more. In this activity, you'll set up a filter in the Filter By Form window.

1. In the BFCustomers table, click the **Filter By Form button** 🔳.

You'll see the Filter By Form window, as shown in Figure 4.3. The characters *Like "*901*"* appear beneath the Phone Number field name. This entry is a holdover from the Filter By Selection you performed in the previous activity.

Figure 4.3
Filter By Form window

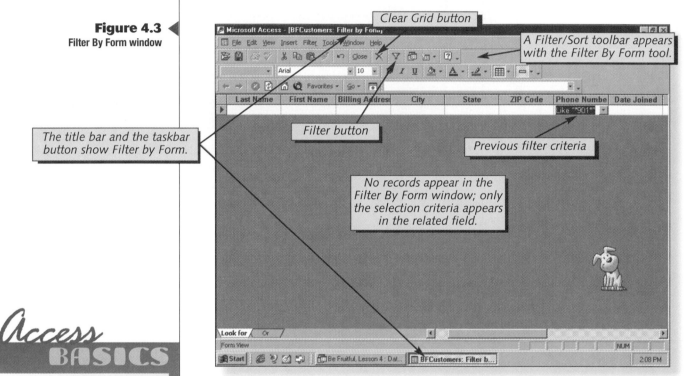

Clear Grid button

A Filter/Sort toolbar appears with the Filter By Form tool.

Filter button

Previous filter criteria

The title bar and the taskbar button show Filter by Form.

No records appear in the Filter By Form window; only the selection criteria appears in the related field.

Access
BASICS

Setting Up the Filter By Form Window

1. Click the Filter By Form button.

2. Delete the previous selection criteria, if necessary.

3. Click the drop-down arrow in the appropriate field and choose the desired selection criteria.

4. Click the Apply Filter button.

You may have noticed several changes to your screen: First, your menu bar now has a Filter option. Second, a new toolbar replaces the one that you have been working with; this new toolbar is called the Filter/Sort toolbar. Finally, the records do not appear in the Filter By Form window—only the field names remain in the top row, and beneath the field names is a row of blank text boxes. You will enter your selection criteria into these boxes.

2. Press ⌦ to remove the previous selection criteria from the Phone Number field.

3. Click the row beneath the Last Name field.

A drop-down arrow appears in the box.

4. Click the **drop-down arrow**.

A list box appears that contains all the last names in the database, as shown in Figure 4.4. The Filter By Form method lets you see the selections in each of the fields, rather than having to search for them as you did in the Filter By Selection method.

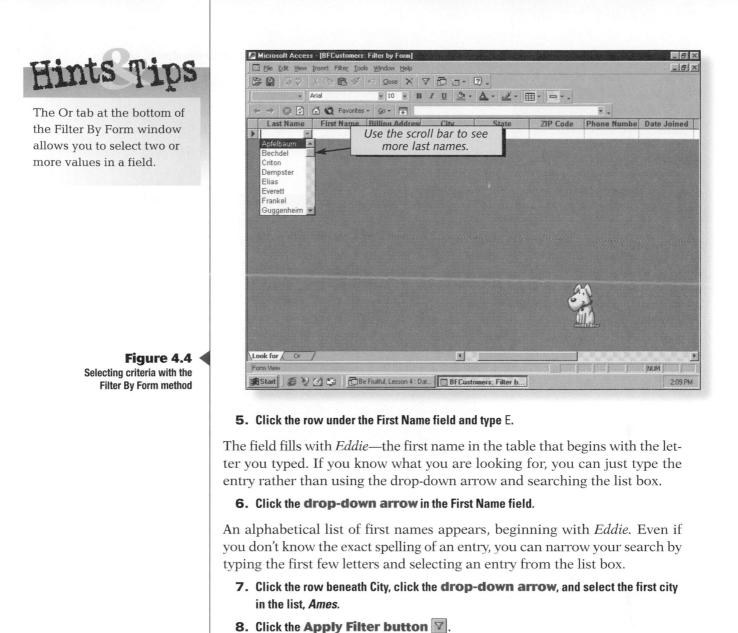

Figure 4.4
Selecting criteria with the Filter By Form method

5. Click the row under the First Name field and type E.

The field fills with *Eddie*—the first name in the table that begins with the letter you typed. If you know what you are looking for, you can just type the entry rather than using the drop-down arrow and searching the list box.

6. Click the **drop-down arrow** in the First Name field.

An alphabetical list of first names appears, beginning with *Eddie.* Even if you don't know the exact spelling of an entry, you can narrow your search by typing the first few letters and selecting an entry from the list box.

7. Click the row beneath City, click the **drop-down arrow**, and select the first city in the list, *Ames.*

8. Click the **Apply Filter button** ▼.

No records appear in the window. This means that no records were found that matched the selection criteria of *Eddie* as the first name in the city of *Ames.* You also may have noticed that your screen has reverted to the previous menu bar and toolbar.

9. Click **Records** on the menu bar, point to **Filter**, and click **Filter By Form**.

You're back to the Filter By Form window. This window only stays active until you apply the selection criteria you have entered.

Selecting Records in Filter By Form

In this activity, you will find some practical uses for the Filter By Form method.

1. Click the **Clear Grid button** ☒ on the Filter/Sort toolbar.

Your previous selection criteria disappear from the screen.

2. Click the row beneath the City field and click the **drop-down arrow**.

The list box contains all of the cities in the table.

3. Scroll down the list and click **New York**.

4. Click the **Apply Filter button** [Y].

You see all the records for the customers who live in the city of New York, as shown in Figure 4.5.

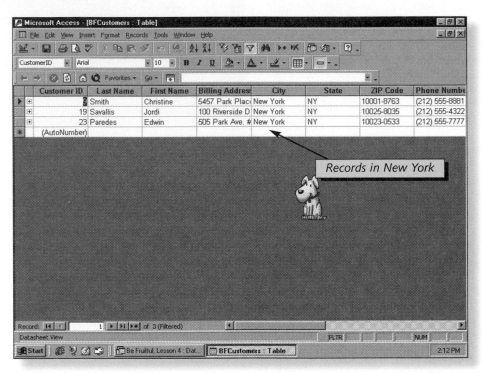

Figure 4.5
Filter showing New York residents

Filtering for Records that Meet One of Several Values

You can also use the Filter By Form method to find any of several values in a field. In a selection criteria, the word *or* means that one or the other must be found. If you want to filter out all records except those containing the names *Elias, Marshall,* or *Ng,* you need to inform Access that one of three names should be displayed. In this activity, you will link these three names together using the Or tab at the bottom of the Filter By Form window.

1. Click the **Filter By Form button** [icon] and click the **Clear Grid button** [X].

2. Click the **Last Name field** and click **Elias** on the drop-down list.

Two tabs appear at the bottom of your screen: *Look for* and *Or*.

3. Click the **Or tab**.

Your first selection criteria—*Elias*—disappears from view.

4. Click the **drop-down arrow** in the Last Name field and click **Marshall**.

5. Click the *second* **Or tab**, click the **drop-down arrow**, and click **Ng**.

You have now informed Access that you want to see records with a last name of Elias *or* Marshall *or* Ng.

6. Click the **Apply Filter button** 🔽.

Figure 4.6 shows that your screen contains three records—one for each of the last names specified in the selection criteria.

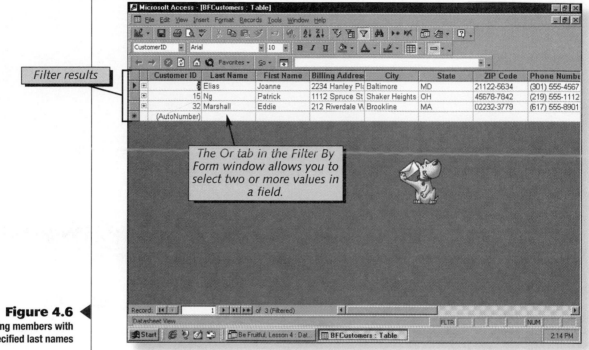

Filter results

The Or tab in the Filter By Form window allows you to select two or more values in a field.

Figure 4.6 ◄
Filter showing members with
specified last names

HANDS On

Access BASICS

Meeting Multiple Criteria

1. Click Filter By Form.

2. Click Clear Grid.

3. Click the drop-down box of the first desired field and choose the selection criteria.

4. Click the drop-down box of one or more additional fields and choose the selection criteria.

5. Click Apply Filter.

Filtering for Records that Meet Multiple Criteria

If, for example, you want to display all customers who live in Venice, California, you have to set up a filter based on two fields: The City field must be Venice and the State field must be CA. You could set up a selection criteria for a state code of CA but that would display records in any city in California. By entering values in both the City and State fields you link the two values in an *and* relationship. The *and* relationship means that both conditions must be met for Access to display a record. In this activity, you will filter for records that meet multiple criteria.

1. Click the **Filter By Form button** 🔳 **and clear your selection criteria.**

2. Click the box below City and click **Venice** on the drop-down list.

3. Click the box below State and click **CA** on the drop-down list.

Your selection criteria should look like that shown in Figure 4.7.

4. Click the **Apply Filter button** 🔽.

You see only one record that meets both conditions.

5. Click the **Remove Filter button** 🔽.

Your unfiltered table reappears.

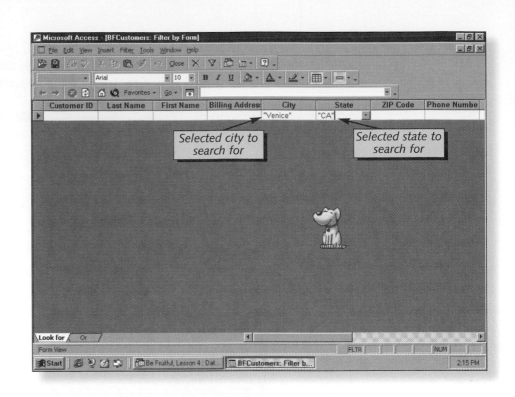

Figure 4.7 ◀
Completed form

1. Right-click the field you wish to filter by.

2. Click Filter For.

3. Type the selection criteria in the Filter For text box and press $\boxed{\text{Enter}}$.

Or

To sort your filter, type the selection criteria in the Filter For box and press $\boxed{\text{Tab}}$; then choose the desired sort option.

Using Filter For Input

Using the Filter By Form method, you can specify criteria by selecting from a list. Using the Filter For Input method, you can quickly access a shortcut menu and type the exact value or expression that you want to use as criteria. You can also use a ***wildcard character*** to search for any number of characters. For example, if you search for *Ma** in the Last Name field, where * is the wildcard character, the filter will return all records for members whose last names begin with *Ma*. In this example, the records for *Marais* and *Marshall* would be included. In this activity, you'll create a filter by typing the exact criteria. You'll also use a wildcard character in a filter.

1. Right-click anywhere in the Last Name field.

A shortcut menu appears.

2. From the shortcut menu, click Filter For.

The insertion point jumps to the Filter For text box. You can use this box to specify filter criteria.

3. Type Smith, **as shown in Figure 4.8, and press** $\boxed{\text{Enter}}$.

The records for all of the customers with the last name of *Smith* appear in the window.

4. Click the Remove Filter button $\boxed{\nabla}$.

Your unfiltered table reappears.

5. Right-click anywhere in the ZIP Code field.

6. Click Filter For on the shortcut menu and type 9*

The asterisk (*) is a wildcard character that finds any number of characters. Typing 9* will find all ZIP Codes that start with 9. You can also use wildcard characters to search for text strings.

7. Press `Tab`.

The records for all of the customers with a ZIP Code beginning with 9 appear in the window. Notice that since you pressed `Tab` instead of `Enter`, the shortcut menu remains on the screen. You may press `Tab` when you want to create another filter, perform a sort, or perform another action on the same field.

8. Click Sort Descending on the shortcut menu.

The shortcut menu disappears and the records are sorted in descending order by ZIP Code, as shown in Figure 4.9.

9. Click the Remove Filter button ▼.

Again, the unfiltered table appears.

Using Advanced Filter/Sort

Using the Filter By Selection, Filter By Form, and Filter For Input methods, you have been able to display records using one or more criteria. You can also sort the data with these methods—but only after you apply the filter. For more complex filters, especially those where you want to sort multiple fields, an Advanced Filter/Sort works well. The Advanced Filter/Sort window allows you to choose criteria for one or more fields to filter as well as choose one or more sort arrangements—all in one window.

With an Advanced Filter/Sort, you can also use an expression as criteria for a filter. An *expression* is a combination of field names, values, and comparison operators that can be evaluated by Access. You can use expressions as criteria not only in the Advanced Filter/Sort method but also in the Filter By

The World Wide Web is a great resource when job searching. Sites such as www.careermosaic.com and www.monster.com provide information on available positions in all kinds of companies.

Figure 4.9
Using a filter and a sort

All ZIP Codes beginning with 9 are sorted in descending order.

Status bar indicates Datasheet view.

Filtered records notation

Using Advanced Filter/Sort

1. Click Records on the menu bar, point to Filter, and click Advanced Filter/Sort.

2. Click the Clear Grid button.

3. Double-click the first field name you wish to use in the Field list.

4. Choose the desired sort option and type the desired criteria below the field name.

5. Click the Apply Filter button.

Form and Filter For Input methods. You can use expressions as criteria in many instances. You may have a situation, for instance, in which you need to see records of customers who have joined the fruit club after 1997. At other times, you might want to show records within a range of values—for example, you might want to find only those customers who joined between 1997 and 1999. In contrast, you might want to exclude particular records, such as when you want to display all records except those of customers in California.

An essential part of most expressions is the comparison operator. A *comparison operator* is a symbol that is used to compare a value or text in the table to characters that you enter. Table 4.1 describes the common comparison operators used in Access.

TABLE 4.1	COMPARISON OPERATORS
Operator	**Description**
=	Equal to
< >	Not equal to
>	Greater than
<	Less than
> =	Greater than or equal to
< =	Less than or equal to
Between...And	Between two specified values

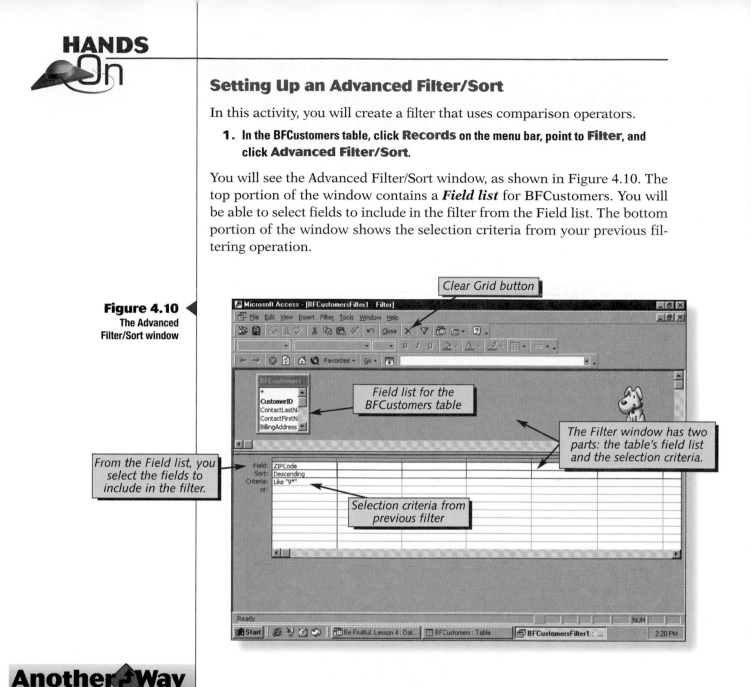
Setting Up an Advanced Filter/Sort

In this activity, you will create a filter that uses comparison operators.

1. In the BFCustomers table, click **Records** on the menu bar, point to **Filter**, and click **Advanced Filter/Sort**.

You will see the Advanced Filter/Sort window, as shown in Figure 4.10. The top portion of the window contains a *Field list* for BFCustomers. You will be able to select fields to include in the filter from the Field list. The bottom portion of the window shows the selection criteria from your previous filtering operation.

Figure 4.10
The Advanced Filter/Sort window

Clear Grid button

Field list for the BFCustomers table

The Filter window has two parts: the table's field list and the selection criteria.

From the Field list, you select the fields to include in the filter.

Selection criteria from previous filter

2. Click the **Clear Grid button** ☒.

3. Scroll the Field list at the top of the window until you see the DateJoined field. Double-click **DateJoined**.

The DateJoined field name is listed in the first Field box in the bottom half of the window.

4. Click the **Sort box** below the DateJoined entry and click the **drop-down arrow** in the Sort box.

You are given the options for sorting the records based on this field.

5. Click **Descending** to sort the records from the most recent to the oldest dates.

Hints & Tips

To cancel both the filter and the sort, click Records on the menu bar, and click Remove Filter/Sort. To keep the records sorted but remove the filter, use the Remove Filter button.

HANDS On

Access BASICS

Filtering Records within a Range

1. Click Records on the menu bar, point to Filter, and click Advanced Filter/Sort.

2. Click the Clear Grid button.

3. Double-click or drag the desired fields from the Field list to the Field box.

4. In the criteria box for one or more fields, type Between XXX And XXX, where XXX is specific criteria.

5. Click the Apply Filter button.

---

6. Click the **Criteria field** below the DateJoined field and type >=3/22/99 in the Criteria box.

You are instructing Access to find all records for customers who joined on or after the date 3/22/99.

7. Click the **Apply Filter button** ▽.

8. Scroll to the right until you can see the DateJoined field. As you can see, Access has displayed the records in descending order for all those who joined on or after 3/22/99.

9. Click **Records** on the menu bar and click **Remove Filter/Sort**.

The table is displayed in its original form.

Filtering Records within a Range

Sometimes you want to specify a range of values between beginning and ending values. In this activity, you will display only those records whose ZIP Codes are between 50000 and 99999 and who have requested extra catalogs.

1. Click **Records** on the menu bar, point to **Filter**, and click **Advanced Filter/Sort**.

The Advanced Filter/Sort window appears.

2. Click the **Clear Grid button** ☒.

The bottom half of the screen is cleared of the previous search and sort criteria.

3. Drag the ContactLastName field from the Field list into the first Field box.

The pointer turns into a small rectangle as you drag the field name into the grid.

4. Click the **Sort box** beneath the ContactLastName field, click the **drop-down arrow**, and click **Descending**.

The display will be in reverse alphabetical order by the last name when you apply the filter. By leaving the Criteria box blank, you will not be excluding any of the last names from the filter.

5. Drag the ZIPCode field from the Field list to the second Field column.

6. Click the **Criteria box** below the ZIPCode field and type Between 50000 And 99999 in the Criteria box.

7. Click the **top box** in the third Field column, click the **drop-down arrow**, and click **ExtraCatalogs** on the list.

8. Type Yes in the Criteria box for ExtraCatalogs.

Typing *Yes* in this Criteria box will display only those customers who have requested extra catalogs (indicated by a check mark in the ExtraCatalogs field check boxes). The Advanced Filter/Sort window should look like the one in Figure 4.11.

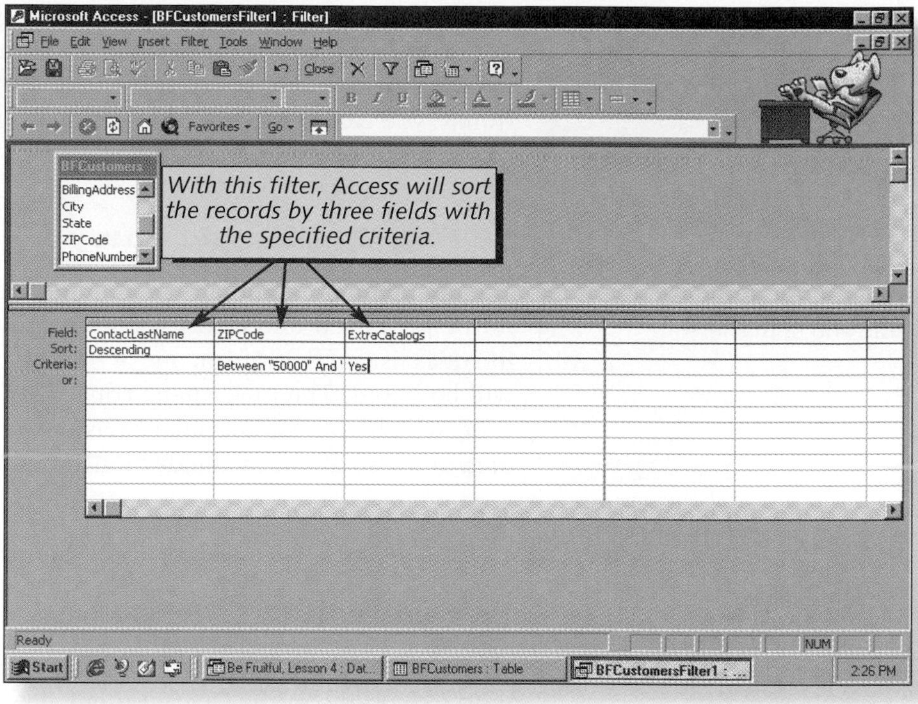

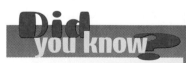

Figure 4.11
The completed Advanced Filter/Sort window

9. Click the Apply Filter button.

Access display 7 records, shown in reverse alphabetical order by last name. All of the records contain ZIP Codes between 50000 and 99999 and contain a check mark in the Extra Catalogs field.

10. Click the Close button to close the BFCustomers table. When you are asked if you want to save changes to the design of your table, click No.

You are back to the Be Fruitful, Lesson 4 Database window.

DESIGNING BASIC QUERIES

Like filters, queries allow you to sort your data in a variety of ways and to extract the data you need by using all types of selection criteria. Queries, however, have several distinct advantages over filters: For one, queries permit you to select the fields that will be displayed. (Remember, filters let you select which fields to sort on but don't enable you to conceal fields.) In addition, you can use queries to perform calculations and to work with data from multiple tables. As you'll discover in Lesson 5, you can also use the results of queries in forms and reports. You can even save your queries so you can use them in the future—getting up-to-the-minute responses to questions about the data in your database.

Access allows you to create several different kinds of queries. This lesson concentrates on the most often-used query type, select queries. You can use ***select queries*** to sort, select, and view records from one or more tables. When you run a query, the result is called a recordset. A ***recordset*** is the portion of your data sorted and selected as spelled out in the query. This portion of data changes to reflect modifications to the data in your tables, so the data in the recordset is always up-to-date. Recordsets are also dynamic in

Did you know?

You can print a query in two different ways. You can select the query name in the Database window and then click the Print button on the Database toolbar. Or, you can open the query and then click the Print button.

Using the Query Design Grid

1. Click the Queries option in the Objects bar of the Database window.

2. Double-click Create a query in Design view.

3. Double-click the table(s) you wish to use in the Show Table dialog box and then close the dialog box.

4. Add the desired fields to the query design grid.

5. Choose the desired options in the Sort and Criteria rows.

6. Click the Run button.

that you often can make changes to them and have those changes reflected in the underlying table(s). When you work with recordsets, you can modify the datasheet much as you can when you work with a table. Among other things, you can move, freeze, and hide columns; change column widths and row heights; and add and edit data.

Setting Up a Simple Query

You set up queries in the Query Design view window, which is very similar to the Advanced Filter/Sort window. This window has an upper pane that includes lists of fields from one or more tables or queries on which the query will be based. The lower pane consists of a grid—called the *query design grid,* which you use to make decisions about how to sort and select your data and also about the fields to include in the recordset.

Using the Query Design Grid

In this activity, you'll experiment with a variety of single-table queries to get used to working in the Query Design view.

1. **In the Be Fruitful, Lesson 4 Database window, click the Queries option in the Objects bar.**

No queries exist in the *Be Fruitful, Lesson 4* database.

2. **Double-click Create query in Design view.**

Access displays the Show Table dialog box, which lists all tables in the open database. You choose tables and/or queries to base your new query on in this dialog box.

3. **Double-click BFCustomers.**

Access adds a Field list for BFCustomers to the Query Design view that you see in the background. You will be able to select fields to include in the query from the Field list of the BFCustomers table.

4. **Close the Show Table dialog box.**

The Show Table dialog box doesn't close automatically, in case you want to create a query that includes multiple tables, as discussed later in this lesson. Access removes the Show Table dialog box from view, leaving you in the Query Design view window. This window closely resembles the Advanced Filter/Sort window, with a Field list at the top and a query design grid at the bottom for entering field names, sorting instructions, and selection criteria.

5. **Double-click the ContactLastName field in the Field list.**

Access adds the field name to the query design grid. Notice that the check box in the Show row is selected automatically, indicating that Access will display the ContactLastName field in the recordset.

6. **Double-click the ContactFirstName field located in the Field list.**

7. Double-click the **State field** and then the **PhoneNumber field** to place them in the next boxes of the Field row in the query design grid.

8. In the Sort row, select **Ascending order** for the ContactLastName and ContactFirstName fields.

The query will display records alphabetically by the last name. If two or more records have the same last name, the records will be alphabetized by the first names.

9. Type CA in the Criteria row under the State field.

Only those records within California will be included in the query. Your Query Design view window should look like that in Figure 4.12.

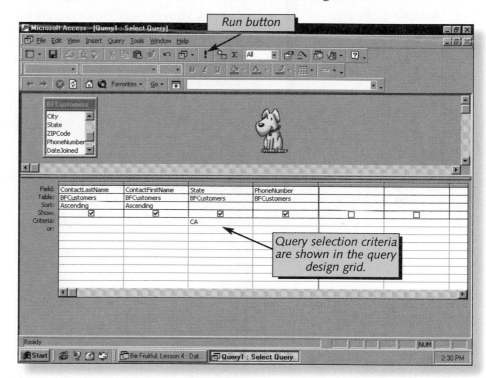

Figure 4.12
The completed Query Design view window

10. Click the **Run button** .

Access displays the recordset; notice that you see only the selected fields, rather than all of the fields in the table. Also note that the fields are displayed in the order in which you arranged them in the query design grid. On both of these counts, queries differ from filters.

Modifying and Saving a Query

You can create, modify, and save queries. Remember, when you create a query, the criteria are saved, not the data in the recordset. If your data changes and you run a query again, the appropriate updated data will appear in the recordset.

Modifying and Saving a Query

1. Open the query you wish to modify in Design view.

2. Modify the query as desired.

3. Click the Run button.

4. Click File on the menu bar and click Save As.

5. Type a query name and click OK.

Hiding the State Field and Naming the Query

In this activity, you'll make a change to the query you just created. Then you'll save the query so you can view the recordset at any time in the future.

1. Click the **View button** ![icon] on the Database toolbar.

Clicking the View button switches to display Query Design view. Notice that after you click the button, the icon changes to indicate that clicking again will switch back to Datasheet view. To check the available views, click the arrow next to the View button or click View on the menu bar. Then make a choice from the available options.

2. Click the **Show check box** under the State field in the query design grid.

Clicking deselects this box. This lets you select records based on state without displaying the State field in the recordset.

3. Click the **Run button** ![icon].

Access displays the new recordset shown in Figure 4.13; all customers in California are displayed as before, but this time the State field does not appear.

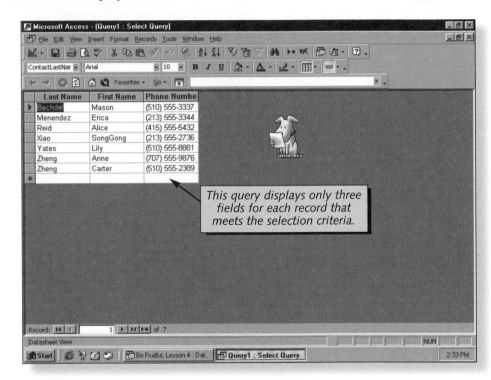

Figure 4.13
Recordset with State field hidden

This query displays only three fields for each record that meets the selection criteria.

4. Click **File** on the menu bar and then click **Save As**.

Remember, saving a query doesn't save the data you currently see in the recordset but instead saves a set of instructions for sorting and extracting a particular set of data. Access displays a Save As dialog box much like the one you saw when you saved your table structure. This time, however, Access requests a query name rather than a table name.

5. Type California Phone Numbers **as the query name and click OK**.

The new query name appears in the title bar and in the taskbar button.

6. Click the **View button** ![icon] to switch to Query Design view.

You can also use the Save button to save a newly created query. When you click the Save button before giving the query a name, Access prompts you for a query name.

Adding and Deleting Fields in Query Design View

After you save a query, you can still make changes. For instance, you can easily add new fields to Query Design view and remove them as well. The changes are reflected in the resulting recordsets. In this activity, you will delete the Phone Number and State fields and add the DateJoined field to the Query Design view window. You will also move a field to a new location and give the revised query a new name.

1. In the query design grid, select the column selectors for the State and PhoneNumber fields and press ⌨Delete.

In the query design grid, the column selectors are the small, blank, gray boxes above the names of the fields. Access deletes the State and PhoneNumber fields from the query design grid.

2. Drag the DateJoined field in the Field list so the field is directly over the ContactLastName field, and then release.

Access adds the DateJoined field to the query design grid, placing the DateJoined field in the ContactLastName field's former position and pushing all other fields to the right.

3. In the Sort row of the DateJoined column, click **Ascending.** Type >12/31/98 in the Criteria row of the DateJoined column.

4. Click the **View button** 📄.

Access runs the query, displaying the names of customers who joined after 12/31/98, as shown in Figure 4.14.

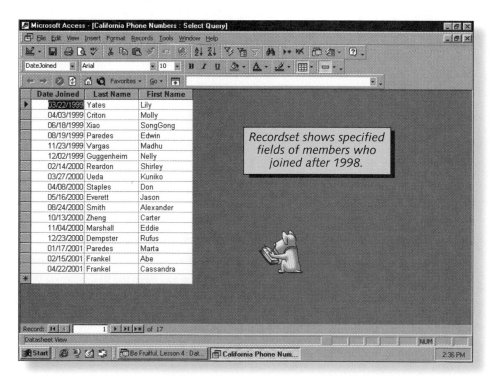

Figure 4.14
Revised query results

5. Click the **View button** to switch to Design view.

6. Click the **column selector** for the DateJoined field to select the field.

You can define sorting and selection instructions based on a field without displaying that field in the recordset.

To build more complex expressions to use as criteria, Access provides a tool called the Expression Builder. Click the Build button to choose from predesigned elements and operators.

HANDS On

Editing Data in a Query

1. Open the query that contains the data you wish to edit.

2. Edit the desired data and close the query.

---

7. With the pointer still over the column selector, drag to the right until the heavy vertical line is just to the right of the ContactFirstName field, and then release.

Access moves the DateJoined field to the right end of the query design grid. Remember, this will change the arrangement of data in the recordset, as well as affect the sort order.

8. Click the **Run button** [!].

Access displays the revised recordset. The same records are included, but now last names are displayed first and the records are then sorted by last name.

9. Click **File** on the menu bar and click **Save As**.

You see the Save As dialog box. This dialog box lets you save your query in the database with a new name. You want to save this new query without overwriting the California Phone Numbers query.

10. In the first text box, type Joined After 1998 **and click OK**.

Access returns you to Datasheet view and displays the new query name in the title bar and the taskbar button.

11. Close the query window.

Access returns you to the Be Fruitful, Lesson 4 Database window, which now includes the two queries—California Phone Numbers and Joined After 1998.

Editing Data in a Query

Being able to save the query to view the recordset at a later date is one of the great benefits of a query. Even when the data in a table changes, the changes are reflected when you reopen a query. In this activity, you will open one of your saved queries and make changes to the data.

1. Double-click the **California Phone Numbers query**.

Access displays the California Phone Numbers query in Datasheet view. (When viewing your queries in the Database window, you can run them either by double-clicking the name or by selecting the query name and clicking the Open button [Open].) Now you'll try changing data in the recordset, noting that your changes are reflected in the underlying table.

2. Change the phone number for Alice Reid to (415) 555-6543. **Then close the datasheet.**

3. In the Be Fruitful, Lesson 4 Database window, click the **Tables option** in the Objects bar and open the BFCustomers table.

4. Scroll to the right until you can see the phone number for Alice Reid.

As you can see, the new number that you just entered through the recordset is reflected in the BFCustomers table.

5. Close the table.

Using HELP

Learning About Other Types of Queries

As you've learned, select queries are the most commonly used queries. Now that you've learned how to create and run a select query, you will use Help in this activity to learn about other types of queries.

1. Click the **Office Assistant**.

2. Type parameter query in the *What would you like to do?* box.

3. Click the **Search button**.

4. Click the **What is a parameter query and when would you use one? option**.

5. Read the text in the Help window to learn about parameter queries.

Figure 4.15
Learning about queries

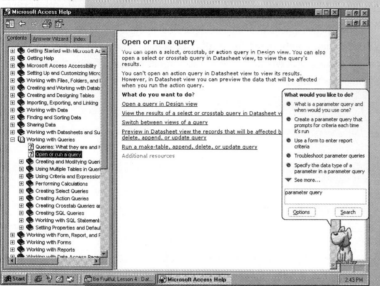

6. Click the **Show button** on the Help window and then click the **Contents tab**.

7. Scroll down and click the **plus sign** before the **Working with Queries topic**.

8. Scroll down and click the subtopic **Open or run a query** (Figure 4.15).

9. Read the new text in the Help window. Then click the appropriate subtopics in the Contents tab to learn about creating action queries and SQL queries.

10. When you are finished exploring, close the Help window.

QUERYING MULTIPLE TABLES

You've just learned how to build queries based on a single table. Now you will create queries that display data from more than one table. Essentially, you add the Field lists for the desired tables to the top of the Query Design window and then choose fields and specify the sort and selection instructions as you do for a single-table query. However, you must also *join* the tables—that is, you must tell Access how to match up records from one table with the appropriate records from any other tables. Otherwise, Access wouldn't know which orders corresponded with which customers, for example.

You can join tables by means of their common fields. In some cases, Access joins the tables for you automatically. This happens if one table has a field of the same name and the same data type as the primary key in the other or if you've already defined a formal relationship between the tables as you did in Lesson 3.

Building a Multi-Table Query

Now you'll build a query that draws data from both the BFCustomers and BFOrders tables. Before you can enter your selection criteria, you need to display Field lists from both tables. Then you can select the fields and values upon which to extract and/or sort your data. In this activity, you'll tell Access to display Field lists from both tables.

1. Select the BFCustomers table in the Be Fruitful, Lesson 4 Database window and click the **drop-down arrow** beside the New Object button 🗿▾ on the far right side of the Database toolbar.

2. Click **Query** from the drop-down list.

Access displays the New Query dialog box, as shown in Figure 4.16.

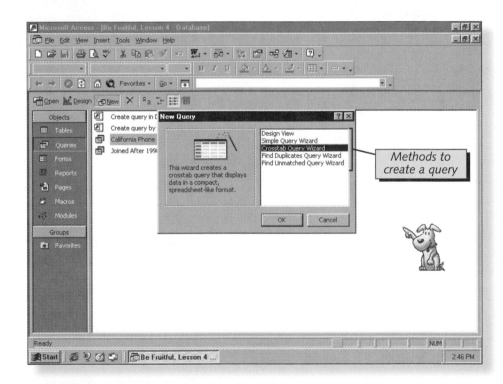

Methods to create a query

Figure 4.16
Revised query results

3. Click the **Design View option** and click **OK**.

Access opens the Query Design window. Since the BFCustomers table was selected when you chose to create the query, its Field list is already displayed; you must add the second Field list.

4. Click the **Show Table button** 🔲 to display the Show Table dialog box.

5. Double-click the **BFOrders table** and then close the Show Table dialog box.

The Field list for the BFOrders table has been added to the Query Design view window. Since a one-to-many relationship was previously assigned to these tables, Access inserts a line showing the joined fields.

Creating Selection Criteria from Two Tables

Now that you have Field lists from both tables in the window and they are joined, you are ready to set up your selection criteria. In this activity, you will create your selection criteria from two tables.

1. **In the BFCustomers Field list, double-click the ContactLastName field and then double-click the ContactFirstName field.**

Access adds both of these field names to the query design grid.

2. **Choose a sort order of Ascending for the ContactLastName field and for the ContactFirstName field.**

3. **Add the FruitType field in the BFOrders Field list to the query design grid and type Apples in the Criteria row for the FruitType field.**

You can expand the selection criteria by joining two or more criteria with the word And. *For instance, if you wanted to list all of the records except those for customers ordering peaches and strawberries, you could type:*
< > Peaches And < > Strawberries

4. **Click the Run button** ⚡.

Access displays the recordset shown in Figure 4.17, which lists records for customers who have ordered apples. Notice that customers who ordered apples more than once are listed more than once.

Figure 4.17
Recordset of customers who have ordered apples

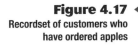

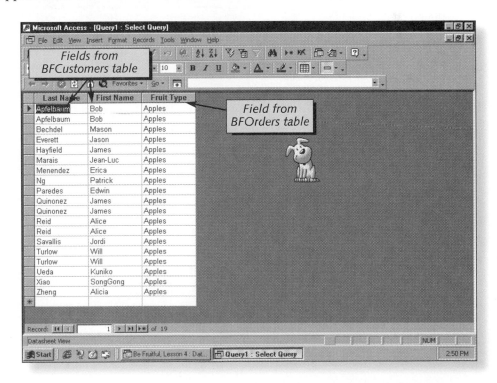

5. Click **File** on the menu bar and click **Save As**. Type Apple Orders **as the query name. Then click OK and close the datasheet.**

You are back to your Be Fruitful, Lesson 4 Database window. Even though you created the new query from the Tables option, you do not see the new query in the Tables list. The query is listed under the Queries option.

6. Click the **Queries option** in the Objects bar to see the Apple Orders query.

Querying for Blank Data

Sometimes you need to set your selection criteria for data that is missing rather than comparing to data that has been entered. For example, in your BFOrders table, a field contains the date the order was paid. In this activity, you will create a query that uses data from two tables and lists records that do not have a date entered in the payment date field. Then you will use the Is Null expression to look for empty fields.

1. Double-click **Create query in Design view**.

2. In the Show Table dialog box, add the BFCustomers and the BFOrders tables to display their Field lists. Then close the Show Table dialog box.

The BFCustomers and BFOrders Field lists should both appear in the Query Design view window. As before, Access displays a join line between the two CustomerID fields.

3. From the BFCustomers Field list, add the ContactLastName and the ContactFirstName fields to the query design grid. Add the PaymentDate field from the BFOrders Field list to the query design grid.

The selected fields should look like those in Figure 4.18.

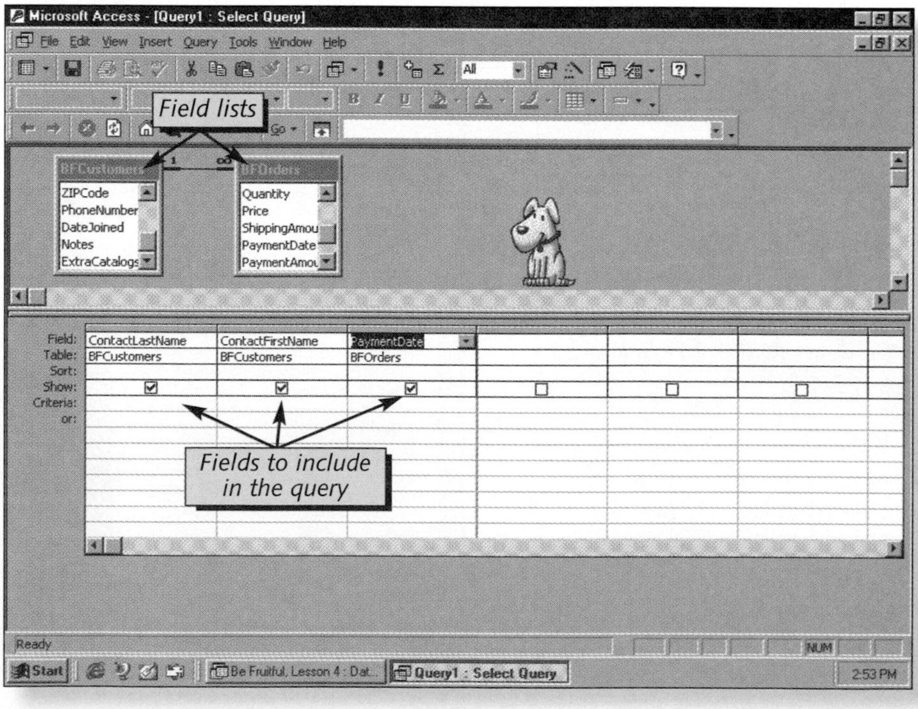

Figure 4.18 ◀
Adding fields to the query design grid

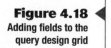

4. Choose an Ascending sort for both the ContactLastName and ContactFirstName fields. Deselect the Show check box for the PaymentDate field.

5. Type Is Null in the Criteria row for the PaymentDate field.

You're going to display all customers who have unpaid orders. *Is Null* is the expression to use to display records where the specified field is empty.

6. Click the **Run button** ▣.

Access displays the recordset of all customers who have ordered fruit but have not yet paid. Note that you can make a selection based on the PaymentDate field without including this field in the recordset.

7. Click **File** on the menu bar, click **Save As**, type the query name Unpaid Orders, and click **OK** to save the query. Then close the query window.

You are back to the Database window. Your queries are saved in the Queries tab and you can view them at any time.

8. Select the query name in the Database window and click the **Print button** ▣ on the Database window to print the query.

9. Click the **Compact on Close option**, if necessary. Close the *Be Fruitful, Lesson 4* database.

Self CHECK

Test your knowledge by matching the following button names with their descriptions. See Appendix D to check your answers.

TERMS	DEFINITIONS
1. Clear Grid	a. Displays only those records that contain the data that you highlight in a field
2. Sort Ascending	
3. Filter By Selection	b. Given the numbers 12, 18, 22, 16, and 3, this button arranges the numbers in the following order: 22, 18, 16, 12, 3
4. Sort Descending	
5. Show Table	c. Deletes the information in the Advanced Filter/Sort window from the previous filter or sort
	d. Displays a list of tables and queries available so that you can open their Field lists
	e. Given the numbers 12, 18, 22, 16, and 3, this button arranges the numbers in the following order: 3, 12, 16, 18, 22

CREATING HYPERLINKS

A hyperlink is a shortcut, or jump, that, when clicked, links you to another object, database, or Web site. If the database is not open, Access automatically opens the file. In forms, you can create hyperlinks that appear as text, graphics, button, or other shapes. In a database, text that contains hyperlinks usually appears in a different color than other items, often blue, and is underlined. Typically, after you click a hyperlink, the text changes color, generally to purple, to remind you that you followed the link. In this activity, you will create hyperlinks to another object in the same database, to another database, and to a Web site.

1. Open the *Be Fruitful, Lesson 4* database in the *Tutorial* folder on your Student Data Disk. Open the California Phone Numbers query in Design view.

2. Replace the text *"CA"* in the Criteria row of the State field with "NC" to find all of the phone numbers for North Carolina customers.

3. Save the new query as North Carolina Phone Numbers **and close the query window.**

4. Open the BFCustomers table, maximize the window, and click the **ZIP Code field selector** to highlight the entire column. Then click **Insert** on the menu bar and click **Hyperlink Column.**

A new column appears between the State and ZIP Code fields and the insertion point moves to the first record within that column. Since the state in the first record is North Carolina, you will create a hyperlink to jump to the query that displays the phone numbers for all of the customers in North Carolina. (You can designate an existing field as a hyperlink field by changing its Data Type in Design view.)

5. Click the **Insert Hyperlink button** 🔗.

The Insert Hyperlink dialog box appears. When you are linking to an object within the current database, filling in the *Type the file or Web page name* box is optional. If you leave this blank, Access assumes that you want to link to an object within the active database.

6. Click the **Bookmark button.**

7. In the *Select Place in Document* dialog box, click the **plus sign** in front of **Queries,** and click the **North Carolina Phone Numbers query.** Then click **OK.**

Access returns to the completed Insert Hyperlink dialog box, as shown in Figure 4.19.

8. Click **OK** to return to the BFCustomers table. Press ⬇ to move the cursor to the next record.

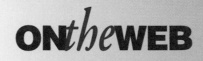

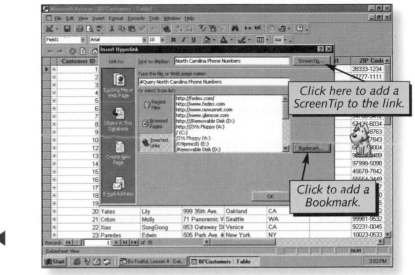

Figure 4.19 ◀
The Insert Hyperlink
dialog box

Note that the hyperlink is now visible in the column labeled Field1. The text, which displays the name of the linked object, appears in blue and is underlined to indicate that a hyperlink exists.

9. Point to the hyperlink and notice that the pointer changes to the shape of a hand. Then click the hyperlink.

Access opens the North Carolina Phone Numbers query. Notice the query name appears in the title bar.

10. Click the **Back button** ⇐ on the Web toolbar to return to the BFCustomers table.

To return to the previously viewed object, you can click the Back button ⇐ on the Web toolbar or you can click the object's taskbar button.

11. Move to the second record and place the insertion point in the Field1 hyperlink column.

You can also type the name of an object in the active database to create a hyperlink. This method will only work if the field (column) has already been designated as a hyperlink field.

12. In Field1 of the fourth record, type California Phone Numbers **and press** Enter↵ . **Then test the hyperlink.**

13. Close the California Phone Numbers and North Carolina Phone Numbers queries and then close the BFCustomers table.

14. In the Database window, click the **Forms option** in the Objects bar and open the BFOrders form.

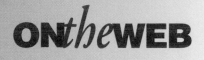
ON_the_**WEB**

15. Add this new record to the form: Order No.: press `Tab`, Order Date: 2/15/01, **Customer ID:** 4, **Fruit Type:** Apricots, **Quantity:** 2, **Price:** 18.95.

Now you need to find the shipping amount charged to a customer who orders two items. To do so, you can create a hyperlink to another database that contains shipping charges.

16. Click the **Shipping Amt. field**. Then click the **View button** to view the form in Design view. Click the **Insert Hyperlink button**, click the **File button** in the Insert Hyperlink dialog box, and navigate to the database named *Shipping Charges* on your Student Data Disk. Click the name and then click **OK** to return to the Insert Hyperlink dialog box.

17. Click the **Bookmark button**, click the **plus sign** in front of **Tables**, select the **Shipping Charges table**, and click **OK**. Click **OK** again.

A hyperlink appears at the top of the Detail section. When you create a hyperlink in a form, the text shows the path and file name of the linked file. However, you can change this text.

18. With the hyperlink selected, as you can tell by the presence of selection handles, click the **Properties button** on the Database toolbar.

19. On the Format tab in the Label dialog box, type Customer Shipping Charges to replace the text in the Caption box. Then close the Label dialog box.

The text for the hyperlink changes to *Customer Shipping Charges*.

20. Point to a border of the hyperlink until the pointer changes to a hand. Then drag the hyperlink to the right of the Shipping Amount label and control. Drag any of the selection handles to resize the hyperlink field, if necessary, so that all of the text is readable.

The hyperlink will look like the one shown in Figure 4.20.

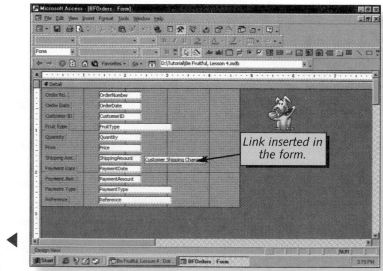

Figure 4.20 ◄
The Customer Shipping
Charges hyperlink

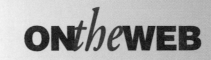

21. Click the **View button** 🔲 to return to Form view.

The new hyperlink appears next to the Shipping Amt. field. Now you're ready to finish entering data for the new record.

22. **Return to the last record and click the Customer Shipping Charges hyperlink.**

To jump to the file linked to the hyperlink, you must be in Form view. Clicking a hyperlink in Design view will select the hyperlink. The Shipping Charges table in the *Shipping Charges* database opens, and you can see that the charge to send two items is $6.50.

23. **Click the Back button** ⬅ **or click the BFOrders taskbar button to return to the BFOrders form. Type 6.50 in the Shipping Amt. field. Complete the record by entering the following information: Payment Date: 2/23/01, Payment Amount: 44.40, Payment Type: Credit Card, Reference: 2222-2222-2222.**

24. **Close the Shipping Charges table and database. Then close the BFOrders form, saving the form.**

25. **Open the Order Type and Quantity form in Design view and click the Insert Hyperlink button** 🖼. **In the *Type the file or Web page name* box, type www.golden-harvest-fruit.com and click OK.**

26. **Drag the new hyperlink to the bottom-center of the form. Then click the View button** 🖼 **to switch to Form view.**

The label *http://www.golden-harvest-fruit.com* becomes a hyperlink. When you click the hyperlink, Access will jump to the site located at the specified URL. A *URL (Uniform Resource Locator)* is the address of a Web site. A URL can be made up of letters, numbers, and special symbols that are understood by the Internet.

27. **Test your new hyperlink. (Connect to the Internet, if necessary.)**

28. **When the Web page for the Golden Harvest Fruit Company appears, explore the link regarding the products the company offers. Click the Back button** ⬅ **to return to the previous page. Explore the fund-raising tips that Golden Harvest offers to users.**

29. **Disconnect from the Internet unless your instructor tells you to remain connected. Close your Web browser. Close your database, saving all changes.**

 You may proceed directly to the exercises for this lesson. If, however, you are finished with your computer session, follow the "shut down" procedures for your lab or school environment.

Lesson Summary & Exercises

SUMMARY

While the data contained in tables can be useful in its raw format, the ability to quickly sort and select records provides great advantages over a manual system. Lesson 4 introduced several methods to sort and select data. You first performed a simple sort of all of your data, sorting by one or more fields using the Sort Ascending and Sort Descending buttons. Then you created filters to display and sort specific records from a table. You also created queries to select and sort specific records and fields from one or more tables. Finally, you added hyperlinks to a database to link to other objects within a database, to another database, and to a Web site.

Now that you have completed this lesson, you should be able to do the following:

- Understand the difference between sorting and selecting data. (Access-164)
- Use the Sort Ascending and Sort Descending buttons to sort one or more fields in alphabetical, numerical, or chronological order. (Access-165)
- Highlight criteria and then select specific records using the Filter By Selection button. (Access-166)
- Choose criteria using the Filter By Form window. (Access-168)
- Use the Filter By Form window to find records that meet one of several criteria. (Access-170)
- Use the Filter By Form window to find records that meet multiple criteria. (Access-171)
- Type text and wildcard characters in the Filter For box to search for and select records. (Access-172)
- Use the Advanced Filter/Sort method to select sort orders and criteria to filter for specific records. (Access-173)
- Type expressions as criteria. (Access-175)
- Use the Between...And expression to specify records that fall within a range. (Access-176)
- Use the query design grid to specify the sort order, criteria, and fields to appear in a query. (Access-178)
- Hide, add, and remove fields in a recordset. (Access-180)
- Save a query with a name. (Access-180)
- Edit data in a query. (Access-182)
- Create a query that uses multiple tables. (Access-184)
- Query for blank data. (Access-186)
- Create hyperlinks to another object, database, or Web site. (Access-188)

CONCEPTS REVIEW

1 TRUE/FALSE

Circle T if the statement is true or F if the statement is false.

T F **1.** A filter allows you to specify the fields that will appear in the results.

T F **2.** The < > comparison operator can be translated as not equal to.

T F **3.** Using the Sort Ascending or Sort Descending button to sort data is somewhat limited as you can only sort on one field at a time.

T F **4.** The Clear Grid button can be used to close the filter window and return to the table or Database window.

T F **5.** Selection criteria are instructions that tell Access exactly which records to gather from the database.

T F **6.** To select data can mean to extract data based on criteria you set.

T F **7.** The set of results of a query is known as a recordset.

T F **8.** To use the Filter For Input method, you must first highlight the character string in the table that you wish to filter.

T F **9.** You can sort data on any type of field except for Memo, Hyperlink, and OLE Object fields.

T F **10.** The Filter By Form window contains a Sort row that allows you to specify how one or more fields should be sorted.

2 MATCHING

Match each of the terms on the left with the definitions on the right.

TERMS

1. sort

2. filter

3. selection criteria

4. recordset

5. join

6. ascending sort

7. query design grid

8. descending sort

9. Is Null

10. Show check box

DEFINITIONS

a. Order in which characters are shown from A to Z

b. Way to link tables in a query so that Access knows how to match up corresponding records

c. Expression used in selection criteria to query a table for empty fields

d. To rearrange records into alphabetical, numerical, or chronological order

e. Area of Query Design view window in which you enter sorting and selection criteria

f. Subset of your data that is the result of a query

g. Area of the query design grid that enables you to choose whether fields are displayed in the recordset

h. To extract a selected subset of your data

i. Instructions used to determine records to be filtered or queried

j. Order in which dates would be listed from most recent to oldest

Lesson Summary & Exercises

3 COMPLETION

Fill in the missing word or phrase for each of the following statements.

1. When you want to extract records and sort them into some order that you can use again in the future, you should use a(n) _____.

2. To remove criteria from the last sort, click the _____ button.

3. To type specific filter criteria, right-click within a field and select _____ from the shortcut menu.

4. Filtering a table based on data you have highlighted in the table is called a Filter By _____.

5. To use a query at a future date, you must _____ the query.

6. To extract and sort records all at once with a filter, you must click the _____ option after clicking Records on the menu bar.

7. To select Field lists for tables in Query Design view, click the _____ button.

8. The symbol used in selection criteria that means greater than or equal to is _____.

9. To filter for records that meet one of several values, use the _____ tab at the bottom of the Filter By Form window.

10. To create a link from a table to another object, click the _____ button.

4 SHORT ANSWER

Write a brief answer to each of the following questions.

1. Name at least two reasons for using a query rather than a filter to sort and/or select data.

2. Describe the purpose of the Show row in the query design grid.

3. List the differences between the Filter By Selection, Filter By Form, Filter For Input, and Advanced Filter/Sort options.

4. Provide the selection criteria you would use to find all customers who joined the club before (but not on) 2/2/2000.

5. Describe how you would change the order in which fields are displayed in the datasheet when you work with a filter. Think about whether this can be accomplished. Then describe two ways to change the order of fields with a query.

6. Describe how you would create an Advanced Filter/Sort in the BFCustomers table that shows all customers living in Massachusetts. Then describe how you would change the filter to show all customers not living in Massachusetts.

7. Describe how you would create a filter using the Filter By Form method to show all customers who joined on 5/18/98 from New York state.

8. Describe how you would modify the filter to show all customers who joined on 5/18/98 and lived in either New York or Illinois.

9. Describe how you would create a query to display the last and first names of customers who have a ZIP Code lower than 45000.

10. Describe how you would create and save a query using both the BFCustomers and BFOrders tables to show all customers who did not order apples, grapefruit, or pears. The query should show the first and last names, in that order.

5 IDENTIFICATION

Label and briefly describe each of the elements of the Query Design window in Figure 4.21.

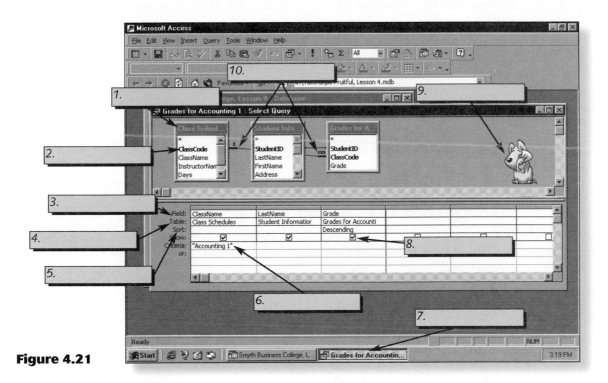

Figure 4.21

SKILLS REVIEW

Complete each of the Skills Review problems in sequential order to review your Access skills to sort, filter, and query data.

1 Sort a Table and Use Filter By Selection

1. Open the **Smyth Business College, Lesson 4** database in the **Skills Review** folder on your Student Data Disk. Open and maximize the Grades for Accounting Classes table.

2. Click anywhere in the Class Code field and click the **Sort Ascending button** ⟨A↓⟩.

3. Drag over the Class Code and Grade column selectors to highlight both fields. Then click the **Sort Ascending button** ⟨A↓⟩.

4. Click anywhere within the Grade field and click the **Sort Descending button** ⟨Z↓⟩.

5. Double-click any occurrence of AC101 in the Class Code field.

6. Click the **Filter By Selection button** ⟨▽⟩ to see a listing of grades for the class.

7. Click the **Remove Filter button** ⟨▽⟩ and double-click any occurrence of 7 in the Student ID field.

Lesson Summary & Exercises

8. Click the **Filter By Selection button** to see the classes and grades of this student.

9. Click the **Remove Filter button** and close the table without saving the changes.

2 Use Filter By Form to Meet Criteria

1. Open the Class Schedules table and click the **Filter By Form button** .

2. Click the row beneath the Days field, click the **drop-down arrow** that appears, and click **TR**.

3. Click the **Apply Filter button** to see the classes offered on Tuesdays and Thursdays.

4. Click the **Remove Filter button** and click the **Filter By Form button** .

5. Click the **Clear Grid button** and type M in the row beneath the Class Code field.

6. Click the **Class Code drop-down arrow** and click **MK101**.

7. Click the **Apply Filter button** to see the details of this class; then click the **Remove Filter button** .

8. Click the **Filter By Form button** and click the **Clear Grid button** .

9. Click the **Instructor Name drop-down arrow**, and click **Berbarg**.

10. Click the **Or tab** at the bottom of the window, click the **Instructor Name drop-down arrow**, and click **Nieves**.

11. Click the **Apply Filter button** to see the details of the classes these two instructors teach. Then click the **Remove Filter button** .

12. Click the **Filter By Form button** and click the **Clear Grid button** .

13. Enter MWF in the Days box and select 10:00-10:50 am in the Time field.

14. Click the **Apply Filter button** to see the classes offered on these days and times.

15. Click the **Remove Filter button** and close the table without saving the changes.

3 Use the Filter For Method

1. Open the Student Information table and right-click anywhere in the Major field.

2. Click **Filter For** on the shortcut menu that appears, type Finance in the Filter For text box, and press Enter⤶ to list all of the students who are finance majors.

3. Click the **Remove Filter button** . Right-click anywhere in the Major field again, and click **Filter For** on the shortcut menu.

4. Type M* in the Filter For box and press Tab.

5. Click **Sort Ascending** on the shortcut menu to show the management, marketing, and mathematics majors in alphabetical order by major.

6. Click **Records** on the menu bar and click **Remove Filter/Sort**.

Lesson Summary & Exercises

4 Filter and Sort

1. With the Student Information table still open, point to **Filter** on the Records menu and click **Advanced Filter/Sort**. Then click the **Clear Grid button** ⊠.

2. Double-click **GradePointAverage** in the Field list, click the **Sort box** below the GradePointAverage entry, click the **drop-down arrow** that appears, and click **Descending**.

3. Type > 3.00 in the Criteria row below GPA. Then click the **Apply Filter button** ▽ to filter the students with grade point averages higher than 3.00 and sort them in descending order by GPA. Navigate the filter to review the data.

4. Click **Records** on the menu bar and click **Remove Filter/Sort**.

5. Click **Records** on the menu bar, point to **Filter**, and click **Advanced Filter/Sort**.

6. Click the **Clear Grid button** ⊠; then double-click **Last Name** in the Field list.

7. Click the **Sort box** beneath the Last Name box and click **Ascending** on the drop-down list.

8. In the Field list, double-click **EstimatedGraduationDate**.

9. Type Between 1/1/01 And 12/31/02 in the Criteria box below EstimatedGraduationDate.

10. Click the **Apply Filter button** ▽ to filter the students who plan to graduate between 1/1/2001 and 12/31/2002 and to sort them in alphabetical order by last name (Figure 4.22).

11. Click **Records** on the menu bar and click **Remove Filter/Sort**. Then close the table without saving changes.

Figure 4.22

5 Create, Modify, and Save a Query

1. Click the **Queries object** in the Smyth Business College, Lesson 4 Database window and double-click the **Create query in Design view option**.

2. In the Show Table dialog box, double-click **Class Schedules** and close the Show Table dialog box.

3. Double-click **ClassName** on the Field list to add the field to the query design grid.

4. Add the InstructorName, Days, and Time fields to the query design grid.

5. Choose Ascending order in the Sort row for ClassName, and type Kellinghaus in the Criteria row under InstructorName.

6. Click the **Run button** 🔘 to view the classes taught by Kellinghaus.

7. Click the **View button** 🔘 and click the **Show check box** under the InstructorName field.

8. Click the **Run button** 🔘 to rerun the query.

9. Click **File** on the menu bar, click **Save As**, and type Classes Taught by Kellinghaus as the query name. Then click **OK**.

10. Click the **View button** 🔘 to switch to Query Design view.

6 Add and Delete Fields

1. Drag across the Days and Time column selectors and press ⌨Delete to delete the fields from the query.

2. Drag the ClassCode field from the Field list to the box in the query design grid where the ClassName field currently appears.

3. In the Sort row of the ClassCode field, click **Ascending**.

4. Type AC* in the Criteria row for the ClassCode field.

5. Delete "Kellinghaus" in the Criteria row of the InstructorName field.

6. Click the **Run button** 🔘.

7. Save the query as Accounting Classes and click **OK**. Then close the query.

7 Use Queries

1. Open the Classes Taught by Kellinghaus query and change the Class Name of Advertising to Principles of Advertising. Then close the query.

2. Open the Class Schedules table and verify that the class name change is reflected in the table; then close the Class Schedules table.

3. Click the **Class Schedules table** in the Database window, click the **New Object drop-down arrow** 🔘, and click **Query** from the drop-down list.

4. Click the **Design View option** and click **OK**.

5. Click the **Show Table button** 🔘.

6. Add the Student Information table and then add the Grades for Accounting Classes table. Close the Show Table dialog box.

7. In the Class Schedules Field list, double-click **ClassName**.

8. In the Student Information Field list, double-click **LastName**.

9. In the Grades for Accounting Classes Field list, double-click **Grade**.

10. Type Accounting 1 in the Criteria row under ClassName.

11. Click **Descending** in the Sort row under Grade.

12. Click the **Run button** 🔘.

13. Save the query as Grades for Accounting 1 and click **OK**. Then click the **Close button** 🔘.

8 Query for Blank Data

1. Open the Class Schedules table and delete the text in the Instructor Name field for AC203. Then close the table and click **Queries** in the Objects bar.

2. Double-click **Create query in Design view**.

3. Double-click all three tables in the Show Table dialog box so that their Field lists appear. Then close the Show Table dialog box.

4. Add the ClassCode, LastName, FirstName, and InstructorName fields to the query design grid.

5. Type Is Null in the Criteria box under InstructorName.

6. Choose an Ascending sort for the LastName field.

7. Click the **Show check box** for the InstructorName field to deselect the field.

8. Click the **Run button** !. The class code and list of students enrolled in that class appear; these students need to be notified that the instructor will no longer be teaching the class.

9. Save the query as No Instructor. Close the query. Close the database.

LESSON APPLICATIONS

1 Use the Sort Buttons

As an employee of Payton Properties, a real estate company, you need to analyze the variety of homes you have for sale. Use the Sort buttons to sort the data in a table in various orders.

1. Open the *Payton Properties, Lesson 4* database in the *Lesson Applications* folder on your Student Data Disk, and open the Homes for Sale table.

2. Use one of the Sort buttons to sort the records by lot size from the largest lot size to the smallest.

3. Use one of the Sort buttons to sort the records in alphabetical order by school district.

4. Use one of the Sort buttons to sort the records by number of bedrooms and bathrooms. The homes with the fewest bedrooms should appear first. Homes with the same number of bedrooms should be sorted with those with the fewest number of bathrooms as a secondary sort. Close the table without saving changes.

2 Use Filter By Selection and Filter By Form

You've received requests from several of the agents for various lists of homes. Use filtering methods to fill these requests.

1. Open the *Payton Properties, Lesson 4* database in the *Lesson Applications* folder on your Student Data Disk, and open the Homes for Sale table.

2. Use the Filter By Selection method to list only homes listed by Priscilla Mayer, agent 1. Print the filter by clicking the Print button 🖨 and then remove the filter.

Lesson Summary & Exercises

3. One of your clients wants to see a list of available homes with four bedrooms. Open the Filter By Form window, clear the previous criteria, and create a filter that displays only homes with four bedrooms. Then remove the filter.

4. Your client has decided that they might also consider a home with five bedrooms. Use the Filter By Form window again to create a filter that displays homes with four or five bedrooms.

5. Another client is looking for a home with at least .70 acres of land and a swimming pool. Use the Filter By Form window to generate an appropriate list. Print and then remove the filter. Close the table without saving changes.

3 Use the Filter For Method

Use the Filter For command to fill additional requests for clients.

1. Open the *Payton Properties, Lesson 4* database in the *Lesson Applications* folder on your Student Data Disk, and open the Homes for Sale table.

2. You've just acquired another new client. He is looking for a home built before 1985. Type an expression in the Filter For box to generate an appropriate list. Then remove the filter.

3. Another client is concerned about the school district in which she purchases a home. Use the Filter For box to list only those homes in the West Avon and West Maple school districts sorted in ascending order. Print and then remove this filter. Close the table without saving changes.

4 Use Advanced Filter/Sort

Use an Advanced Filter/Sort to help a client find available homes in her price range.

1. Open the *Payton Properties, Lesson 4* database in the *Lesson Applications* folder on your Student Data Disk, and open the Homes for Sale table.

2. Open the Advanced Filter/Sort window. Remove the previous selection criteria.

3. Create a filter that lists all homes priced more than $100,000. Sort the homes by price in ascending order. Run and then remove the filter.

4. When your client sees the list, she asks you to narrow the filter a bit. Create another filter using the Advanced Filter/Sort window that lists the homes priced between $100,000 and $150,000. Again, sort the homes by price in ascending order. Run and print the filter. Then remove the filter. Close the table without saving changes.

5 Create, Modify, and Run a Query

Now that you've filtered for records to find appropriate homes for clients, your manager would like you to generate some facts about homes that have been sold through Payton Properties.

1. Open the *Payton Properties, Lesson 4* database in the *Lesson Applications* folder on your Student Data Disk. Click Queries on the Object bar.

2. Create a new query in Design view.

3. Add the Homes Sold Field list and close the Show Table dialog box.

4. Add the following fields in the order shown to your query design grid: AgentID, PropertyAddress, ListingPrice, SellingPrice, and YearBuilt.

5. Type an appropriate criteria in the AgentID field to show only those homes listed by Brian Matthews, agent 3.

6. Sort the records in descending order by SellingPrice and run the query (Figure 4.23).

7. View the query in Design view again and choose the option to hide the AgentID field. Run the query again.

8. Save the query as Homes Sold by Matthews. Then close the query.

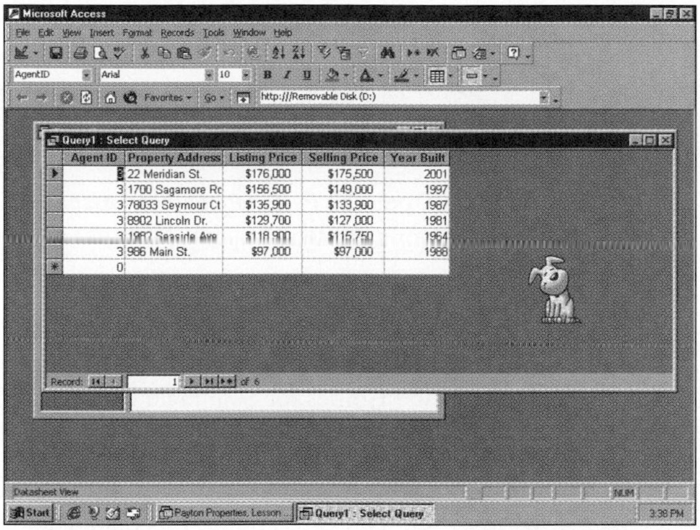

Figure 4.23

6 Add and Delete Fields and Edit Data

Edit the Homes Sold by Matthews query to include more pertinent fields and data.

1. Open the ***Payton Properties, Lesson 4*** database in the ***Lesson Applications*** folder on your Student Data Disk. Open the Homes Sold by Matthews query and switch to Design view.

2. Add the PercentofListingPrice field to the query before the YearBuilt field.

3. Delete the YearBuilt field from the query. Then run the query.

4. Edit the address of the home on Sagamore Rd. to 1702 Sagamore Rd.

5. Close the query, saving the changes, and open the Homes Sold table to verify that the address change is reflected. Then close the Homes Sold table.

7 Query Two Tables

Your manager has asked you to generate a list of homes for sale priced over $120,000. Your list should only include homes that have swimming pools and be sorted by the sales agents' last names.

1. Open the ***Payton Properties, Lesson 4*** database in the ***Lesson Applications*** folder on your Student Data Disk.

2. Create a new query and add Field lists for the Homes for Sale and Employees tables.

3. Add the following fields to the query design grid: LastName, Address (from the Homes for Sale Field list), Bedrooms, Baths, Price, and Pool.

4. Sort the records in alphabetical order by LastName.

5. Issue a secondary sort by Price in descending order.

6. Type criteria that will limit the query to homes priced over $120,000.

7. Type No in the Pool Criteria box to eliminate homes with swimming pools. Hide the Pools field. Then run the query.

8. Save the query as Homes over $120,000 without Pools and close the query.

8 Look for Empty Fields

As you are updating the Homes for Sale database, you notice that some of the Occupancy data is incomplete. You need to contact the sales agents to see if their clients have yet determined how soon after the sale of their home they will be able to move.

1. Open the *Payton Properties, Lesson 4* database in the *Lesson Applications* folder on your Student Data Disk.

2. Create a new query and add Field lists for the Homes for Sale and Employees tables.

3. Add the following fields to the query design grid: LastName, Address (from the Homes for Sale Field list), and Occupancy.

4. Sort the records in alphabetical order by LastName.

5. Use the Is Null expression in the Occupancy Criteria box to find homes with no data entered into this field. Hide the Occupancy field. Then run the query.

6. Save the query as Need Occupancy Information and then close the query.

7. Click the Compact on Close option, if necessary, and close the *Payton Properties, Lesson 4* database.

PROJECTS

1 The Effects of Merging Stores

You work as a manager for Electro Shop, a retail store that sells home electronics. Two of your stores recently merged and you need to familiarize yourself with the new employee data. Open the *Electro Shop, Lesson 4* database in the *Projects* folder. Open the Employees table. Sort the employees by last name in ascending order. Then sort the records in descending order by hourly rate. How much do the highest and lowest paid employees earn? Lastly, sort the records by last name again; however, this time, use the first names as a secondary sort. Close the table without saving changes.

2 Checking Up on the Salespeople

Next you'd like to see how a few specific employees are doing so far this month. Open the December Sales table in the *Electro Shop, Lesson 4* database in the *Projects* folder on your Student Data Disk. Use the Filter By Selection method to filter sales for Justin Murdock, employee 8. Then use the same method to check sales for Lydia Ramos, employee 13, and Mitchell Aicholz, employee 27. Which employee of the three has the most sales so far this month? Which has the least? Close the table without saving changes.

3 Looking at Your Products in a Variety of Ways

Now you want to review the products you currently sell. Open the Products table in the **Electro Shop, Lesson 4** database in the **Projects** folder on your Student Data Disk and review the data. Use the Filter By Form method to show only information on VCRs that you sell. Then use another Filter By Form window to check stock for a customer who wants a stereo made by either Keiko or RML.

Later in the day, a representative from Wiley/Markle calls you. Use a Filter For method to quickly check all of the products of this brand that you sell. Are any TVs or video cameras included in the list? Lastly, a customer wants information on all of the VCRs and video cameras that you sell. Use the Filter For method to generate a list that provides this information. Close the table without saving changes.

4 Finding a Group of Employees

Some of Electro Shop's employee benefits changed in 1996, but all employees hired before 1996 were grandfathered into the old program. You need to send a memo to these employees regarding their retirement program. Use the Employees table in the **Electro Shop, Lesson 4** database in the **Projects** folder on your Student Data Disk and an Advanced Filter/Sort to filter all of the full-time employees who are affected, sorting them by their hire dates.

Also, this year the company is recognizing those employees hired in 1995 for their service to the company. Use an Advanced Filter/Sort to filter all employees, both full time and part time, hired during 1995. Print and remove the filter. Close the table without saving changes.

5 Should We Keep This Product?

Open the **Electro Shop, Lesson 4** database in the **Projects** folder on your Student Data Disk. As manager, you like to track sales of each product sold to analyze whether you should continue stocking. In the past few months, two products—products 5 and 18—have not been selling well. Create a query that lists the sales for the ClearPict television (product 5). Include the ProductID, SaleID, EmployeeID, and DateSold fields. Sort the records by DateSold and hide the ProductID field. Name the query ClearPict TVs Sold. Create another query with the same information except use this query to analyze the Wiley/Markle VCR (product 18). Name the second query Wiley/Markle VCRs Sold. How many of each product were sold this month? Do you think you should consider removing either item from your product list?

Open each of the queries you just created and add the QuantitySold field. Remove the Employee ID field from each. In the Wiley/Markle VCRs Sold query, edit the quantity sold to 2 for sale number 75. Print the queries. Close the queries, saving the changes, and open the December Sales table. Was your edit incorporated? Close the December Sales table.

6 Recognizing the Best

Create a new query that uses the December Sales, Products, and Employees tables in the *Electro Shop, Lesson 4* database in the *Projects* folder on your Student Data Disk. Include the following fields in the order given: DateSold, LastName, ProductType, Brand, Model, Price, and QuantitySold. Sort the records in ascending order by DateSold. Set the criteria to show only sales made by Marta Fuentes, one of your past sales leaders, and hide the LastName field. Run the query and save the query as Sales by Fuentes. Print the recordset and close the query.

7 What's in the Stockroom?

You are about to tell your stockroom employees to perform a manual inventory count. First, you'd like to see what items are out of stock according to your computer. In the *Electro Shop, Lesson 4* database in the *Projects* folder, create a query with the following fields: ProductID, ProductType, Brand, Model, and InStock. Sort the records in ascending order by the ProductType and query for records whose InStock field contains no data. Hide the InStock field. Save the query as Out of Stock Items. Close the query and the table. Click the Compact on Close command, if necessary, and close the *Electro Shop, Lesson 4* database.

8 Linking Your Data

Some of the new employees at Electro Shop haven't yet memorized all of the product codes, making it difficult for them to use the December Sales table in the company database. They find themselves switching back and forth between the Sales table and the Products table to look up product IDs. To help them out, open the *Electro Shop, Lesson 4* database in the *Projects* folder and open the December Sales AutoForm. Add a hyperlink next to the Product ID field that links to the Products table. Test the hyperlink to verify it opens the Products table.

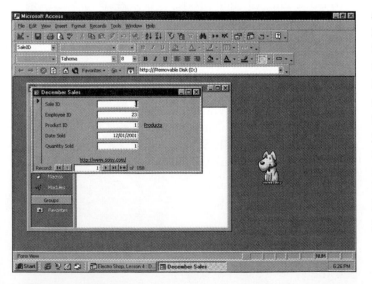

Also, you've been talking with a representative from Sony, a manufacturer of electronics, about selling their products. To learn more about Sony, add a hyperlink to the bottom of the December Sales AutoForm that links to Sony's Web site at www.sony.com (Figure 4.24). Test the hyperlink. Close the *Electro Shop, Lesson 4* database. Then close your browser and disconnect from the Internet unless your instructor tells you to remain connected.

Figure 4.24

Project in Progress

9 Contacting the Boss

Open the **I-Comm** database in the **Projects** folder and open the Customers table. Since you'd like to sort your customers by the area in which they live, select the City, State, and ZIP Code fields and sort them all at once in descending order. Then sort the customers again in ascending order by company name.

Next, you'd like to see how many owners of companies are used as your main contact. Use the Filter By Selection method to filter the records to display only those where the contact is the owner. Remove the filter and then issue an Advanced Filter/Sort to find companies where the contact is either an owner or a marketing person (use a wildcard after marketing); sort the Advanced Filter/Sort in ascending order by company name. Print and then remove the filter. Close the Customers table without saving the changes.

Lastly, create a query that uses all three tables. Include the CompanyName (Customers table), ItemDeveloped (Projects table), ServicesPerformed (Projects table), I-CommProjectManager (Projects table), and LastName (Employees table) fields (Figure 4.25). In your query, include only brochures, advertisements, and Web sites developed. Sort the recordset by company name and print it. Save the query as Brochures, Ads, and Web Sites. Close the query, make sure the Compact on Close option is selected, and close the **I-Comm** database.

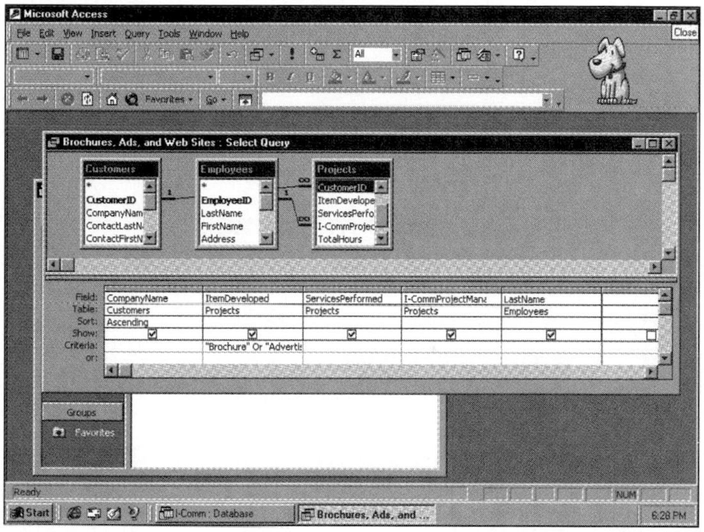

Figure 4.25

Using Forms and Reports

CONTENTS

OBJECTIVES

After you complete this lesson, you will be able to do the following:

- Create an AutoForm.
- Use a Form Wizard to create a columnar and a tabular form.
- Add and edit data with forms and subforms.
- Preview and print forms and reports.
- Create an AutoReport.
- Use the Report Wizard to create a columnar report, a tabular report, and a report with totals.
- Use the Control Toolbox to add controls in forms and reports.
- Modify format properties in Form and Report Design view.
- Use sections in forms and reports.
- Create a calculated field.
- Use a calculated control on a form and a report.
- Move and resize controls.
- Save a table, query, and form as a Web page.
- Create a data access page.

Now that you have learned how to create a database, design tables, enter data, and use queries to obtain the data you want, Lesson 5 teaches you how to use forms and reports. Using Microsoft Access forms and reports, you can improve the appearance of your data in many ways. Through the Form Wizard, you'll produce a wide variety of form layouts, edit your data using the forms and subforms, view groups of data using forms and preview and print forms. Additionally, you'll discover how to generate AutoReports to create columnar reports, tabular reports, and reports with totals and subtotals. Finally, you'll print these reports.

WHEN AND WHY TO USE FORMS

As you probably remember from Lesson 1, Access forms are electronic versions of paper forms. You can use forms to view, edit, and enter data into your tables. For the most part, you've only used the datasheet to work with your data. Although this setting provides a fine overview, generally it doesn't permit you to see all fields at once—making assessing or editing your data awkward. To create a more comfortable working environment, you can create a custom form and determine how the form will present the data from a table or query. Among other things, you can build forms that display a single record at a time as well as forms that reveal only selected fields from the chosen table or query. Forms are particularly helpful when you want to simplify data entry or when you need to control which data is displayed.

You can create a basic form easily with Access and the many Form Wizards. Like the Table Wizard you used in Lesson 2, the Form Wizards enable you to build several standard forms with minimal effort. However, once created you may want to adjust or change the form. When making these changes, you work in Design view and adjust the controls. ***Controls*** are the objects that display the raw data, perform the actions upon the data and also allow you to format the data. Because controls are responsible for the manipulation of data, controls are only used in Form Design view, Report Design view, or Data Access Page Design view. You access these controls by using the Control Toolbox. Some controls are available in all three views, while others are view specific. Table 5.1 lists the names of the controls and shows the toolbox button.

When using the Control Toolbox controls, you must also decide not only the type but the function. To use controls to fulfill certain functions, you must select a bound, unbound, or calculated control. A ***bound control*** is linked to a field in another table. Using bound controls you can display, enter, and edit values. An ***unbound control*** does not have a data source and is used to display information or graphical elements such as lines, rectangles, or pictures. A ***calculated control*** uses an expression as the source of data. Calculated controls cannot be edited in the actual form or report.

Controls are also the source for determining the appearance of your text in the form or report. You can modify the text that appears in the control; the background of the control; the line width and color; the font, size, and color; among other format options.

In forms, you move through fields and records much as you do in Datasheet view. In fact, you can switch any time to the form's Datasheet view to see multiple records at once. (This view is identical to the Datasheet view of the table but displays only the information that you would see in the form.) And, since you already know how to add, edit, delete, sort, and select data in the datasheet, you'll soon learn that the procedures are much the same for forms.

TABLE 5.1		CONTROL TOOLBOX ITEMS
Button	**Name**	**Description**
	Select Objects	Selects the object or control.
	Control Wizards	Initiates the wizard for creating controls.
	Label	Displays descriptive text. These are always unbound.
	Text Box	Displays data from an underlying source. Typically this is a bound control.
	Option Group	Displays choices, but only one value can be selected. Typically this is a bound control.
	Toggle Button	Shows a Yes/No value from an underlying source. Typically this is a bound control.
	Option Button	Displays a Yes/No value from an underlying source. Typically this is a bound control.
	Check Box	Shows Yes/No values from an underlying source. Typically this is a bound control.
	Combo Box	Lists values from an underlying source and allows you to also enter data. Can be bound or unbound.
	List Box	Lists values from an underlying source. Can be bound or unbound.
	Command Button	Used to store commands to perform another action or set of actions. (Used only on forms and data access pages.)
	Image	Inserts an image in your form, report, or data access page.
	Unbound Object Frame	Frames your unbound object.
	Bound Object Frame	Frames your bound object.
	Page Break	Inserts a page break in your form, report, or data access page.
	Tab Control	Used to present several pages of information as a single set.
	Subform/ Subreport	Displays data that has a one-to-many relationship. The "one" side is the form or report, and the "many" side is the subform or subreport.
	Line	Creates a line on your form, report, or data access page.
	Rectangle	Creates a rectangle on your form, report, or data access page.
	More Controls	Provides a list of additional controls.

CREATING AN AUTOFORM

To create an AutoForm, you must choose the table or query on which you want to base the form and then click a single button. An *AutoForm* is actually a specialized type of Form Wizard that doesn't request any special choices on your part but instead gathers the information it needs by examining the selected table or query. The wizard builds a very basic form that includes every field from the table or query arranged in columns. The field names (or captions) appear on the left side of the form to identify the fields, and the name of the table or query appears at the top as a heading. Most fields are displayed as text boxes; Memo fields are displayed as slightly larger text boxes, and Yes/No fields appear as check boxes that you can click to either select or deselect.

Exploring an AutoForm

In this activity, you'll create an AutoForm based on the BFCustomers table, and you'll view and move through your data using the form. Since the records in the BFCustomers table contain subdatasheets, Access will automatically create a subform for each record. A *subform* is a form within a form that displays related records.

Creating and Exploring an AutoForm

1. Select the table you want to base the form on, click the New Object drop-down arrow, and click AutoForm.

2. Click the navigation buttons to move from record to record.

3. Click the View drop-down arrow and click the appropriate option to change views.

1. Open the *Be Fruitful, Lesson 5* database in the *Tutorial* folder on your Student Data Disk and select the BFCustomers table.

2. Click the **New Object drop-down arrow** 🗗▾ on the Database toolbar and click **AutoForm**, as shown in Figure 5.1.

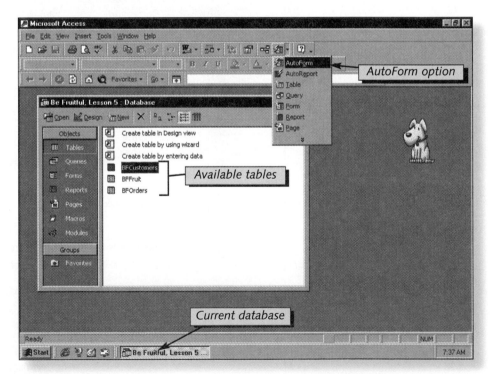

Figure 5.1
Choosing an option from the New Object drop-down arrow

Access creates a form based on the BFCustomers table. Notice that the form displays the data for the first record in the BFCustomers table. The form will include all of the fields for a single record. The subform created by Access is displayed at the bottom of the form.

3. Click the **Maximize button** 🔲, if necessary, to be able to see more fields on your screen.

4. Click the **Last Record navigation button** ▶️❙.

Access displays the information for the last record in the table as shown in Figure 5.2. All the navigation buttons at the bottom of the form work as they do in the datasheet.

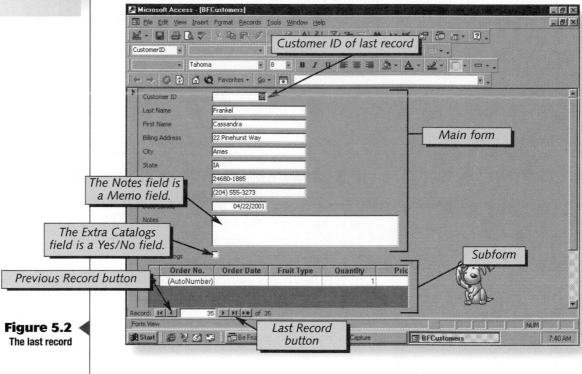

Figure 5.2
The last record

5. Click twice on the **Previous Record button** ◀.

Access moves up two records in the table. The Notes field has a larger text box because it's a Memo field, and the Extra Catalogs field is displayed as a check box because it's a Yes/No field. You can click this check box to turn it on or off.

6. Click the **View drop-down arrow** 📷▾ and click **Datasheet View**.

Access displays the form in Datasheet view. You'll see the portion of the data that you were viewing in Form view. In the Datasheet view, the data appears in columns and rows. If you like, you can also scroll your data up and down (and left and right), as you can when working on a table in Datasheet view.

7. Click the **View drop-down arrow** 📷▾ and click **Form View**.

Access returns you to Form view. In the Form view, the data appears like a paper form.

8. Click the form's **Close button** ❎.

Because you haven't saved the form, Access displays a warning box.

9. Click **Yes**.

10. In the Save As dialog box, type BFCustomers AutoForm **as the form name and click OK**.

You can add a subform at any time. Open the form in Design view and click the Subform/Subreport tool in the toolbox. Click the form where you want the subform to appear and follow the directions.

Access saves and then closes the form, returning you to the Be Fruitful, Lesson 5 Database window. The form you just created becomes one of the objects under the Forms option in the Objects bar.

CREATING A FORM WITH THE FORM WIZARD

If you have uncomplicated needs and simple tables, AutoForms might do the job. Often, however, you'll want more control over your forms—you might want to choose their layout, decide the fields to include, and more. If so, you can use the Form Wizard. Using the Form Wizard is much like using the Table Wizard; the Form Wizard prompts you for information, and Access builds a form based on your responses. When using a wizard, remember that you can click the Back button any time you want to move back one step.

Creating a Columnar Form with the Form Wizard

A *columnar form* is one that displays each field on a separate line with the label or caption to the left of the field. In this activity, you'll use the Form Wizard to create a columnar form that incorporates most of the fields from the BFCustomers table.

1. Click the **Forms option** in the Objects bar of the Database window, and double-click **Create form by using wizard**.

2. In the first Form Wizard dialog box, click the **Tables/Queries drop-down arrow** and click **Table: BFCustomers**.

As shown in Figure 5.3, the list of available fields changes to reflect those in the BFCustomers table. You can choose the fields to include in the form, as well as the order in which to display them. This dialog box works much like the first Table Wizard dialog box, although in this case, you can only choose fields from the selected table or query.

3. Click the **Add All Fields button** >> .

Access moves all of the field names to the Selected Fields list box. If you want to include all or most fields in the form, this button quickly adds them all at once, and then you can remove a few with the Remove Field button < .

4. Click the **DateJoined field** and click the **Remove Field button** < .

Access removes the DateJoined field from the list of fields to be included in the form and returns the field to the Available Fields list box. Notice that the Notes field is selected.

5. Double-click the **Remove Field button** < to remove the Notes field, and then remove the ExtraCatalogs field.

6. Click **Next**.

This dialog box allows you to choose the type of form you want to create. When you click a layout option button, you will see a preview of the layout.

7. Click the **Columnar button** and click **Next**.

Creating a Columnar Form

1. Double-click Create form by using wizard in the Forms option.

2. Select the desired table in the Tables/Queries box of the Form Wizard dialog box.

3. Select the fields to include in the form and click Next.

4. Click Columnar and click Next.

5. Click the desired style and click Next.

6. Type a name for the form and click Finish.

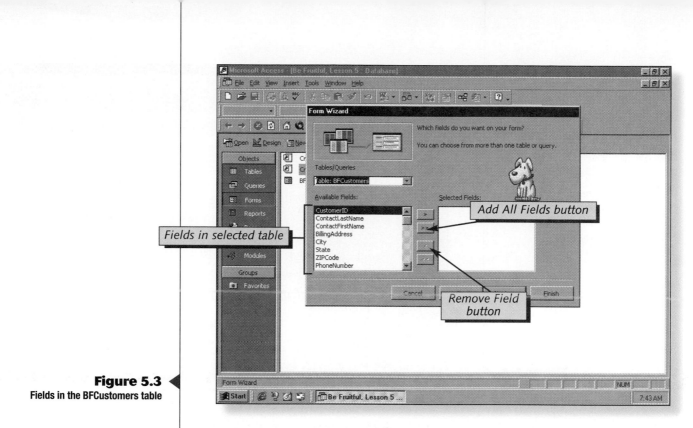

Figure 5.3
Fields in the BFCustomers table

The next Form Wizard dialog box lets you choose a style for your form. Styles include pictures, shading, and colors to give a special look to the form. When you select an option button, a preview of the style appears in the dialog box.

8. Click International, look at the preview, and click Next.

Access displays the final Form Wizard dialog box. Access uses the name of the table as a suggestion for a form title. In this dialog box you supply a title for your form and decide whether to open the form with data or edit the form's design. In either case, you can choose to view helpful information while you work with the form.

9. Type BFCustomers Names and Addresses as the title for the form.

10. Click the Open the form to view or enter information. option and click Finish.

In a moment, Access displays the form you just created, as shown in Figure 5.4. The form contains data from the BFCustomers table that you selected via the Form Wizard. Also, note that the form displays only the designated fields.

Even though only some of the table's data is displayed in this form, all the data is still there in the underlying table. Always remember that a form only displays your data, the form does not hold your data. You might want to think of a form as a window to your data.

11. Close the form.

You return to the Be Fruitful, Lesson 5 Database window.

The order of fields in the Selected Field list box determines their order in the form itself. If you want to change the existing order of fields, you must use the Add Field button to add them one by one in the desired order.

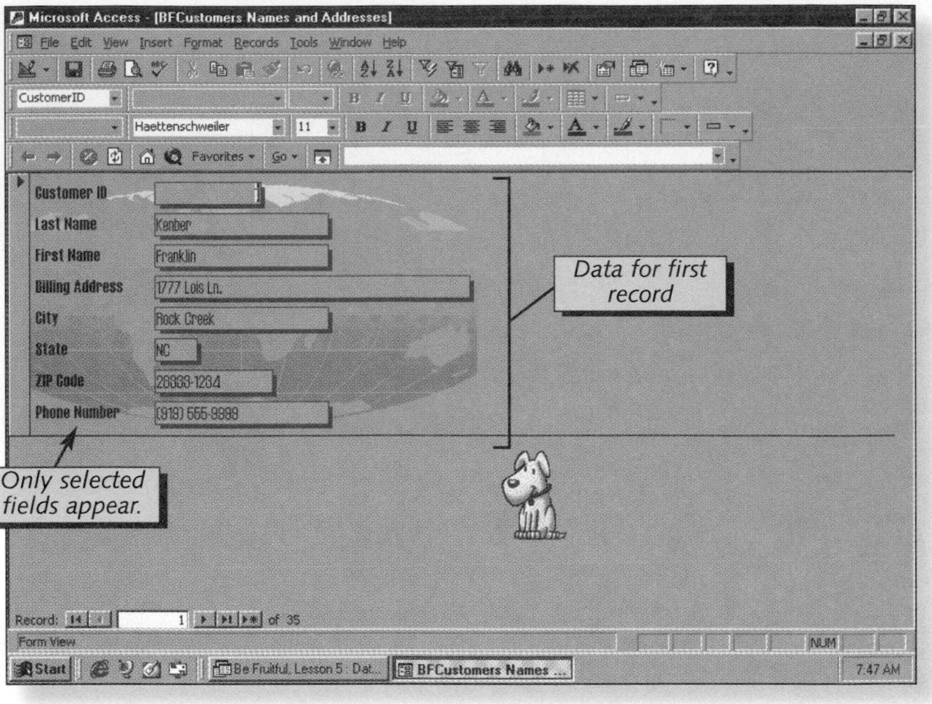

Figure 5.4 ◀
The BFCustomers Names
and Addresses form

HANDS On

Creating a Tabular Form with the Form Wizard

The two forms you've created so far display the fields in columns and show only one record at a time. On some occasions, however, you might want to see multiple records at once but not in Datasheet view. If so, you might want to use a tabular form. A *tabular form* displays all of the fields for a single record in one row and displays multiple records at once. You see field names or captions displayed as column headings—much as they are in Datasheet view. These forms work particularly well for tables or queries that don't include many fields. In this activity, you will use the Form Wizard to create a tabular form based on the Joined After 1998 query.

1. **In the Be Fruitful, Lesson 5 Database window, click the Queries option in the Objects bar. Select the Joined After 1998 query.**

Remember, this query sorts customers in ascending order by last name and displays only records whose Date Joined field is greater than 1998.

2. **Click the New Object drop-down arrow 🖼️ ▾ and click Form.**

Access displays the New Form dialog box. The Joined After 1998 query is already selected in the *Choose the table or query where the object's data comes from* box.

3. **Click Form Wizard in the list box and click OK.**

The initial Form Wizard dialog box appears for you to choose the fields to include in the form.

Another Way

To create a form, click Insert on the menu bar and click Form.

Creating a Tabular Form

1. In the Queries option of the Database window, click the query on which the form should be based.

2. Click the New Object drop-down arrow and click Form.

3. Click Form Wizard and click OK.

4. Select the appropriate form or query name in the Tables/Queries box, and select the fields to include in the form. Then click Next.

5. Click Tabular as the layout and click Next.

6. Click a desired style and click Next.

7. Type a name for the form and click Finish.

4. Click the **ContactFirstName field** and then click the **Add Field button** [>].

The field moves to the Selected Fields list box.

5. In the same manner, move the ContactLastName and DateJoined fields, in that order, to the Selected Fields list box.

Warning *In this instance, you can't just use the Add All Fields button* [>>] *to select all these fields because you need to change the order in which they appear.*

6. Click **Next** and click **Tabular** as the layout option. Then, click **Next**.

7. In the next dialog box, click the **Blends option** and then click **Next**.

Access displays the final Form Wizard dialog box. As when you created a columnar form, you now can enter a title for the form, and you can choose to view data with the form or to view the form's design.

8. Type Joined After 1998 Tabular Form **as the form's title; make sure the** *Open the form to view or enter information.* **option is selected, and click the Finish button**.

You see the tabular form, as shown in Figure 5.5, which displays the data from your Joined After 1998 query in a tabular layout.

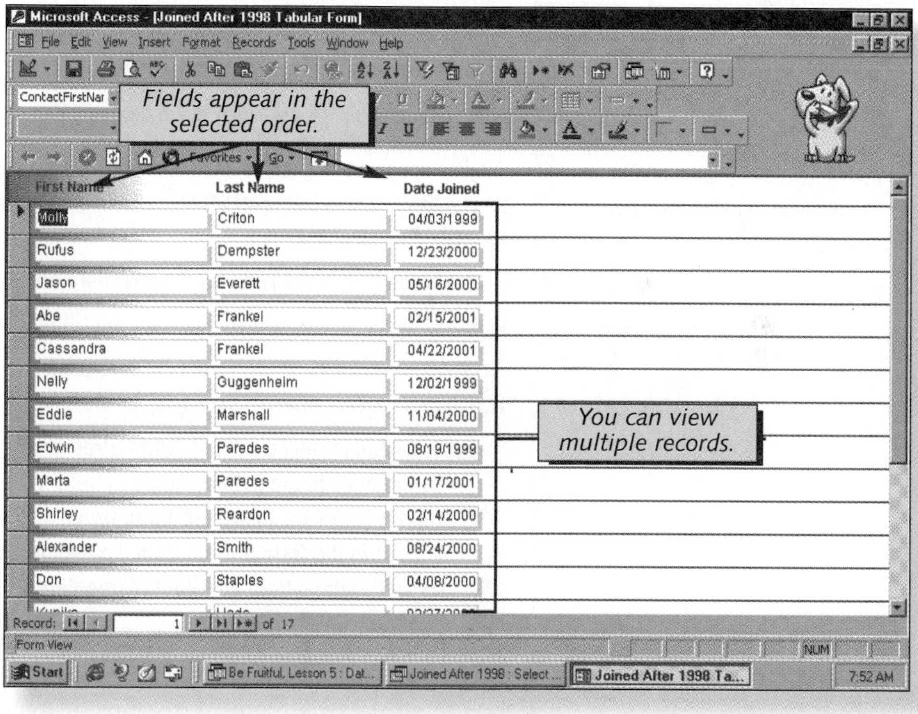

Figure 5.5
The Joined After 1998
Tabular Form

First Name	Last Name	Date Joined
Molly	Criton	04/03/1999
Rufus	Dempster	12/23/2000
Jason	Everett	05/16/2000
Abe	Frankel	02/15/2001
Cassandra	Frankel	04/22/2001
Nelly	Guggenheim	12/02/1999
Eddie	Marshall	11/04/2000
Edwin	Paredes	08/19/1999
Marta	Paredes	01/17/2001
Shirley	Reardon	02/14/2000
Alexander	Smith	08/24/2000
Don	Staples	04/08/2000

Fields appear in the selected order.

You can view multiple records.

Record: 1 of 17

Form View

9. Scroll the data to view the available records and close the form.

Access returns you to the Be Fruitful, Lesson 5 Database window.

ADDING AND EDITING DATA BY USING FORMS AND SUBFORMS

Sometimes you may want to use forms to browse your data. The real purpose of forms, however, is to facilitate the entering and editing of data. In forms, as in the datasheet, you need to know how to find the records that you want to edit. Once you're there, you need to know a few editing strategies. Fortunately, the techniques for navigating in forms are basically the same as those for moving around in the datasheet. (Refer to Lesson 3 if you need to review how to navigate or how to edit data.)

Adding Data Using a Form and Subform

When you add data in a form or subform, the change is automatically reflected in the appropriate table. The data you add to the main form affects one table, while the data you add to the subform may affect a different table. In this activity, you'll use the BFCustomers AutoForm to add a new customer and order.

1. Click the Forms option in the Objects bar of the Database window and then double-click BFCustomers AutoForm.

Access displays the selected form and shows the first record for the underlying table.

2. Click the New Record button ▶∗.

Access presents you with a new, blank record. As in Datasheet view, Access also saves any changes to the record you were working on when you moved to another record.

3. Press ⌨Tab to move to the Last Name field. Type Myrianthopoulos and press ⌨Tab.

Notice that Access automatically enters the next record number in the Customer ID field. (If you're confused about why there are more customer IDs than customers, don't forget that you deleted a record in Lesson 3.)

4. Type Zoe in the First Name field. Pressing ⌨Tab to move from field to field, type 1357 Birch St. #7 in the Billing Address field, Woodstock in the City field, NY in the State field, 11223-4432 in the ZIP Code field, (917) 555-1234 in the Phone Number field, and 4/22/01 in the Date Joined field. Leave the Notes field blank for now, and leave the Extra Catalogs field deselected (the default).

You now have a new record in the table. This new customer placed an order. Rather than entering the order data in the BFOrders table, you can enter it in the subform currently displayed. Access will automatically change the BFOrders table to reflect the new order.

5. Press ⌨Tab until you get to the Order Date field of the subform.

6. Type 4/22/01 and press ⌨Tab.

As shown in Figure 5.6, once you start typing in the Order Date field, the Order Number is automatically assigned.

7. Pressing ⌨Tab to move among fields, type Pears in the Fruit Type field, 1 in the Quantity field, 18.50 in the Price field, and 4.50 in the Shipping Amt. field.

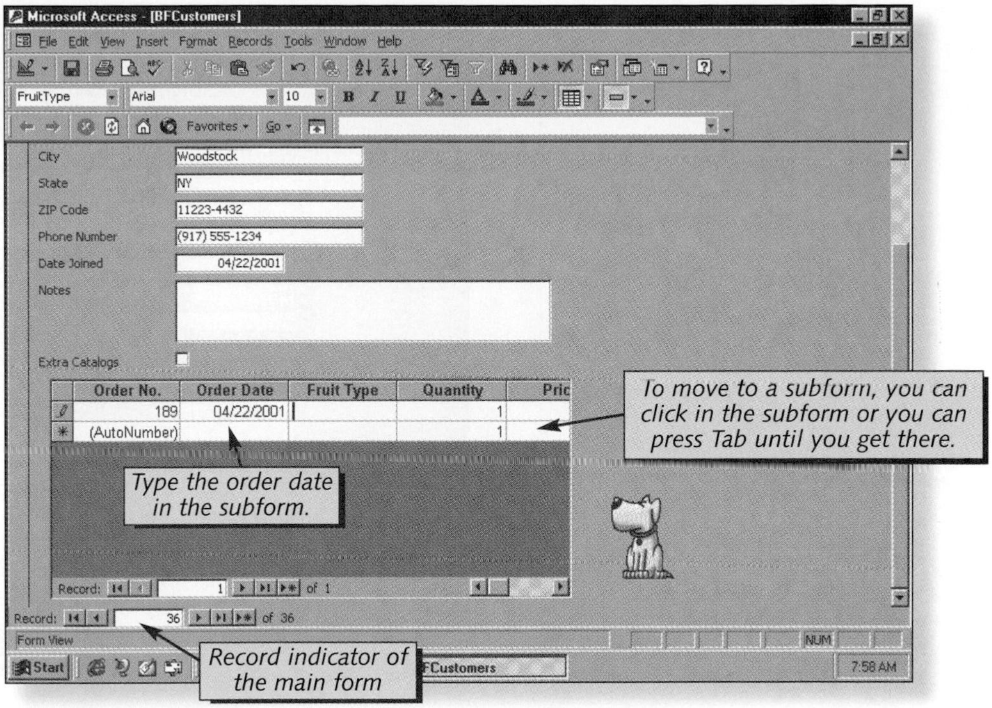

Microsoft Access - [BFCustomers]

File Edit View Insert Format Records Tools Window Help

FruitType | Arial | 10 | B I U

	City	Woodstock
State	NY
ZIP Code	11223-4432
Phone Number	(917) 555-1234
Date Joined	04/22/2001
Notes	
Extra Catalogs	

	Order No.	Order Date	Fruit Type	Quantity	Pric
	189	04/22/2001		1	
*	(AutoNumber)			1	

To move to a subform, you can click in the subform or you can press Tab until you get there.

Type the order date in the subform.

Record: 14 ◄ 1 ► ►I ►* of 1

Record: 14 ◄ 36 ► ►I ►* of 36

Form View NUM

Start FCustomers 7:58 AM

Figure 5.6
Entering data in a subform

Record indicator of the main form

HANDS On

Editing Records Using a Form

You can also make changes to data already in the table with the use of a form. Once the record you want to edit is displayed, you can change the record with the same basic steps you used in Lesson 3. In this activity, you'll edit one record and delete another.

1. **Type 7 in the record indicator of the main form and press** Enter ↵ .

Access moves you to the seventh record in the table—the record for Mason Bechdel.

2. **Click the box for the Notes field.**

Although there's no text, Access places the insertion point within the field and adds a vertical scroll bar.

3. **Type the following text:**

7/15/00: Mr. Bechdel reported not receiving his order of pears, although the fruit was delivered to his front door. Please send him a replacement box, rush delivery, and include a half dozen extra pears. Leave all packages at the back door in the future.

4. **Move to record 35—the record for Cassandra Frankel.**

5. **Click the record selector—the long vertical bar on the left side of the window.**

The record selector should turn a darker shade of gray, which indicates that this entire record is selected. You can see this effect in Figure 5.7.

6. **Press** Delete **to remove the record.**

Access displays a warning to verify that you want to delete the record; you see an identical warning when you delete records in Datasheet view.

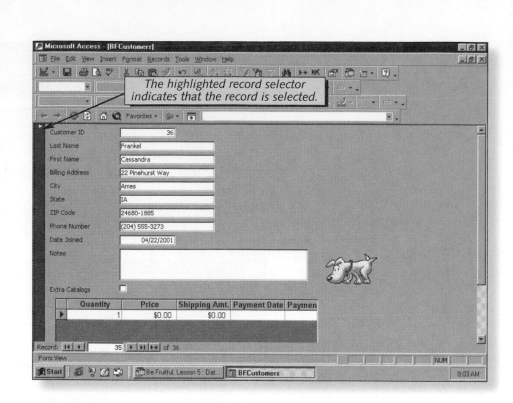

The highlighted record selector indicates that the record is selected.

Figure 5.7 ◀
Selecting a record in Form view

With Microsoft Access, you can quickly access frequently used commands by using keyboard shortcuts. Access also lets you view and print the list of all available keyboard shortcuts.

7. Read the warning and click **Yes** to delete the record. Then close the form.

The BFCustomers AutoForm is closed and you return to the Database window.

 You can sort and filter records in a form using the same methods you learned to sort and filter records in a table.

MODIFYING CONTROLS IN FORMS

Databases, as you learned in Lesson 1, are storehouses of information. In this lesson, you have been creating forms and manipulating raw data because of controls. Controls act as the holding place for the raw data you have stored in your table. Using controls, you can retrieve data from the underlying source, adjust the appearance of the data, and use the data in calculations.

Modifying and Adding Controls in a Form

In this activity, you will open a form in Design view and use the Control Toolbox to add a label to your form. You will also add a bound control from the Field list.

1. Open the *Best of the Orchard, Lesson 5* database in the *Tutorial* folder on your Student Data Disk and click **Forms**.

2. Click **Customers** and click **Design** ⬚ Design ⬚.

The Customers form opens with the Orders subform also displayed. A field list box is also available.

3. Examine the displayed toolbars. If the Control Toolbox toolbar is not displayed as shown in Figure 5.8, click **View** on the menu bar and click **Toolbox**.

Figure 5.8
The Toolbox toolbar

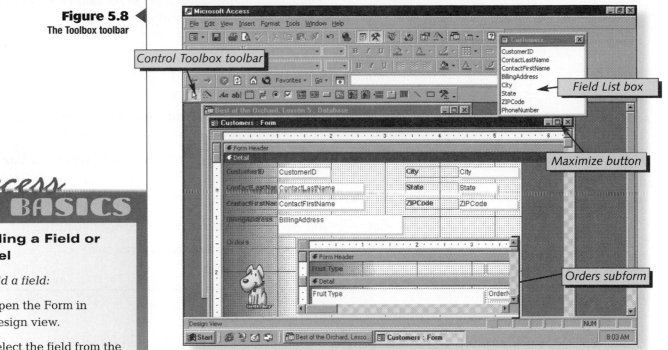

Figure 5.8 ◄
The Toolbox toolbar

Adding a Field or Label

To add a field:

1. Open the Form in Design view.

2. Select the field from the Field list box.

3. Drag to the desired location.

To add a label:

1. Open the Form in Design view.

2. Click the Label button.

3. In the desired location, click and drag to create a box.

4. Type your label.

4. Click the **Maximize button** 🔲 to maximize the form window.

5. Click and drag PhoneNumber from the Field list to the space below the ZIPCode field, as shown in Figure 5.9

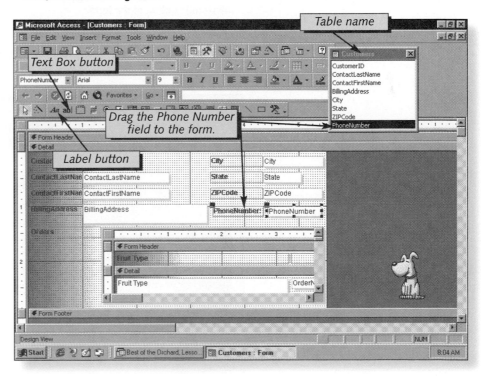

Figure 5.9 ◄
Using the Field List

Note *If you want to move the PhoneNumber field, point to the label box border. When the pointer changes to an open hand, click and drag the label to the desired location and release. You'll learn more about moving and resizing controls later in this lesson.*

The PhoneNumber field has been added to the Customers form. This control is bound to the Customers table field, PhoneNumber. You can edit the PhoneNumber data or create new records using this form.

6. Click the **Label button** Aa. Then click and drag below the caption *Orders*, approximately the same width and twice the height, to place a control.

The label appears as a white rectangle with the insertion point inside the label.

7. **Type** Orders received by 11 a.m. are shipped the same day.

Notice that while you type, the label box automatically adjusts the size.

8. Click the **Save button** 🖫 to save the changes to your form.

Creating a Calculated Control

In this activity, you will add a calculated control to your form to show the total charges for each customer order.

1. **With the Customers form open in Design view, scroll to the last field (Quantity) of the subform.**

2. **Click the Text Box button** abl **and click immediately after the Quantity field in the Detail section of the form.**

The label and control text box appear in your form. Note that the text box currently displays on top of the Quantity field with text indicating the unbound status, as shown in Figure 5.10.

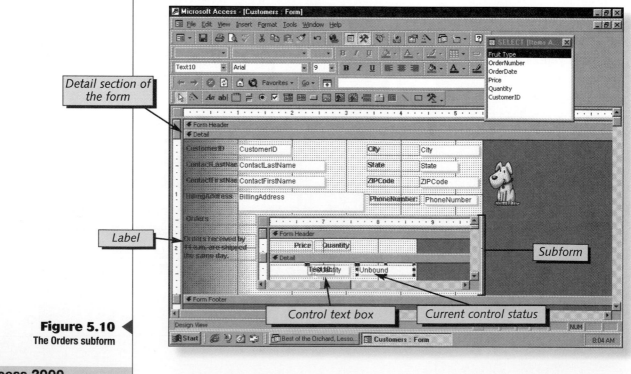

Figure 5.10 ◀
The Orders subform

Another Way

To open the Properties dialog box, click the Properties button on the Database toolbar.

3. Right-click the unbound text box and click **Properties** from the displayed menu.

A Properties dialog box appears with five tabs.

4. Click the **All tab** to view all the properties for the text box.

5. Click the **Control Source field** and click the **Build button**.

The Expression Builder dialog box appears with the Orders subform field list displayed in the second column.

6. Double-click the **Price field** in the second column (not the Price label). Then, in the row of operator buttons, click the **asterisk**. Finally, double-click the **Quantity field**.

The fields appear above in the Expression box.

7. Click the **asterisk** and type 1.08, as shown in Figure 5.11. Then, click **OK**.

Figure 5.11
The Expression Builder

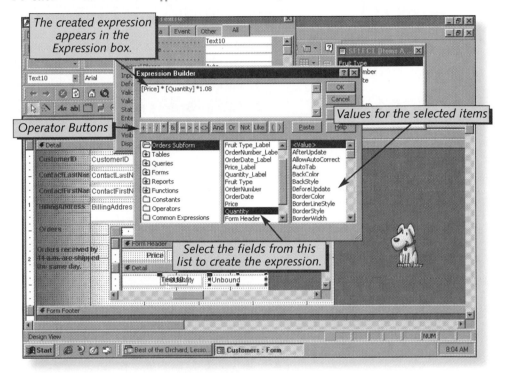

Creating a Calculated Control

1. Open the Form in Design view.

2. Add a text box.

3. Click the Properties button.

4. Click the Build button and create an expression.

5. Close the Expression Builder.

6. In the Properties dialog box, rename the field.

7. Close the Properties dialog box.

8. Switch to Form view to verify.

You have now created an expression that multiples the Price, Quantity and Shipping costs (8 percent). In addition, by using the figure *1.08*, you are determining the total for the order (including the shipping costs). The Expression Builder closes and returns you to the Properties dialog box.

8. Click the **Format field**, click the **drop-down arrow**, and click **Currency**.

9. Click the **Decimal Places drop-down arrow** and click **2**. Then type Total Cost in the **Name field**.

Setting the field properties to Format:Currency and Decimal Places:2 will adjust the way the calculated value appears. These settings will allow the value to appear as a monetary figure with the label Total Cost.

10. Scroll the Properties dialog box to review the other options you can control and then click the **Close button** ☒.

The Properties dialog box closes and you can now see the calculation expression in the text box.

11. In the Detail section of the form, click the label for the calculated control you just created and press ⌨Delete.

The label field is removed from the subform.

12. Click the **Label button** 🔤 and insert a label in the Form Header section immediately to the right of the Quantity label.

13. Type Total Cost in the label box and click the **Save button** 💾.

You have now created a calculated field in your form and saved your work.

14. Switch views and view your form in Form view verifying the calculations in the subform field, Total Cost.

Changing the Appearance of Your Data

In this activity, you will modify the format properties of your controls in order to change the appearance of your data.

1. Click the **View button** 🔳 to return to Design view.

2. Click the **Orders received by 11 a.m. are shipped the same day label**.

3. Click the **Font drop-down arrow** `Abadi MT Condensed` and click **Times New Roman**. (If Times New Roman is not available, select another font.)

4. Click the **Font size drop-down arrow** `10` and click **12**.

Some of the words disappear, as shown in Figure 5.12.

Modifying Format Properties

1. Open the form in Design view.

2. Click the control to modify.

3. Click the desired formatting button.

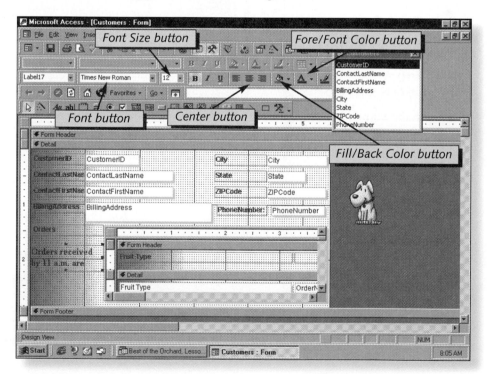

Figure 5.12
Formatting changes

5. Resize the label box to display all words.

6. Click the **Fill/Back Color button** 🎨 to change the background color to dark green.

The information, however, is still visible because the text is blue.

7. Click the Center button ▦ **. Then save your changes and close the form.**

USING SECTIONS IN FORMS

Sections help increase your ability to accurately and effectively enter data in forms. Sections include the header, footer, and detail section. A **_header_** is the information that appears at the top of each page. The **_footer_** is the information that appears at the bottom of each page. **_Detail_** includes all the raw data or calculations derived from the raw data. The forms with which you have been working have these sections. Using sections helps make the information easier to read and understand. You can even create additional headers and footers to increase efficiency.

HANDS On

Using the Header and Footer Sections

In this activity, you will open the Customers form and use the headers and footers.

1. Open the Customers form in Design view.

Access opens the form in Design view, as shown in Figure 5.13.

Figure 5.13
Customers form in Design view

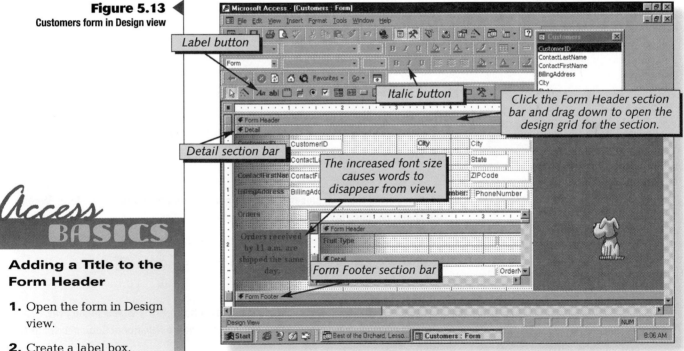

Access BASICS

Adding a Title to the Form Header

1. Open the form in Design view.

2. Create a label box.

3. Type the appropriate text.

4. Format the text as desired.

2. Click the Detail section bar and drag down to open the design grid under the Form Header section.

3. Create a label in the Form Header section and type Best of the Fruit - Order Form **in the box. Italicize the text and increase the font size to 20, resizing the label, if necessary.**

4. Click **Insert** on the menu bar and click **Date and Time**.

The Date and Time dialog box appears.

5. Click **OK** to accept the default choices.

The date and time information is inserted in the Form Header section.

6. Drag this information to the Form Footer section at the left margin.

The Form Footer section automatically expands to just enough space for the field.

7. With the date and time information still selected, click the **Special Effect button** and change the effect from Shadowed to Flat.

8. Switch views and review your data in Form view. Then save your changes and close the form.

PREVIEWING AND PRINTING FORMS

Usually, when you want printed output, you create a report; you'll do this later in this lesson. Sometimes, though, you may want to print some of the forms you've created. Also, often you might want to see an on-screen preview of the form before you print—to get a sense of what it will look like when printed. Previewing a form before printing can help you save time and paper. While previewing, you may notice errors that you can fix before printing.

Generating a Printout of a Form

In this activity, you will preview and then print a form.

1. Open the *Be Fruitful, Lesson 5* database and select the BFCustomer Names and Addresses form.

2. Click the **Print Preview button**. Maximize the window, if necessary.

You should see a preview of your form, much like the one shown in Figure 5.14.

3. To view part of the form closely, move the cursor over any portion of the form. When the shape changes to a magnifying glass, click.

4. To return to the full-page view, click anywhere in the form again.

5. To view two pages at once, click the **Two Pages button**.

Two pages of the form appear.

6. Click **Print** on the File menu. In the Print dialog box, click **Pages** in the Print what box. Set the print range from 1 to 1. Verify that the Number of Copies is set to 1. Click **OK**.

Page 1 of the form will be printed.

7. Click the **Close button** to close the Print Preview window and return to the Database window.

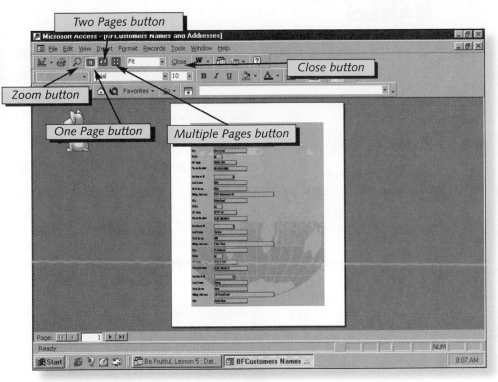

Figure 5.14 ◄
Previewing a form

WHEN AND WHY TO USE REPORTS

You generally use reports when you need professional-looking printed output. You might have to provide handouts for a presentation. Or, perhaps you need to share information with someone who isn't familiar with Access, doesn't have access to a computer, or prefers to spread pages out on a desk rather than view them on a computer screen. Although you can print datasheets and forms, reports look more polished and provide much more control over how your data is presented. In addition, from reports you can automatically generate summary data, such as totals and grand totals. When you create reports, as with forms, you will be able to do much of what you need by using the Report Wizard.

CREATING AN AUTOREPORT

AutoReports are basic reports generated automatically by Access. To create an AutoReport, you choose the table or query on which to base your report and then click the New Object drop-down arrow and click Report. Like the AutoForm, the AutoReport tracks the required information by examining the selected table or query—without asking you for any input. Access builds a basic report that includes every field from the table or query arranged in columns. The field names (or captions) appear on the left, to identify the fields. You can also create a second type of AutoReport that contains a header and a footer. In this type of report, the name of the table or query appears as a report header. A header is text information printed at the top of every page of the report; a report header appears at the top of the first page only. A report footer appears at the bottom of every page and includes the date on which the report is printed, the page number, and the number of pages in the entire report.

Creating a Columnar AutoReport

In this activity, you'll create an AutoReport based on the BFCustomers table.

1. Select the BFCustomers table. Then click the New Object drop-down arrow ![] **and click Report.**

The New Report dialog box appears.

2. Double-click the AutoReport: Columnar option in the list box.

In a few moments, Access displays a print preview of the report similar to the one shown in Figure 5.15. All fields in the table appear in a single column to the left of the field contents. The table name is the report header. Notice that you're looking at the data for the first record in the BFCustomers table. In an AutoReport, records always occur in the same order as in the underlying table or query.

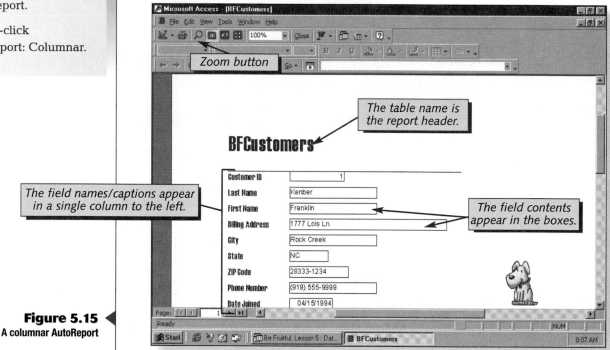

Figure 5.15
A columnar AutoReport

Note Depending on the actions taken by others who have used Access before you, the style of the text in your AutoReports may be different than the style of the text in the illustrations shown in this tutorial. However, the actual text (the labels, record data, and headings) should be the same.

3. Scroll the report using the vertical scroll bar.

You'll see the second record in the table. Access shows as many records as possible on a single page.

4. Scroll to the end of the page and to the right, if necessary, to see the report footer.

Navigating a Report

At the bottom of this Print Preview window are navigation buttons. These navigation buttons allow you to move from page to page in the report, rather than from record to record (as they did in Form view). In this activity, you'll explore a report by navigating the pages and zooming in and out of it.

1. Click the **Last Page navigation button** ▶︎❙, and then scroll to see the data on this page.

Access displays the last page of the report, and you can verify that the records are in the same order as in the underlying table.

2. Click twice on the **Previous Page button** ◀︎.

Access moves up two pages in the report.

3. Press `F5` or double-click the **Current Page indicator**, type 6 and press `Enter⏎`.

Access moves to the sixth page of the report, as shown in Figure 5.16.

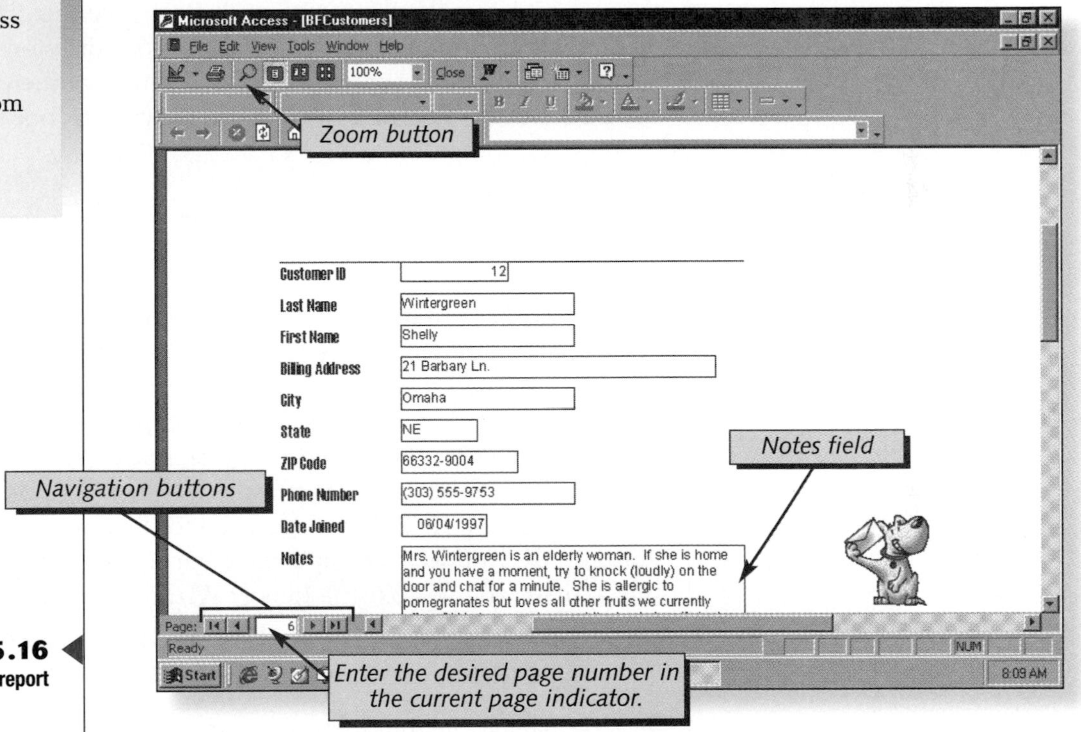

Access BASICS

Navigating a Report

- To move to a different page of a report, click a navigation button.

- To move to a specific page, press `F5`, type a page number, and press `Enter⏎`.

- To zoom, click the Zoom button or click on the report itself.

Figure 5.16 ◀︎
Moving among pages of a report

[Screenshot: Microsoft Access - [BFCustomers] window showing Print Preview with labels: "Zoom button", "Navigation buttons", "Notes field", "Enter the desired page number in the current page indicator."]

Customer ID: 12
Last Name: Wintergreen
First Name: Shelly
Billing Address: 21 Barbary Ln.
City: Omaha
State: NE
ZIP Code: 66332-9004
Phone Number: (303) 555-9753
Date Joined: 06/04/1997
Notes: Mrs. Wintergreen is an elderly woman. If she is home and you have a moment, try to knock (loudly) on the door and chat for a minute. She is allergic to pomegranates but loves all other fruits we currently

4. Scroll until you see the Notes field for Shelly Wintergreen.

The Notes text is wrapped and appears in several rows.

5. Point to the report and click when the pointer changes to the shape of a magnifying glass.

Access shrinks the report so that you can see an entire page on the screen at once. As you can see, this page contains a footer, but no header appears on this page.

6. Click the **First Page navigation button** ❙◀︎.

Both the header and footer appear on the first page.

7. Click the **Zoom button** 🔍 or click the report again.

Did you know?

You can change the margins of a report by clicking Page Setup on the File menu.

Access returns the report to the original magnification. The portion of the page that you see enlarged depends on where you click.

8. Click the report's **Close button** ⊠ to close the report. Click **Yes** to save the report.

Access displays a Save As dialog box that prompts you for a report name.

9. Save the report as BFCustomers AutoReport.

10. Click the **Reports option** in the Objects bar of the Database window.

Access displays the name of the report you just created: BFCustomers AutoReport.

USING THE REPORT WIZARD

If you need a basic report, an AutoReport might do the job. If, however, you want to choose the layout, decide the fields to include and their order, determine the text layout on the page (columnar, tabular, or justified), and more, then you can use the Report Wizard. Using the Report Wizard is similar to using the Form Wizard: Access prompts you for information and then constructs a report based on your replies. As in any other wizard, you can click the Back button any time you want to move back one step.

HANDS On

Creating a Columnar Report

The Report Wizard allows you to choose the layout and orientation of the report. The columnar layout displays the records one after another. The tabular layout shows the fields of each record in rows. The justified layout displays each record in its own small box. In *portrait orientation,* pages print down the long side of the page. In *landscape orientation,* pages print across the wide side of the paper. If you want a *columnar report*—as in a columnar *form*—all of the fields for a record are displayed vertically on the page. Actually, the AutoReport you created earlier is a simple columnar report. In this activity, you will use the Report Wizard to create a columnar report.

1. Select the **BFCustomers table** and click the **New Object drop-down arrow** 🔲▾. Click **Report** and then double-click **Report Wizard**.

Access displays the first Report Wizard dialog box, as shown in Figure 5.17. The selected table name appears in the Tables/Queries text box.

2. Click the **Add All Fields button** ⧽⧽ .

Access moves all of the field names to the Selected Fields list box.

3. Click the **CustomerID field** in the Selected Fields list and click the **Remove Field button** ⦁ .

Access removes the CustomerID field from the list of fields.

4. Select the **DateJoined field** and click the **Remove Field button** ⦁ . Click the **Remove Field button** ⦁ two more times.

Access removes the DateJoined, Notes, and ExtraCatalogs fields from the list of fields to include in the report.

Hints & Tips

To change the existing order of fields, remove the fields and then add the fields one by one in the desired order.

Figure 5.17
The Report Wizard dialog box

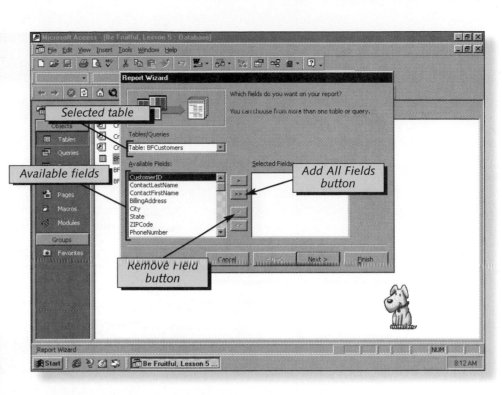

Using the Report Wizard

1. Click the table or query name on which you want to base the report.

2. Click the New Object drop-down arrow and click Report.

3. Double-click Report Wizard.

4. Select the table or query name in the Tables/Queries box.

5. Select the fields to include in the report and click Next.

6. Click Next twice if you don't want to group or sort the records.

7. Click the desired layout and orientation options and click Next.

8. Click the style and click Next.

9. Type a name for the report and click Finish.

5. Click **Next** to move to the dialog box that allows you to group the records. (You will learn more about grouping for reports later in this lesson.)

6. Click **Next** to move to the dialog box that allows you to sort records by up to four fields. (You will learn more about sorting for reports later in this lesson.)

7. Click **Next** to move to the dialog box that allows you to choose the report layout and the orientation.

8. Click the **Columnar** and **Portrait option buttons**. Then, click **Next** to move to the dialog box that allows you to choose a style for your report.

9. Click **Corporate** and click **Next**.

In the final Report Wizard dialog box, you enter the title of the report and tell Access what you want to do next.

10. Type Customer Names and Addresses **in the title text box and click the Preview the report. option**. Then click **Finish**.

In a moment, Access displays the first page of the report you just created, as shown in Figure 5.18. The report contains data from the selected BFCustomers table. Unlike the AutoReport you created previously, this report displays only designated fields from the underlying table.

 *You can rename your report later by selecting it in the Database window. Click the name again. When you see the insertion point, press* Backspace *or* Delete *to delete the existing name and type a new one. If you want to create a copy of the same report using a different name, open the report, click Save As on the File menu, and type a name for the copy of the report.*

11. Click the **Last Page navigation button** ▶|.

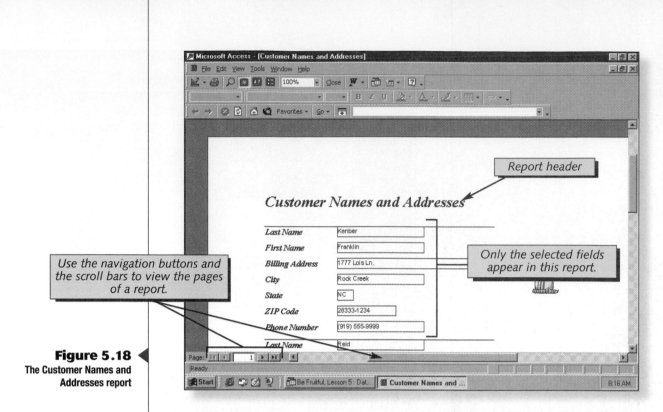

Figure 5.18
The Customer Names and Addresses report

Callouts in figure:
- Report header
- Only the selected fields appear in this report.
- Use the navigation buttons and the scroll bars to view the pages of a report.

Window title: Microsoft Access - [Customer Names and Addresses]

Customer Names and Addresses

Last Name	Kenber
First Name	Franklin
Billing Address	1777 Lois Ln.
City	Rock Creek
State	NC
ZIP Code	28333-1234
Phone Number	(919) 555-9999
Last Name	Reid

Access shows the last page in the report. Note that you see the report title on the first page only.

12. Scroll to the bottom of the page.

The date and page number appear as a report footer.

13. Click the report's Close button ☒ to close the report.

Access closes the report and returns you to the Be Fruitful, Lesson 5 Database window.

Creating a Tabular Report

If you have a large amount of data to display in a relatively small amount of space, use a tabular report. Like a tabular form, a *tabular report* displays the fields for a single record in one row and presents multiple records at once. Field names or captions appear near the top of the report as column headings. Realize that tabular reports don't work well with long Text or Memo fields or with too many fields to fit on a single page.

HANDS On

Creating a Query for a Report

In this activity, you will create a query to select the portion of the data that you want a report to print.

1. Click the BFOrders table in the *Be Fruitful, Lesson 5* database. Click Query on the New Object drop-down list.

Access displays the New Query dialog box.

2. Click Design View and click OK.

Access displays the Query Design view window.

3. Double-click the title bar of the BFOrders Field list.

As shown in Figure 5.19, Access selects all of the fields in the Field list.

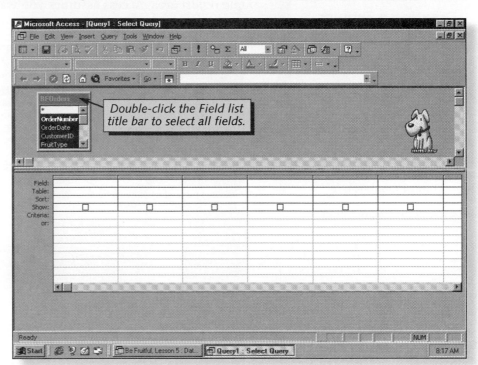

4. Drag the selected list of fields to the first column in the query design grid.

Access inserts all fields into the query design grid.

5. In the Sort row of the OrderDate field, click Ascending.

6. Type >12/31/99 and <= 12/31/00 in the Criteria row of the OrderDate field.

You're selecting all orders after 12/31/99 and on or before 12/31/00—that is, all orders in the year 2000.

7. Click the Run button [!].

Access displays a Recordset that includes only the orders from 2000.

8. Save the query as 2000 Orders. Then close the query.

HANDS On

Creating a Tabular Report Based on a Query

In this report, you will use the Report Wizard to create a report for the 2000 Orders query.

1. In the Reports option, double-click Create report by using wizard.

Access displays the initial Report Wizard dialog box, where you can choose the fields to include in the report.

2. Click Query: 2000 Orders from the Tables/Queries box, if it is not already selected.

Creating a Tabular Report

1. Click Reports in the Objects bar.

2. Double-click Create report using wizard.

3. Select the query or table on which to base the report in the Tables/Queries box.

4. Add the desired fields and click Next.

3. Add the **OrderDate, FruitType, Quantity, Price, ShippingAmount,** and **PaymentAmount** fields to the Selected Fields list, in that order. Then, click **Next**.

The first dialog box should look like the one in Figure 5.20. As shown in the sample report area, Access assumes you want the records grouped by fruit type.

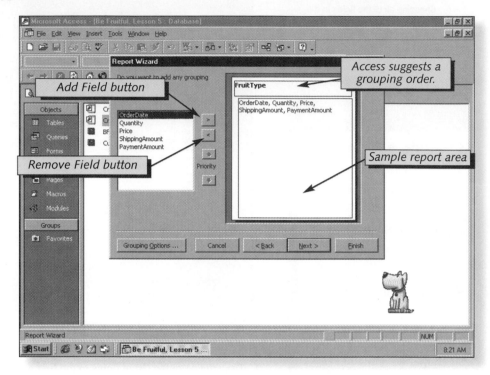

Figure 5.20
The Report Wizard dialog box with grouping settings

Grouping and Sorting Records in a Tabular Report

Groups, as the name implies, are collections of records with like information. Examples of groups include records with a city field of Philadelphia or records with the same order date. You can group records by any field in the report. In this activity, you will create a report that groups the orders by the month.

1. Since you don't want to group records by fruit type, click the **Remove Field button** `<` .

Access removes the FruitType heading from the sample area.

2. Click **OrderDate** and click the **Add Field button** `>` .

The sample area now shows OrderDate by Month.

3. Click **Next** to move to the dialog box that allows you to control the order in which records appear within each group.

In this case, you want the records to be in chronological order within each month.

4. Click the **drop-down arrow** beside the number 1 field, and click the **OrderDate field**.

The OrderDate field will determine the sequence of the records within each group. As shown in Figure 5.21, the button beside each field allows you to sort in ascending or descending order. Ascending order is the default.

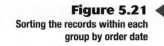

Grouping and Sorting Records

1. If you want to change a grouping level, click the Remove Field button.

2. Click the field on which you want to group and click the Add Field button. Click Next.

3. Click the first field's drop-down arrow and click the field on which you want to sort.

4. Click the button beside the field name to change the sort order, if desired. Then click Next.

5. Click the desired layout and orientation options and click Next.

6. Click the desired style and click Next.

7. Type a report name and click Finish.

5. Click Next to move to the dialog box to choose the layout for the tabular report.

As you can see, when you create a report that groups and sorts the records, a tabular report is selected automatically. The preview box inside the dialog box illustrates what the Stepped layout looks like.

6. Click the Align Left 1 option button, and look at the layout in the preview box.

7. Click Landscape in the Orientation box, and click Next to move to the dialog box to choose a style.

8. Click Soft Gray as the style, and then click the Next button to move to the final Report Wizard dialog box.

9. Type Be Fruitful 2000 Orders as the title and click Finish.

In a moment, Access displays the tabular report, as shown in Figure 5.22; it shows the data from your 2000 Orders query in a tabular layout.

Previewing a Tabular Report

In this activity, you will preview your report.

1. Scroll the report.

Access has grouped the records by month and sorted each month's records by order date, as shown in Figure 5.23.

Figure 5.22
The Be Fruitful 2000 Orders report

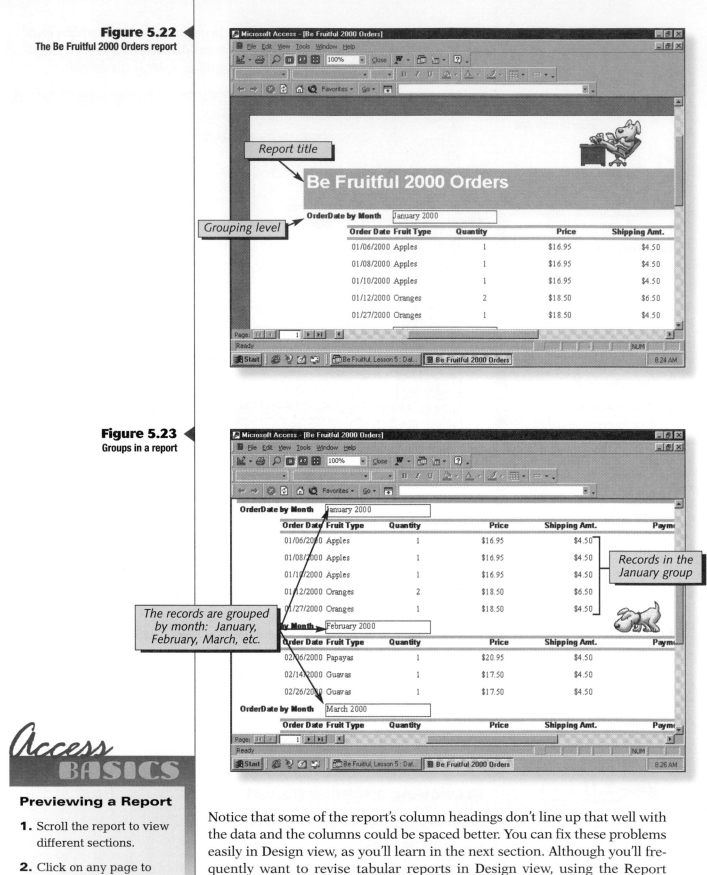

Report title

Grouping level

Figure 5.23
Groups in a report

The records are grouped by month: January, February, March, etc.

Records in the January group

Access
BASICS

Previewing a Report

1. Scroll the report to view different sections.

2. Click on any page to zoom.

Notice that some of the report's column headings don't line up that well with the data and the columns could be spaced better. You can fix these problems easily in Design view, as you'll learn in the next section. Although you'll frequently want to revise tabular reports in Design view, using the Report Wizard is the quickest way to create the basic report.

2. Click anywhere on the page to zoom out.

Although much of the text is not readable, you can use this view to preview the layout of an entire page.

3. Close the report and return to the Be Fruitful, Lesson 5 Database window.

Modifying Reports and Forms

The spacing and alignment of data in reports and forms doesn't always look perfect. And, depending on the page layout, some column labels may not be entirely visible. Use Help to learn how you can modify a report or form in Design view.

1. Click the Office Assistant.

2. Type resize a control **in the** *What would you like to do?* **box and click Search.**

3. Click Move, size, align, and format text boxes or controls in a form or report.

4. Click Move a control and its label. Maximize the window and read the Help information to learn how to work with controls in Design view (Figure 5.24).

5. Explore for answers to these questions: What view do you use to move a text box or other control? What shape does the pointer have when you are dragging the control? How do you maintain vertical or horizontal alignment with other controls?

Figure 5.24
Learning about moving controls

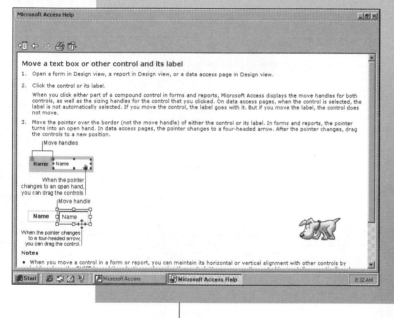

6. Click the Show button on the Help window and then click the Contents tab.

7. Scroll and click the plus sign before the Working with Controls on Forms, Reports, and Data Access Pages topic.

8. Open the Creating, Manipulating, and Formatting Controls topic. Explore for information on aligning controls.

9. Open the Be Fruitful 2000 Orders report and look for controls that need to be resized or moved. Switch to Design view and fix the report's appearance.

10. Close the Help window.

Just as a form can contain a subform, a report can contain a subreport that provides details of the main report.

CREATING TOTALS IN REPORTS

Access can easily group records in tabular reports. Sometimes, however, you may want to include totals of the numeric fields in the report as well. In the Be Fruitful 2000 Orders report, you might want subtotals for each month's orders and a grand total for all of the records in the query or table. You might also like to see the total sales per year rather than only the entire sales over the life of the company. In such cases, you can add totals to a report.

HANDS On

Access BASICS

Creating a Report with Totals

1. Double-click Create report by using wizard.

2. Select the table or query on which to base the report in the Tables/Queries box.

3. Select the fields to include in the report and click Next.

4. Select one or more fields on which to group.

5. Click the Grouping Options button and select the intervals for the grouped fields. Click OK.

6. Click Next and select one or more fields on which to sort.

Building a Report with Totals

In this activity, you will use the Report Wizard to create a report that sorts and totals orders by year.

1. Double-click **Create report by using wizard in the Reports option** of the *Be Fruitful, Lesson 5* database.

In the first Report Wizard dialog box, you will choose the tables, queries, and fields you want to include in the report.

2. Click **Query: 2000 Orders** in the Tables/Queries box, if necessary.

3. Use the **Add Field button** `>` to include the OrderDate, FruitType, Quantity, Price, ShippingAmount, and PaymentAmount fields, in that order. Then, click **Next**.

In this dialog box you will choose up to four fields to use as the basis for grouping data in your report. Access sorts on the first designated field first and then on each designated field in the order you choose them.

4. Click the **Remove Field button** `<` to remove the FruitType heading as the grouping level.

5. Click **OrderDate** and click the **Add Field button** `>`.

6. Click **FruitType** and again click the **Add Field button** `>`.

Both fields are added to the list box on the right as shown in Figure 5.25, indicating that you want the records in the table grouped by OrderDate. Then, within each group, you want the orders grouped by FruitType.

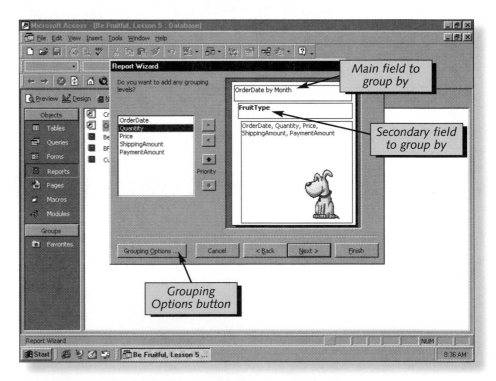

Figure 5.25
Adding groups and subgroups to a report

7. Click the **Grouping Options button**.

8. In the Grouping Intervals dialog box, click **Year** for the Grouping intervals of the OrderDate field, as shown in Figure 5.26.

9. Click **OK** to group the records by the year in which the orders were placed. Then click **Next** to move to the dialog box to choose the fields to sort by.

Access provides many ways to group data in the group by fields. For example, you can group by the first letter (or first several letters) of a Text field; you can group Date/Time fields by year, quarter, month, and more; and you can group Number fields by ranges (by tens, fifties, hundreds, and so on).

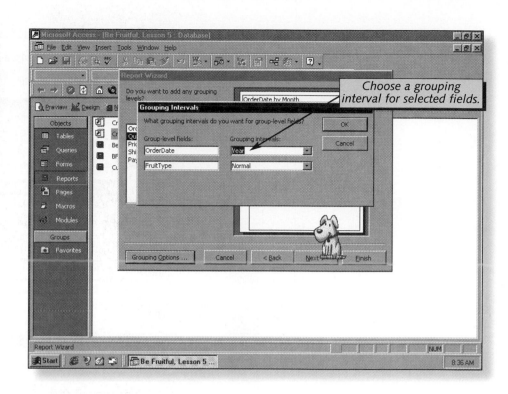

Choose a grouping interval for selected fields.

Figure 5.26
The Grouping Intervals dialog box

10. Click **Quantity** in the Field 1 box.

Access will use the Quantity field to sort records that have the same order year and type of fruit.

HANDS On

Access BASICS

Adding Totals and Subtotals to a Report

1. Click the Summary Options button.

2. Click the desired boxes to sum, average, show the minimum, or show the maximum for the desired fields. Click OK and then click Next.

3. Select a layout and an orientation. Click Next.

4. Select a style. Click Next.

5. Type a report name and click Finish.

Adding Totals and Subtotals to a Report

In this activity, you will continue using the Report Wizard. You will add totals and subtotals for the numeric fields in your report. Because you have created a group within a group, Access will display totals for each year's order and totals for each type of fruit ordered within each year. In addition, you will calculate a total at the end of the report.

1. Click the **Summary Options button**.

In the Summary Options dialog box, you can select from four different types of summary information—totals (Sum), average (Avg), minimum value (Min), and maximum value (Max)—for each numeric field. The option buttons on the right allow you to choose between Detail and Summary or Summary Only. If you choose Detail and Summary, you will see the data for each record as well as summary information for each group, subgroup, and final totals. If you choose Summary Only, you will see the summary information for each group, subgroup, and final totals, but you will not see the data for individual records.

2. Click the **Sum check boxes** for the Quantity, ShippingAmount, and PaymentAmount fields.

3. Click **OK**; then click **Next** to choose the layout and orientation for the report.

4. Click the **Outline 1 layout** and **Landscape orientation**. Then click **Next**.

5. Click **Compact style** and click **Next**.

6. Type Orders by Year and Fruit Type **as the title of the report and click Finish.**

After a few moments, the Report Wizard displays a preview of your report.

7. Scroll the report to see the totals and subtotals, as shown in a portion of the report in Figure 5.27. Then close the preview.

Subtotals for Strawberries group

Totals for one order date

Figure 5.27
A report with totals and subtotals

MODIFYING CONTROLS IN REPORTS

In Reports, controls determine how you can manipulate the raw data to create an impressive and effective presentation. As with Forms, you use the Control Toolbox to create and edit controls in Report Design view. Controls must be bound to perform calculations in reports. Unbound controls can provide a general note or message, or hold graphical elements. Calculated controls take the raw data and perform the manipulation, and the result appears in the report. You can also create a calculated field. A calculated field appears in the query or table and uses the raw data to create a new field. Because reports are based on queries and tables, you can perform your calculation in the query or table, and then allow the wizard to create the report.

HANDS On

Modifying and Adding Controls in Your Report

In this activity, you will open a report in Design view and use the Control Toolbox to add a label to your report. You will also add a bound control from the Field list.

1. Open the *Best of the Orchard, Lesson 5* database in the *Tutorial* folder on your Student Data Disk, and open the Customers Purchases report in Design view.

The Customers Purchases report opens and a field list box is displayed.

2. Click **View** on the menu bar and click **Toolbox**, if necessary, to display the Control Toolbox. Maximize the window.

To add a label:

1. Open the report in Design view.

2. Select the Label button.

3. Click in the appropriate spot and drag to create a box.

4. Type your label.

To add a field:

1. Open the report in Design view.

2. Select the field from the Field list box.

3. Drag to the desired location.

3. Drag State from the Field list to the CustomerID Header section. Position the control to the right of the ContactFirstName field at about 4.5" on the design grid.

The State field is added to the Customers Purchases report. This control is bound to the Orders Placed query, field State.

4. In the Report Header section, insert a label starting at the 4" mark and going toward the right margin. Type Prepared by: Student Name as the label (using *your* name instead of *Student Name*).

The report design should appear as shown in Figure 5.28.

5. Save and close your report.

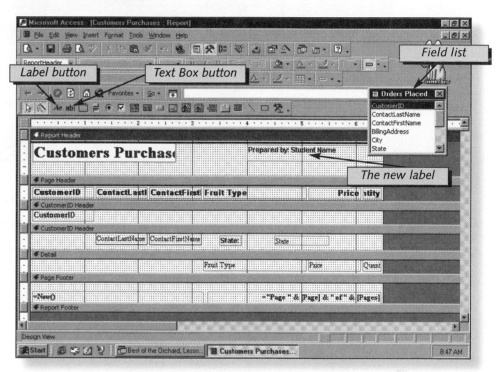

Figure 5.28
Report Design view

Creating a Calculated Field

In this activity, you will create a calculated field in the Orders Placed query to determine the total price, including an eight percent shipping fee. Then you will use the Report Wizard to generate a report.

1. Open the Orders Placed query in Design view.

2. Scroll to the first blank field and click in the Field row.

3. Right-click, and then click **Build**.

The Expression Builder dialog box opens with the Orders Placed folder open and the fields available displayed in the second column as shown in Figure 5.29.

4. Double-click the **Tables folder** and click the **Items Available folder**.

The list of fields from the Items Available table appears in the second column.

Figure 5.29
Expression Builder dialog box

Expression will appear here.

Additional commands

Available fields in the open folder

5. Double-click the **Price field** in the second column.

Access inserts *Price* as part of the expression in the Expression box.

6. Click the **asterisk button** in the row of operator buttons.

An asterisk appears in the Expression box.

7. Open the Orders folder and double-click the **Quantity field**.

Access adds *Quantity* to the Expression box.

8. Click the **asterisk button** again and type 1.08.

This calculation will allow you to obtain the total cost (Price x Quantity) plus the 8 percent shipping charge. Multiplying by 8 percent would just give the shipping charge, whereas 1.08 provides the total cost including the shipping charge.

9. Click **OK**.

The Expression Builder dialog box closes and the expression you just created is inserted in the field.

10. Click the **Properties button** 📷.

The Field Properties dialog box displays.

11. Select **Currency** in the Format field. Type Total Plus Shipping in the Caption field; then close the dialog box.

The field name is *Expr1,* but the caption will appear when you view the data.

12. Save and close the query.

13. Click **Reports** and double-click **Create report by using wizard**.

14. Select the query *Orders Placed* as the source for the report.

Access
BASICS

Creating a Calculated Field to Use in a Report

1. Click Queries in the Objects bar.

2. Open the query in Design view.

3. Type the expression in the Field row.

4. Save the query.

15. In the Report Wizard dialog boxes, select the following fields: **OrderDate, Fruit Type, and Expr1. Add grouping with OrderDate by Month. Select the Stepped Layout, Landscape Orientation, and Bold style. Name the report** Summary of Orders. **Then, finish the report.**

Access opens the report in Print Preview, as shown in Figure 5.30.

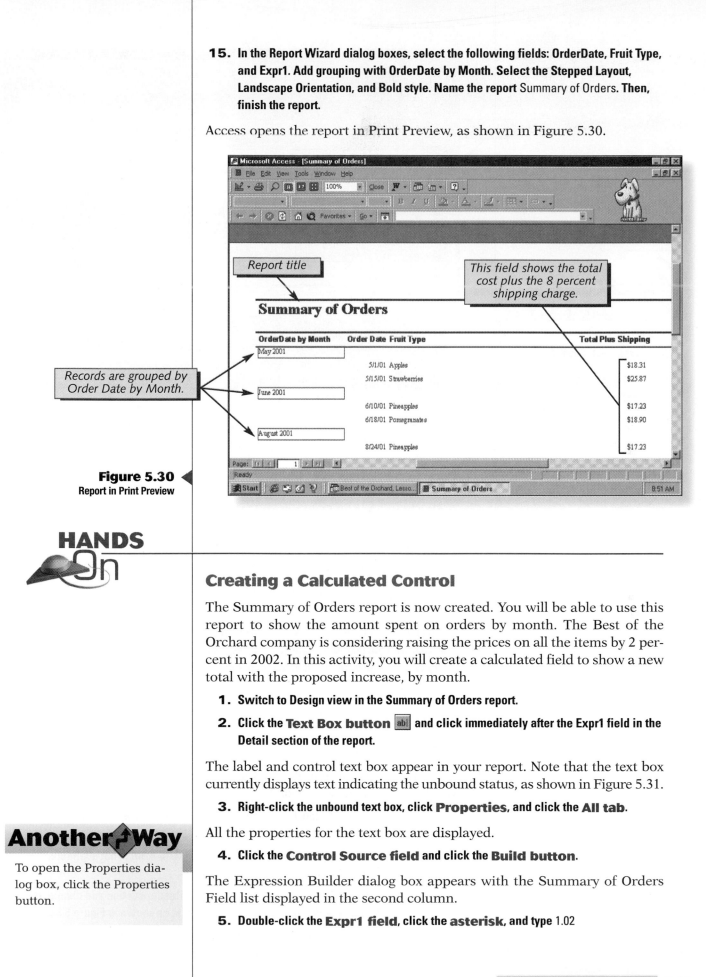

Report title

This field shows the total cost plus the 8 percent shipping charge.

Records are grouped by Order Date by Month.

Summary of Orders

OrderDate by Month	Order Date	Fruit Type	Total Plus Shipping
May 2001			
	5/1/01	Apples	$18.31
	5/15/01	Strawberries	$25.87
June 2001			
	6/10/01	Pineapples	$17.23
	6/18/01	Pomegranates	$18.90
August 2001			
	8/24/01	Pineapples	$17.23

Figure 5.30
Report in Print Preview

HANDS On

Creating a Calculated Control

The Summary of Orders report is now created. You will be able to use this report to show the amount spent on orders by month. The Best of the Orchard company is considering raising the prices on all the items by 2 percent in 2002. In this activity, you will create a calculated field to show a new total with the proposed increase, by month.

1. Switch to Design view in the Summary of Orders report.

2. Click the **Text Box button** [abl] **and click immediately after the Expr1 field in the Detail section of the report.**

The label and control text box appear in your report. Note that the text box currently displays text indicating the unbound status, as shown in Figure 5.31.

3. Right-click the unbound text box, click **Properties**, and click the **All tab**.

All the properties for the text box are displayed.

4. Click the **Control Source field** and click the **Build button**.

The Expression Builder dialog box appears with the Summary of Orders Field list displayed in the second column.

5. Double-click the **Expr1 field**, click the **asterisk**, and type 1.02

Another Way

To open the Properties dialog box, click the Properties button.

Figure 5.31 ◀
Report in Design view

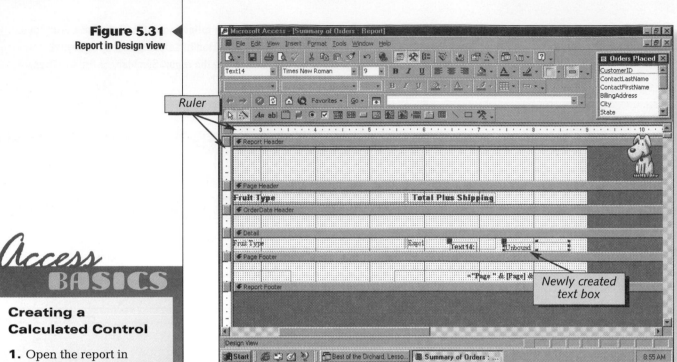

**Creating a
Calculated Control**

1. Open the report in
   Design view.

2. Add a text box.

3. Click the Properties
   button.

4. Click the Build button
   and create an
   expression.

5. Close the Expression
   Builder.

6. In the Properties dialog
   box, rename the field.

7. Close the Properties
   dialog box.

The completed expression appears in the Expression Builder dialog box.
This expression will multiply the calculated field you created earlier with the
proposed 2 percent increase.

6. Click OK to close the Expression Builder dialog box.

The dialog box closes and you return to the Properties dialog box for the text
box.

7. Click the Format drop-down arrow and click Currency. Type With
Proposed Increase **in the Name field; then close the Properties dialog box.**

The Properties dialog box closes and you can now see the expression in the
text box.

**8. Delete the label for the calculated control and create a label in the Page Header
section with the text** *With Proposed Increase.* **Resize and move the label as necessary to best align with the other labels in the Page Header.**

9. Save the report.

Modifying the Report

In this activity, you will modify the format properties of your controls to
change the appearance of your data.

**1. Resize the Summary of Orders label in the Report Header section so the entire label
shows.**

**2. Change the font to Arial, size 22. Resize the label again. (If Arial is not available,
select another font.)**

**3. Change the font size to 8 for all the items in the Page Header section and change the
font color for the label** *With Proposed Increase* **to black, as shown in Figure 5.32.**

**4. Preview the report to see whether other changes are needed. Switch views and
make necessary changes. Save your changes.**

Modifying Format Properties

1. Open the report in Design view.

2. Click the control to modify.

3. Click the desired formatting button.

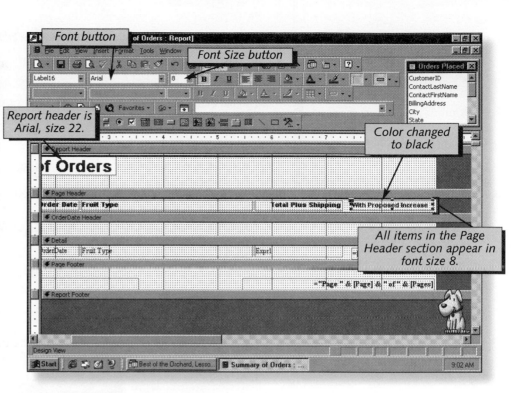

Figure 5.32 ◀
Changes to Report Design view

USING SECTIONS IN REPORTS

Sections, as you can see in the Summary of Orders report, increase your ability to accurately and effectively understand the data presented. Sections in reports are used for grouping and calculating and can provide critical information as to when the report was printed and who prepared the report. Sections in reports, like forms, include the header, footer, and detail section. The reports with which you have been working have these sections. Using sections makes the information easier to read and understand.

Using the Header and Footer Sections

Now that you have added the additional calculation to your Summary of Orders report, you are ready to make the final changes before your 2002 projections meeting. In this activity, you will continue working with the Summary of Orders report and modify the report sections.

1. Create a label at 4.5" in the Report Header section and type 2002 Projections Meeting.

2. Italicize the text and increase the font to 16, resizing the label, if necessary, to keep the text on one line.

3. Click Insert on the menu bar and click Date and Time.

The Date and Time dialog box appears.

4. Click OK to accept the default choices.

The date and time information is inserted in the Report Header section at the left margin.

Adding a Title to the Report Header

1. Open the report in Design view.

2. Create a Label box.

3. Type the appropriate text.

4. Format the text as desired.

5. Drag the date and time information below the *2002 Projections Meeting* label.

Now, the date and time information will print directly below the *2002 Projections Meeting* label.

6. In the Detail section, click the **calculated control** you created in the last activity and click **Bold** 🅱.

The calculated field will now appear bold.

7. Right-click the Detail section bar and click **Sorting and Grouping**.

The Sorting and Grouping dialog box appears as shown in Figure 5.33.

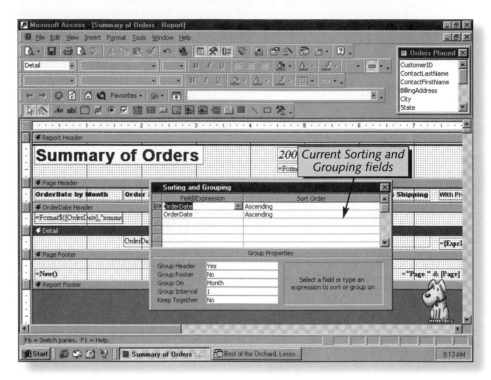

Figure 5.33
Sorting and Grouping dialog box

8. In the Field/Expression column of the second row, select **Fruit Type** from the drop-down list. Then close the Sorting and Grouping dialog box.

9. Create a label in the Report Footer section and type Prepared by: Your Name **(using your name). Align the footer at the left margin.**

10. Save and close the report.

PRINTING REPORTS

Although you can print forms and even datasheets, you'll usually use reports when you want to present professional-looking printed output. When you printed forms earlier in this lesson, you first previewed them to get a sense of how they would look when printed. When you work with reports, though, they are displayed in Print Preview mode by default. As you learned, you can use the Zoom feature for either an overview or a close-up view of the report before you decide to go ahead and print.

 *You can quickly and easily generate mailing labels using Access. Click Insert on the menu bar, click Report and double-click Label Wizard in the New Report dialog box that appears. Then follow the instructions provided by the wizard. You can use labels to mail items, create file folder labels, or generate name tags.*

Printing a Report

1. Open the report you wish to print.

2. Click Print on the File menu.

3. Change the settings in the Print dialog box, if desired, and then click OK.

Printing the Orders by Year and Fruit Type Report

In this activity, you'll print the Orders by Year and Fruit Type report that you created earlier in this lesson.

1. In the *Be Fruitful, Lesson 5* database, open the Orders by Year and Fruit Type report and click the **Zoom button** 🔍.

Access displays a reduced view of the report, so you can see what an entire page looks like.

2. Click **Print** on the File menu.

Note that you can print while viewing the report in Print Preview mode, and you can also select the report name in the Database window and print from there. In the Print dialog box, you can choose to print only selected pages of the report; you also can choose to print multiple copies of the pages or the full report.

3. Click **Pages** in the Print Range box, and type 1 in the From and To boxes. Verify that the Number of Copies is set to 1. Click **OK**.

Access will display a message to tell you that it is printing the first page of your report.

4. Close the report.

5. Click the **Compact on Close option**, if necessary, and close the *Be Fruitful, Lesson 5* database.

Self CHECK

Test your knowledge by answering the following questions. See Appendix D to check your answers.

T   F   1. When Access creates an AutoForm, it gathers information by checking the table or query on which it is based rather than asking you for preferences.

T   F   2. A tabular report usually shows data for one record per page.

T   F   3. A report header is printed only on the first page of a report.

T   F   4. In a database that contains student information, all of the students who chose Finance as a major could be considered a group.

T   F   5. When you print a report by clicking the Print button, a dialog box appears allowing you to change the number of copies printed.

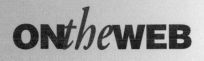

CREATING YOUR OWN WEB PAGE

After you create a database, you may want to share some of the information with others. You can share your data with millions of people by publishing your page on the Web. Before you can publish your page, though, you must save the page in a format that is readable by the Web. This format, called *Hypertext Markup Language (HTML),* tags a document so that you can publish the document and allow others on the Web see your work. As you learned in Lesson 1, you can also create data access pages, which are saved in an HTML format, and then view them through a Web browser. (Data access pages display information in records, allowing you to sort, search and filter the information.)

After you've created Web pages, you may want to share them with other Web users. To make your work accessible to others, you can publish it on an intranet or the World Wide Web. To add your work to an intranet or a network, contact your network administrator or your instructor. The process will vary depending on the type of system on which you are working. To publish your work on the World Wide Web, you'll need to contact your local Internet service provider. Each service provider has unique requirements and will likely charge a fee for the space you use. Ask your instructor for additional details on publishing your Web page.

In this activity, you will learn how to save a table, query, and form in HTML format so others can view your work from the Web. You will also create a data access page.

1. Open the *Best of the Orchard, Lesson 5* database in the *Tutorial* folder on your Student Data Disk. Open the Items Available table and maximize the window.

2. Click the **File menu** and click **Export**.

The Export Table "Items Available" As dialog box appears.

3. In the Save in box, navigate to your *Tutorial* folder and type Items Available in the File name box. In the Save as type box, click **HTML Documents**. Click the **Save formatted option** to save the table in a format that is similar to the Datasheet view. Click **Autostart** to have Access automatically open your newly created HTML document, as shown in Figure 5.34. Then click **Save All**.

The HTML Output Options dialog box appears, which allows you to enhance the appearance of your HTML documents by using HTML template files. If you specify an HTML template file in the Output Options dialog box, Access merges the HTML template file with the output file.

4. Verify that the HTML Output Options dialog box is empty and click **OK**.

Access opens your browser and displays the Items Available table as an HTML document.

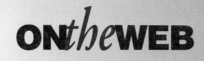

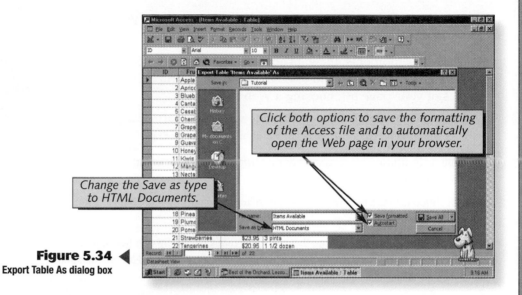

> Click both options to save the formatting of the Access file and to automatically open the Web page in your browser.

> Change the Save as type to HTML Documents.

Figure 5.34 ◄
Export Table As dialog box

5. Click the *Best of the Orchard, Lesson 5* taskbar button to return to your database and open the Orders Placed query.

6. Click the **File menu** and click **Export**.

7. In the Export Query "Orders Placed" As dialog box, save the file in your *Tutorial* folder as *Orders Placed*. Change the Save as type to **HTML Documents**. Click the **Save formatted option** and click **Autostart**. Click **Save All**.

8. Verify that the HTML Output Options dialog box is empty and click **OK**. Maximize the browser window and view your Web page.

9. Click the *Best of the Orchard, Lesson 5* taskbar button to return to the Database window and open the Customers form.

10. Click the **File menu** and click **Export**.

11. Save the file as *Customers* in your *Tutorial* folder. Change the Save as type to **HTML Documents**. Click **Autostart**; then click **Save All**.

12. Verify that the HTML Output Options box is empty and click **OK**. View your Web page in your browser and then close the document.

13. Open the *Fruit Information, Lesson 5* database in the *Tutorial* folder. Click **Pages** and double-click **Create data access page by using wizard**.

14. In the Page Wizard dialog box, select the **Table: Nutritional Information option** in the Tables/Queries box.

15. Click the **Add All Fields button** ⧈ to add all of the fields to the Selected Fields box and click **Next**.

16. Without selecting a grouping level in the next dialog box, click **Next**.

17. Select **FruitType** in the field 1 box. Click **Ascending**, if it is not selected. Then click **Next**.

18. Accept the name *Nutritional Information* and select the **Do you want to apply a theme to your page? box**. Then click **Finish**.

After a few moments, the data access page and then the Theme dialog box appear. Access allows you to change the color, graphics, fonts, and font sizes of your page by choosing a Web theme.

19. In the Choose a Theme box, click **Blends** and look at the sample. (Choose a different theme if Blends is not available.) Then click **OK**.

Your data access page changes to the selected theme and displays in Design view.

20. Maximize the data access page window. Close the Toolbox if it is in your way.

21. Click the title of the page that currently reads *Click here and type title text* and type Be Fruitful. **Click just above the Header:** *Nutritional Information* **and type this text:**

The following database contains nutritional information on fruit that we sell. Use the navigation buttons to find the fruit in which you are interested. For more information on Be Fruitful's fruit-of-the-month club, please call 1-800-555-3000.

22. Switch to Page view.

As you can see in Figure 5.35, the data for the first record appears. The toolbar below the data allows you to perform several functions, such as scrolling, sorting, and filtering records.

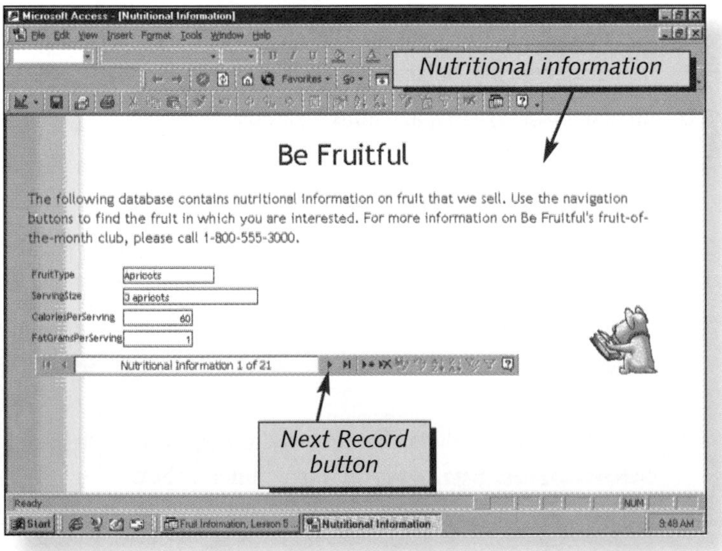

Figure 5.35 ◄
Page view of the data access page

23. Click the **Next Record button** [▶] on the toolbar below the data a few times.

Access displays the next few records, one at a time. As you specified in the Page Wizard dialog box, the records are sorted in alphabetical order by fruit type. Using the data access page toolbar, you can use Sort Descending [Z↓A], Sort Ascending [A↓Z], Next Record [▶], and Filter By Selection [▼] commands to control the appearance of the data.

24. Click the **Save button** [💾] on the Page View toolbar. Save the Web page as *Nutritional Information*.

25. Click **Web Page Preview** on the File menu. (If the Web Page Preview option is grayed, close the Nutritional Information data access page and then reopen it from the Database window. Then try issuing the command again.)

Access launches your Web browser and displays a preview of the data access page.

26. Maximize the window to view your page. Then close your browser.

27. Close the Nutritional Information data access page to return to the Database window. Click the **Compact on Close option**, if necessary, and close the *Fruit Information, Lesson 5* database.

You may proceed directly to the exercises for this lesson. If, however, you are finished with your computer session, follow the "shut down" procedures for your lab or school environment.

Lesson Summary & Exercises

SUMMARY

In Lesson 5, you created, modified, and saved forms and reports. Forms are useful for entering and editing data as well as viewing data. They allow you to see one or more records at a time and to choose specific fields to view. Reports display selected data in an organized, professional format. You can calculate totals and subtotals in your reports, and you can print them. You can easily modify format properties and work with sections of a form or report. You also learned how to save a table, query, and form as an HTML document, how to create a data access page, and how to view all Web documents in your browser.

Now that you have completed this lesson, you should be able to do the following:

- Explain the purposes and uses of forms. (Access-208)
- Explain controls and the Control Toolbox. (Access-208)
- Create an AutoForm. (Access-210)
- Use the Form Wizard to create a columnar form. (Access-212)
- Use the Form Wizard to create a tabular form. (Access-214)
- Add and edit data in forms and subforms. (Access-216)
- Add and modify a control in a form. (Access-218)
- Create a calculated control on a form. (Access-220)
- Modify control format properties in a form. (Access-222)
- Work with form sections. (Access-223)
- Preview and print forms. (Access-224)
- Explain the purposes and uses of reports. (Access-225)
- Create an AutoReport. (Access-226)
- Navigate a report. (Access-227)
- Use the Report Wizard to create a columnar report. (Access-228)
- Create a query for a report. (Access-230)
- Create a tabular report. (Access-231)
- Group and sort records in a report. (Access-232)
- Preview a report. (Access-233)
- Use Help to modify reports and forms. (Access-235)
- Create a report with totals. (Access-236)
- Add totals and subtotals to a report. (Access-237)
- Add and modify control format properties in a report. (Access-238)
- Create a calculated field in a report. (Access-239)
- Create a calculated control in a report. (Access-241)
- Work with report sections of a report. (Access-243)
- Print a report. (Access-245)
- Save a query, table, and form as an HTML document and create a data access page. (Access-246)

CONCEPTS REVIEW

1 TRUE/FALSE

Circle T if the statement is true or F if the statement is false.

T F **1.** Headers, footers, and detail sections can only be used in reports.

T F **2.** You can create a form using the AutoForm, Form Wizard or in Design view.

T F **3.** Calculated fields can be created in queries or tables.

T F **4.** You cannot move or resize fields and controls.

T F **5.** The Report Wizard generates reports, but does not allow customization.

T F **6.** A tabular form displays all the fields for a single record in one row.

T F **7.** Subforms can be used to add and edit data.

T F **8.** Controls can be bound, unbound, or calculated.

T F **9.** You can create reports that generate totals.

T F **10.** Forms are often used to simplify data entry.

2 MATCHING

Match each of the terms on the left with the definitions on the right.

TERMS

1. groups

2. Design view

3. landscape orientation

4. zoom

5. record selector

6. Datasheet view

7. portrait orientation

8. footer

9. style

10. wizard

DEFINITIONS

a. Text that is printed at the bottom of each page in a report

b. View in which data in any type of form is laid out in a series of columns and rows

c. Printing setup in which report text is printed horizontally across a page

d. View in which you can modify a form's layout

e. Vertical bar at the left side of a form that you can use to activate a designated record

f. An Access tool that creates a form or report based on your responses to a series of questions

g. Collections of records with similar information

h. To enlarge or decrease the size of a form or report so you can see less of it in more detail or more of it in less detail

i. Pictures, shading, and colors that give forms and reports a special look

j. Printing setup in which report text is printed vertically across a page

Lesson Summary & Exercises

3 COMPLETION

Fill in the missing word or phrase for each of the following statements.

1. Click the _____ Options button in the Report Wizard dialog box to change the way records are collected.

2. Clicking the _____ buttons will move you from page to page in a report.

3. The AutoForm option on the New Object drop-down list automatically creates a(n) _____ form.

4. _____ forms display all fields in a single row.

5. Click the _____ Options button in the Report Wizard dialog box to display totals and subtotals.

6. Reports can use data from tables or _____.

7. The _____ button increases or decreases the amount of the form or report that you can preview in one screen.

8. A(n) _____ displays text information at the top of each page in the report.

9. _____ is a system for tagging a document so that you can publish the document and allow others on the Web to view your information.

10. Before you print a hard copy of a form, you should display it on the screen using the _____ button.

4 SHORT ANSWER

Write a brief answer to each of the following questions.

1. Describe briefly what Access does for you when you click the AutoForm button. What type of form does it create? What fields are included? What is used as the form title?

2. What type of form do you use to display multiple records at once? Does this type of form work well for tables or queries that contain many fields? Explain your answer.

3. Describe the exact steps involved in first previewing and then printing a form. Why should you preview forms before printing them?

4. Describe the differences between using AutoForms and Form Wizards.

5. Describe the benefit of creating a form for data entry. What are the advantages over working on the table in the Datasheet view?

6. List two limitations of an AutoReport.

7. Describe the differences between a tabular and a columnar report.

8. What must you do to display totals in a report? What option would you choose if you want individual records displayed as well?

9. If you created a report with the following fields and records, would you likely want to group any of the records? If so, which field(s) would you choose to group? Explain your answer.

First Name	Last Name	Address	City	State
Mary	Martin	11890 Oakwood Drive	Cincinnati	OH
Charles	Parker	909 State Street	Cleveland	OH
Suzanne	Casper	34 Greens Farm Lane	Columbus	OH
Mia	Sanchez	899 Merwin Drive	Cincinnati	OH
Gunnar	Hopkins	2028 Kitchen Place	Columbus	OH
Grace	Jaehnen	7889 Reinders Street	Youngstown	OH
Clark	Martin	11890 Oakwood Drive	Cincinnati	OH
Penny	Mitchell	77 First Street	Cleveland	OH

10. Describe the difference between landscape and portrait orientations.

5 IDENTIFICATION

Label each of the elements of the form in Figure 5.36.

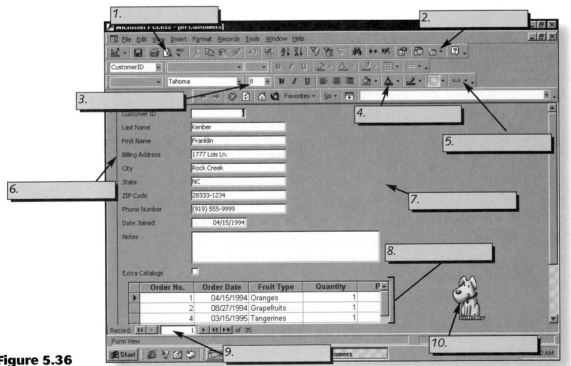

Figure 5.36

Lesson Summary & Exercises

SKILLS REVIEW

Complete each of the Skills Review problems in sequential order to review your Access skills to create, modify, preview, and print forms and reports.

1 Create a Form

1. Open the *Smyth Business College, Lesson 5* database in the *Skills Review* folder on your Student Data Disk.

2. Click the **Instructor Information table**, click the **New Object drop-down arrow** 📇, and click **AutoForm**. Then maximize the form.

3. Click the **Next Record button** ▶ several times to move through the records.

4. Click the **View drop-down arrow** 📈 and click **Datasheet view**.

5. Return to Form view and close the form.

6. Click **Yes** to save the form; type Instructor Information AutoForm as the form name. Then click **OK**.

7. Click **Forms** and double-click **Create form by using wizard**.

8. Click the **Tables/Queries drop-down arrow** in the Form Wizard dialog box and click **Table: Student Information**.

9. Click the **Add All Fields button** ⏩ to add all of the fields to the Selected Fields box.

10. Click the **Major field** and click the **Remove Field button** ◀ to remove this field from the list. Then remove the GradePointAverage and EstimatedGraduationDate fields. Click **Next**.

11. Click **Columnar** and click **Next**.

12. Click **SandStone** as the style and click **Next**.

13. Type Student Addresses as the title, make sure the *Open the form to view or enter information.* option is selected, and click **Finish**.

14. View the form, navigate a few records, and then close the form.

15. In the Tables option, click the **Grades for Accounting Classes table**, click the **New Object drop-down arrow** 📇, and click **Form**.

16. Click **Form Wizard** in the list box and click **OK**. Verify that the Grades for Accounting Classes table appears in the Tables/Queries box.

17. Add all of the fields to the Selected Fields box and click **Next**.

18. Click **Tabular** in the next dialog box and then click **Next**.

19. Click **Sumi Painting** as the style and click **Next**.

20. Type Accounting Grades Tabular Form as the title, make sure the *Open the form to view or enter information.* option is selected, and click **Finish**.

21. View the form, scroll a few records, and then close the form.

Lesson Summary & Exercises

2 Add and Edit Data

1. Open the Instructor Information AutoForm and click the **New Record button** ▶*.

2. Type Little in the Instructor Name field.

3. Press [Tab] to move through the remaining fields, typing General Business in the Department field, 8/15/99 in the Start Date field, General Business in the Undergraduate Degree field, Education in the Graduate Degree field, and PT in the FT/PT field.

4. In the Class Code field of the subform, type BU202; type Business Ethics in the Class Name field; type TR in the Days field; and type 10:00-11:30 am in the Time field. Access will automatically add the new class data to the Class Schedules table.

5. With the Instructor Information AutoForm still open, navigate to the record for the instructor named Kellinghaus.

6. Since the time for the marketing class taught by Kellinghaus has been changed, replace the 2:00-2:50 pm time currently indicated for the MK201 class with 3:00-3:50 pm.

7. Navigate to the record for the instructor named Franklin, click the **record selector** for the record, and press [Delete].

8. Click **Yes** to delete this record. Then click **Close** on the File menu.

3 Adding and Modifying Controls

1. Click the **New button** ▯ to create a new database.

2. Name the database *Fruit Works* and save it in the *Skills Review* folder on your Student Data Disk.

3. Import all the information (tables, queries, forms, and reports) from the *Best of the Orchard, Lesson 5* database.

4. Click **Forms** and double-click **Create form in Design view**.

5. Click **Properties** 🖻 and click the **All tab**.

6. Click the **Record Source drop-down arrow** and select the **Orders Placed query**. Then close the Form dialog box.

7. Add the ContactLastName field to the design grid at the left margin.

8. Delete the label and move the control to the left margin.

9. Add ContactFirstName, OrderDate, Fruit Type, and Price in the same row, deleting the label for each one.

10. Click the **Text Box button** 🔲 and insert a box to the right of Price in the first row.

11. Delete the label, right-click the control, and click **Properties**.

12. Click the **Build button** beside the Control Source row in the All tab.

13. In the Expression Builder dialog box, create an expression to calculate a 20 percent price increase.

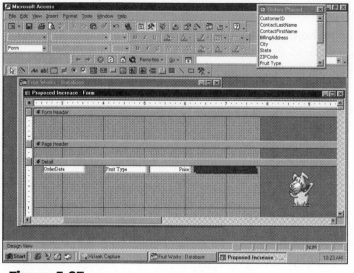

Figure 5.37

14. Click **OK** and close the Expression Builder; then close the Properties dialog box.

15. Save the form as Proposed Increase.

16. Click each field and change the font to Times New Roman.

17. Change the background color of the calculated field to red.

18. Click the **Special Effect button** and change the calculated field to Shadowed (Figure 5.37).

19. Format the control to always print and display in Currency format.

20. Save the changes.

4 Use Form Sections

1. With the Proposed Increase form still open in Design view, right-click anywhere in the grid.

2. From the menu, click **Page Header/Footer**. Right-click again and click **Form Header/Footer**.

3. Add a label in the Page Header and type Proposed Increase.

4. Format the text to be Times New Roman, 26 point.

5. Insert the **Date and Time** and drag the date and time control to the Page Footer.

6. Save the changes and close the form.

5 Preview and Print a Form

1. Open the *Smyth Business College, Lesson 5* database in the *Skills Review* folder and click the **Instructor Information AutoForm** in the Forms option.

2. Click the **Print Preview button**. Maximize the window.

3. Click any part of the window to view it closely.

4. Click the **Two Pages button** to preview two pages.

5. Click the **Multiple Pages button** and drag to select four pages.

6. Click the **File menu** and click **Print**. Set the print range to print one copy of page 1.

7. Close the form.

Lesson Summary & Exercises

6 Create and Navigate a Report

1. Select the **Class Schedules table**, click the **New Object drop-down arrow** 🔲, and click **Report**. Then, double-click **AutoReport: Columnar** in the list box.

2. When the AutoReport is created, scroll to see the bottom of the first page of the report.

3. Click the **Next Page button** ▶ three times to scroll the first few pages.

4. Click the **Previous Page button** ◀.

5. Double-click the **current page indicator**, type 4, and press ⏎.

6. Scroll to see the record for the MK201 class.

7. Click within the page to zoom out.

8. Click the **Zoom button** 🔍 to zoom in again.

9. Close the report.

10. Click **Yes** to save the report; then type Class Schedules AutoReport and click **OK**.

11. Click the **Student Information table**, click the **New Object drop-down arrow** 🔲, click **Report**, and double-click **Report Wizard**.

12. Click **Table: Student Information** in the Tables/Queries box, if it is not already selected.

13. Add all of the field names to the Selected Fields box.

14. Remove the Major, GradePointAverage, and EstimatedGraduationDate fields.

15. Click **Next**. Since you don't want to group records in this report, click **Next** when the next dialog box appears. Since you don't want to sort records, click **Next** once again.

16. Click the **Columnar** and **Landscape options**. Click **Next**.

17. Click the **Casual style** and click **Next**. Then type Student Addresses Columnar Report and click **Finish**. Scroll and then close the report.

7 Create a Query and a Tabular Report

1. Click the **Instructor Information table**. Click the **New Object drop-down arrow** 🔲, and click **Query**.

2. Click **Design View** and click **OK**.

3. Double-click the **title bar** of the Instructor Information Field list to select all of the fields, and then drag the selected fields to the first column in the query design grid.

4. In the Sort row of the InstructorName field, select **Ascending**.

5. Type FT in the Criteria row of the FullTime/PartTime field, and click the **Show button** to hide the field.

6. Click the **Run button** 🔳.

7. Save the query as Full Time Instructors and click **OK**. Then close the query.

8. Click the **Reports option** and double-click **Create a report by using wizard**.

9. Click **Query: Full Time Instructors** in the Tables/Queries box.

10. Add the InstructorName, Department, UndergraduateDegree, GraduateDegree, and StartDate fields, in that order. Then click **Next**.

8 Group and Sort Records and Preview the Report

1. In the dialog box that requests a grouping field, click **Department** and click the **Add Field button** 🔲. Then click **Next**.

2. Click the **drop-down arrow** beside the first field in the Sorting dialog box and click **InstructorName**. Click **Next**.

3. Click the **Align Left 1 option** and then click **Portrait**. Click **Next**.

4. Click **Bold** as the style and click **Next**.

5. Type Full Time Instructors by Department and click **Finish**.

6. Scroll the first page of the report.

7. Click anywhere on the page to zoom out.

8. Close the report.

9 Build and Use a Report with Totals

1. Double-click **Create report by using wizard** in the Reports option.

2. Click **Table: Student Information** in the Tables/Queries box and add the LastName, FirstName, Major, GradePointAverage, and EstimatedGraduationDate fields to the Selected Fields list. Then click **Next**.

3. Select **Major** as the grouping field.

4. Click the **Grouping Options button** and select **Normal** in the Grouping Intervals box, if it is not already selected. Click **OK**.

5. Click **Next** and click **GradePointAverage** in the Field 1 box.

6. Click the **Summary Options button** and click the **Average (Avg) check box** for the GradePointAverage field.

7. Click **OK**, click **Next**, and click the **Outline 1 layout** and **Portrait orientation**. Then click **Next**.

8. Click the **Formal style** and click **Next**.

9. Type GPAs of Students by Major and click **Finish**.

10. Scroll the report to see the subtotals for the majors. Then close the report.

10 Modify Controls in a Report

1. Open the *Fruit Works* database in the *Skills Review* folder of your Student Data Disk.

2. Open the Summary of Orders report in Design view.

3. Drag the right margin to 9.5".

4. In the Page Header section, change the label *With Proposed Increase* to With Proposed Increase (Including Shipping).

5. Add a text field to the With Proposed Increase field in the Detail section.

6. Delete the label and right-click the field. Click **Properties** and click the **All tab**.

7. Click the **Control Source drop-down arrow**, click **Price**, and close the dialog box.

8. In the Page Header section, insert a label for the Price field called *Current Price*.

9. Save the changes and close the report.

11 Create a Calculated Field

1. Open the Orders Placed query in Design view.

2. Right-click the first blank field and click **Build**.

3. In the Expression Builder dialog box, create an expression that multiples the Expr1 field and the six percent sales tax to achieve the final total.

4. In the field, press ⌑Home⌑ and type With Tax: directly in front of the first bracket.

5. Modify the properties to calculate as currency.

6. Save and close the query.

12 Create and Modify Controls and Use Report Sections

1. Open the Summary of Orders report in Design view; add a text box next to the Price field in the Detail section.

2. Create an expression using the Price field from the Items Available table. Multiply Price and the 20 percent increase to get the new total cost and click **OK**.

3. Select **Currency** as the format for the field and close the Properties dialog box.

4. Delete the label that appears in the Detail section, and create a label in the Page Header section with the text *20% Increase Proposal*.

5. With the Summary of Orders report open in Design view, change all the fields in the Detail section to a blue font color and bold.

6. Right-click the Detail section bar and click **Sorting and Grouping**.

7. Click **Fruit Type**, and in the Group Properties section, change the Group Header to **Yes** and close the dialog box.

8. In the Fruit Type Header section, insert the Fruit Type field from the Field List at the left margin. (Hint: Click Field List on the View menu, if necessary.) Then, delete the label.

9. Save and close the report.

13 Print a Report

1. Open the GPAs of Students by Major report in the *Smyth Business College, Lesson 5* database in the *Skills Review* folder, and click the **Zoom button** 🔍.

2. Click **Print** on the File menu. Set the print range to print only one copy of the last page of the report.

3. Close the report.

4. Click the **Compact on Close option**, if necessary, and close the *Smyth Business College, Lesson 5* database.

LESSON APPLICATIONS

1 Create Forms

As a manager at Payton Properties, Inc., you decide to create some Access forms to ease data entry for all employees. You will create an AutoForm that displays employee addresses and other information, a columnar form based on a query, and a tabular form to display the data in a table.

1. Open the *Payton Properties, Lesson 5* database in the *Lesson Applications* folder on your Student Data Disk.

2. Click the Employees table and click the New Object drop-down arrow 🔳 to create an AutoForm. Maximize the form and navigate all of the records.

3. View the form in Datasheet view; then return to Form view and close the form, saving the form as Employees AutoForm.

4. Use the Create form by using wizard option to create a new form. Base the form on the Homes Sold by Matthews query and include all of the fields in the form.

5. Choose the columnar layout and Ricepaper style. Save the form as Homes Sold by Matthews Columnar Form and then view and close the form.

6. Use the Form Wizard to create a form based on the Agent Statistics table. Include the AgentID, Commissions, Listings, and HomesSold fields, in that order. Assign a tabular layout and the Blends style.

7. Save the form as Agent Statistics Tabular Form and then view the records. Close the form.

2 Add and Edit Data and Print a Form

Now you'll really start using the forms you created. First, you'll add two new employees to the database using the Employees AutoForm. You'll also add some new listings by one of the agents. Last, you'll use the form to edit and delete existing data.

1. In the *Payton Properties, Lesson 5* database in the *Lesson Applications* folder, open the Employees AutoForm.

2. Add two new records in the Employees AutoForm that contain the data in Table 5.2.

TABLE 5.2	EMPLOYEES AUTOFORM DATA	
Field	**1st New Record**	**2nd New Record**
Last Name:	Kaplin	Sallinger
First Name:	Robert	Pat
Address:	29 Mainview Rd.	18 Blossom Dr.
City:	Dallas	Dallas
State:	TX	TX
ZIP Code:	75226-4993	75226-1872
Home Phone:	(214) 555-2567	(214) 555-1334
Date Hired:	9/1/00	9/1/00

3. In the subform for Pat Sallinger, add the following homes for sale, as listed in Table 5.3.

TABLE 5.3	PAT SALLINGER SUBFORM DATA	
Field	**1st Home for Sale**	**2nd Home for Sale**
Address:	1800 Twiggs Ln.	20398 Sycamore St.
Bedrooms:	5	3
Baths:	3	1.5
Sq. Feet:	2,095	1,700
Rooms:	8	6
Year Built:	1999	1999
Price:	$172,000	$105,500
Lot Size:	1.3	1.0
School District:	West Avon	Milfort
Pool:	No	No
Occupancy:	30 days	30 days

4. Robert Kaplin has changed his mind and decides to take a job with a different company. Delete his record while in Form view.

5. Move to the record for Benji Eto and change his telephone number to (214) 555-0053.

6. Preview the revised form. Zoom to see the details of one record. Then use the Two Pages button 🔳 to view two pages at once.

7. Print and then close the form.

Lesson Summary & Exercises

3 Create and Navigate Reports

Now that you've created several forms in the database, you want to generate some reports for your agents. First, create a columnar AutoReport to show each sales agent how she or he is doing so far this year. You'd also like to practice using the Report Wizard to create a simple report based on the Homes Sold table and a tabular report based on a query.

1. In the **Payton Properties, Lesson 5** database in the **Lesson Applications** folder, use the New Object drop-down arrow to create a report based on the Agent Statistics table. In the New Report dialog box, choose the AutoReport: Columnar option. Scroll the first page of the report.

2. Zoom out to view an entire page at once. Close the report, saving it as Agent Statistics Columnar AutoReport.

3. Start the Report Wizard. In the first dialog box, tell the wizard to base your report on the Homes Sold table and to include the PropertyAddress, Bedrooms, Baths, SquareFeet, Rooms, YearBuilt, SellingPrice, and AgentID fields.

4. Do not change the default grouping, and do not add any grouping or sorting levels. Choose the Align Left 1 layout, portrait orientation, and the Corporate style. Save the report as Homes Sold Columnar Report.

5. Navigate some of the pages and then close the report.

6. Create a query based on the Homes for Sale table. In the query, include the Address, Bedrooms, Baths, SquareFeet, Rooms, YearBuilt, Price, LotSize, and Pool fields. Sort the recordset in ascending order by square feet and only include homes that measure 2,000 or more square feet. Save the query as Homes with 2,000+ Square Feet.

7. Create a tabular report based on the query you just created. Include the Address, SquareFeet, Bedrooms, Baths, LotSize, and Price fields, in that order.

8. Group the records in the report by number of bedrooms. Within each group, sort the records in ascending order by price.

9. Assign the Align Left 1 layout, portrait orientation, and the Casual style. Save the report as Homes with 2,000+ Square Feet. Zoom in to see a full page of the report. Then print and close.

4 Create and Print a Report that Calculates Totals

You'd like to create a report that shows how your agents are doing as a team. Create a report that sums the total listings, homes sold, and commissions earned by your agents.

1. In the **Payton Properties, Lesson 5** database in the **Lesson Applications** folder, use the Report Wizard to create a report based on the Agent Statistics table. Include all of the fields in the table in the report.

2. Group the records by Agent ID. In the Summary Options dialog box, choose to sum the HomesSold, Listings, and Commissions fields. Choose the Summary Only and the Calculate percent of total for sums options. Then click OK.

3. Choose the Stepped layout, portrait orientation, and the Bold style.

4. Save the report as Combined Sales, Listings, and Commissions.

5. Preview and then close the report.

5 Create and Print a Report that Calculates Averages

Your last activity for the day requires you to generate a report about the homes that have been sold through Payton Properties. Your report should list all of the homes that were sold, grouping them by the number of bedrooms in each. Within each group, the records should be sorted by selling price and the average list and selling prices should be averaged within each group.

1. In the **Payton Properties, Lesson 5** database in the **Lesson Applications** folder, use the Report Wizard to create a columnar report based on the Homes Sold table. Include the PropertyAddress, Bedrooms, Baths, ListingPrice, SellingPrice, and AgentID fields in the report.

2. Group the records by the number of bedrooms in each home. Sort the records in each group in descending order by selling price.

3. In the Summary Options dialog box, choose to average the ListingPrice and SellingPrice fields. Choose the Detail and Summary option.

4. Choose the Align Left 1 layout, landscape orientation, and the Corporate style.

5. Save the report as Average Listing and Selling Prices and view the report.

6. Print and then close the report.

7. Click the Compact on Close command, if necessary, and close the **Payton Properties, Lesson 5** database.

PROJECTS

1 New Products and New Sales

As the sales manager at Electro Shop, you are using Access to create several forms to better input and review data on your employees, sales, and products. Start by opening the **Electro Shop, Lesson 5** database in the **Projects** folder on your Student Data Disk. Then create an AutoForm based on the Products table. Add two new records to the AutoForm to represent new products your store is carrying. Include the information in Table 5.4 in the main forms for the records.

TABLE 5.4	RECORD DATA TO ADD	
Field	**1st New Record**	**2nd New Record**
Product ID	(AutoNumber)	(AutoNumber)
Product Type	TV	VCR
Brand	Keiko	Keiko
Model	KS650	KS6100
Price	$1,299.95	$359.95
In Stock	5	5
Notes	52" screen	

Lesson Summary & Exercises

So far, your sales associates have sold two of the new TVs and three of the new VCRs. Record the data in Table 5.5 in the subform for each of the products. Close the AutoForm, saving it as Products AutoForm.

TABLE 5.5	SUBFORM DATA TO ADD	
Keiko KS650 TV		
Sale ID	(AutoNumber)	(AutoNumber)
Date Sold	12/19/01	12/20/01
Employee ID	3	23
Quantity Sold	1	1
Keiko KS6100 VCR		
Sale ID	(AutoNumber)	(AutoNumber)
Date Sold	12/20/01	12/20/01
Employee ID	7	16
Quantity Sold	2	1

2 Updating the Staff

In the *Electro Shop, Lesson 5* database in the *Projects* folder, use the Form Wizard to create a columnar form based on the Employees table. Include all of the fields in the form and use a style of your choice. Save the form as Employees Columnar Form. After you create the form, you find you need to update some of your employee information. While in Form view, delete employee 26, Kathleen Feldman, since she recently resigned. Next, employee 11, Sonya Mitter, has just been promoted to a sales associate. Change her position appropriately. Lastly, add the new employee that you hired to fill Sonya's open position, using the data in Table 5.6. Preview the Employees Columnar Form, viewing multiple pages at once. Then print and close the form.

TABLE 5.6	EMPLOYEE DATA
Field	**Data**
Employee ID	(AutoNumber)
Last Name	Hester
First Name	Gail
SS#	282-82-8282
Hourly Rate	$8.00
FT/PT	FT
Position	Cashier
Hire Date	12/20/01

3 Seeing the Sales Data in a Table

You'd like to create a form that allows you to see many records of sales data at one time. In the *Electro Shop, Lesson 5* database in the *Projects* folder, use the Form Wizard to create a tabular form based on the December Sales table. Include the DateSold, ProductID, EmployeeID, and QuantitySold fields, in that order. Use a style of your choice and name the form December Sales Tabular Form. Preview, print, and then close the form.

4 Should I Use a Form or a Report?

You've decided that you'd also like to generate a report in the *Electro Shop, Lesson 5* database in the *Projects* folder from the December sales data, rather than viewing the information in a form. You'd like your report to contain a report header and a footer. Create a columnar AutoReport based on the December Sales table. Navigate several pages of the report. Preview and then print the report. Close the report, saving it as December Sales AutoReport. In what ways does the AutoReport vary from the tabular form? In what circumstances would each presentation of the data be useful?

5 Submitting a Printout of Employee Updates

You need to submit an updated copy of employee information to your payroll department. In the *Electro Shop, Lesson 5* database in the *Projects* folder, use the Report Wizard to create a columnar report that contains the HireDate, First Name, Last Name, Hourly Rate, and Position fields from the Employees table. Sort the report in descending order by hire date. Choose portrait orientation and a style of your choice. Save the report as Employees by Hire Date. Preview, print, and close the report.

6 Analyzing Big Ticket Items

You are analyzing the prices of some of your products, specifically those priced over $350 in the *Electro Shop, Lesson 5* database in the *Projects* folder. To generate a list of products that meet the criteria, first create a query based on the Products table. Include all of the fields in the query and sort the records in the query in ascending order by price; include only those that sell for more than $350. Name the query Products Priced Over $350.

Create a tabular report based on the query you just created. In the report, include only the ProductType, Brand, Model, and Price fields. Group the records by product type and sort the records within each group by price. Choose landscape orientation, Align Left 2 layout, and a style of your choice. Name the report Products Over $350 Grouped by Product Type. Preview, print, and close the report.

Lesson Summary & Exercises

7 Totaling the Sales

Your district manager wants you to provide a report that lists and totals sales so far this month by product. In the **Electro Shop, Lesson 5** database in the **Projects** folder, create a report that includes all of the fields from the December Sales table except for the Sale ID field. Group the records by Product ID and sort the records within each group by the date sold. Calculate totals for the QuantitySold field as well as a grand total for the month. Choose the Align Left 1 layout, portrait orientation, and the Corporate style. Name the report December Sales by Product. Preview, print, and then close the report.

8 Products Online

Electro Shop wants you to create HTML documents and a data access page. In the **Electro Shop, Lesson 5** database in the **Projects** folder, create a form based on the Products table. Include the ProductID, ProductType, Brand, Model, and Price fields. Save the form as Available Products. Then, save the form as an HTML document with the same name and view the document in your browser. Using the Products table, create a data access page with the same fields as the form. Save the data access page as Product Offerings. Apply a Web theme of your choice. In Design view, replace the temporary text with *Electro Shop Available Products*. View the data access page in Page view and navigate the records. Then view the data access page in your Web browser. Close the page, saving the changes, and close the browser. Click the Compact on Close option, if necessary, and close the **Electro Shop, Lesson 5** database.

Project in Progress

9 Who's Accountable for the Most Projects?

As an employee of I-Comm, you use forms and reports to input and edit data and generate printouts of information. First, you'd like to generate a form to enter data for customers. Open the **I-Comm** database in the **Projects** folder on your Student Data Disk, and create an AutoForm named Customers and Projects based on the Customers table. Add the new customer and the new project information in Table 5.7.

TABLE 5.7	NEW CUSTOMER INFORMATION

Main Form

Customer ID:	(AutoNumber)
Customer Name:	The Door Store
Contact Last Name:	Rivera
Contact First Name:	Carmen
Contact Title:	Owner
Billing Address:	1800 Lakeside Dr.
City:	Memphis
State:	TN
ZIP Code:	38112-8344
Phone Number:	(901) 555-1000

Subform

Project ID:	(AutoNumber)
Item Developed:	brochure
Services Provided:	writing, editing, design
I-Comm Project Mgr.:	14
Total Hours:	83
Fee:	$4,980

Lock-All Security Systems (customer 19) Subform

Project ID:	(AutoNumber)
Item Developed:	project proposal
Services Provided:	writing, editing, design
I-Comm Project Mgr.:	8
Total Hours:	139
Fee:	$8,340

Next, your manager has asked you to generate a report that displays all of the projects completed so far this year grouped by the employee who acted as project manager on each. Use the Report Wizard to generate a tabular report using all of the fields in the Projects table. Group the records by the project manager and sum the hours and fees for each group. Use a layout and style of your choice. Save the report as Projects by Manager. Print the report and then close. Click the Compact on Close option, if necessary, and close the *I-Comm* database.

Overview: Congratulations! You have completed all the lessons in the Access tutorial and now have the opportunity in this capstone project to apply the Access skills you have learned. You have opened a daycare and want to use a database to track employees, students, and classes. As you create and use the database, try to incorporate the following skills:

- Plan and create a new database.
- Create tables and add data to them.
- Assign appropriate data types to fields.
- Determine the primary keys.
- Establish relationships among tables and enforce referential integrity.
- Search for particular strings of characters in a table.
- Change column widths in a datasheet.
- View data in subdatasheets.

- Sort and filter data.
- Create a multi-table query.
- Create an AutoForm.
- Add data to a form.
- Sort data in a form.
- Create a report with groups and totals.
- Modify format properties.
- Preview and print a report.
- Create a data access page.
- Compact and close a database.

Instructions: Follow these instructions to create your database for this project.

1. Create a new database and save it as *Tiny Tots Daycare* in the *Projects* folder on your Student Data Disk.

2. Create three new tables, assigning appropriate primary keys, data types, field sizes, captions, and other field properties.

   - Name the first table *Employees* and create fields to include the following information: employee ID number, employee last name, employee first name, Social Security number, hourly pay rate, and full-time or part-time status. Enter the data in Table CS.1 in the Employees table.

   - Name the second table *Classes* and create fields to include the following information: class ID, class name, room number, head teacher, age range of students, teacher-to-student ratio, and weekly fee. Enter the data in Table CS.2 in the Classes table.

   - Name the third table *Students* and create fields to include the following information: student ID number, student last name, student first name, birth date, class name, guardian name, guardian phone number, and allergies/special needs. Enter the data in Table CS.3 in the Students table.

TABLE CS.1   DATA FOR EMPLOYEES TABLE

Employee ID	Employee Name	SS#	Hourly Rate	FT/PT
1	Betty Strickley	111-11-1111	$9.50	FT
2	Robert McVey	222-22-2222	$9.25	FT
3	Lorna Williams	333-33-3333	$7.75	PT
4	Mario Delgado	444-44-4444	$8.75	FT
5	Eric Huffman	555-55-5555	$8.00	FT
6	Arthur Hughes	666-66-6666	$8.00	FT
7	Maria Dugan	777-77-7777	$8.25	FT
8	Stacey Renning	888-88-8888	$8.25	FT
9	Tatsu Iwasaki	999-99-9999	$8.75	PT
10	Matthew Milton	101-01-0101	$7.75	FT
11	Donna Wolfe	110-11-0011	$7.50	FT
12	Mary Levine	121-21-2121	$7.75	FT
13	Dale Shepherd	131-31-3131	$7.50	FT
14	Gordon Crofts	141-41-4141	$7.50	PT
15	Chris Gregg	151-51-5151	$7.25	FT

TABLE CS.2   DATA FOR CLASSES TABLE

Class ID	Class Name	Room Number	Head Teacher	Age Range	Ratio	Fee
1	Infants	1	13	2 to 18 months	1:4	$165
2	Toddler 1	2	11	19 to 28 months	1:6	$155
3	Toddler 2	5	6	29 to 36 months	1:7	$145
4	Young Threes	7	8	37 to 42 months	1:7	$140
5	Old Threes	8	14	43 to 48 months	1:7	$135
6	Four Year Olds	4	4	49 to 60 months	1:7	$130
7	Five Year Olds	9	7	61 to 72 months	1:7	$125

TABLE CS.3   DATA FOR STUDENTS TABLE

Student ID	Student Name	Birth Date	Class ID	Guardian	Guardian Phone	Allergies/ Special Needs
1	Lauren Johnson	8/2/95	7	Gary Johnson	(402) 555-3111	
2	Marie Rappold	5/28/97	6	Sylvia Rappold	(402) 555-4893	
3	Roger Stephenson	7/28/97	5	Mia Stephenson	(402) 555-2093	
4	Michael Kroger	12/13/95	7	Doug Kroger	(402) 555-8026	
5	Michelle Goodwin	3/23/97	6	Cary Goodwin	(402) 555-6339	allergic to penicillin

Student ID	Student Name	Birth Date	Class ID	Guardian	Guardian Phone	Allergies/ Special Needs
6	Chi-luan Kuo	5/19/99	2	Yu-lan Kuo	(402) 555-8349	
7	Joey Buhr	8/3/97	5	Marti Buhr	(402) 555-3902	
8	Morgan Adams	5/27/98	4	Samantha Rye	(402) 555-4456	
9	Ashley Sohngen	3/3/96	7	Sarah Sohngen	(402) 555-7987	
10	Kenneth Feingold	8/18/98	3	Kenneth Feingold	(402) 555-1902	
11	James Danson	3/2/99	2	Marianne Danson	(402) 555-5893	prone to ear infections
12	Mitchell Tepe	12/24/96	6	Mark Tepe	(402) 555-6592	vegetarian diet
13	Violeta Torres	6/1/98	4	Vincente Torres	(402) 555-2569	
14	Courtney Morris	7/9/99	2	Drew Morris	(402) 555-7670	
15	Carl Carson	6/23/96	6	Angela Carson	(402) 555-4023	
16	Abby Simms	1/10/99	3	Ginny Simms	(402) 555-9833	
17	Allison Kuhlman	4/23/96	7	Jennifer Kuhlman	(402) 555-3990	
18	Marcus Matracia	10/31/99	2	Andrew Matracia	(402) 555-6847	
19	Aaron Potter	10/3/97	5	Bert Potter	(402) 555-5389	
20	Anna Hartlaub	3/16/98	4	Amy Hartlaub	(402) 555-7227	
21	David Yeager	9/30/97	5	Bob Yeager	(402) 555-1455	
22	Alan Bockenstette	11/3/98	3	Sue Bockenstette	(402) 555-8600	
23	Stephanie Roberts	10/7/00	1	Sharon Roberts	(402) 555-2784	allergic to milk
24	Kathy Zerkle	6/26/01	1	Patrick Zerkle	(402) 555-9324	
25	Mason Jasper	1/5/98	4	Anne Jasper	(402) 555-5203	
26	Elizabeth Finke	2/1/99	3	Martin Finke	(402) 555-1288	

3. Assign relationships among the tables, relating the Employees table to the Classes table by joining the Employee ID field to the Head Teacher field. Then relate the Classes and Students tables by joining the Class ID fields. Establish referential integrity in both relationships.

4. Adjust the widths of columns of each table, if necessary.

5. Open the Classes table and use the subdatasheets to view the names of the students enrolled in each class. How many students are enrolled in the Toddler 2 class? How many students are enrolled in the Five Year Olds class?

6. Sort the Employees table in ascending order by the employees' last names. Then, sort the employees in descending order by their pay rate.

7. A potential customer has asked if you have any openings in the Infants classroom. Use the Find feature to find out how many students are currently enrolled in this class.

8. Your supervisor would like to know how many full-time employees earn over $7.75 per hour. Use a filter to generate a list of employees that meet these criteria, sorting them so that the highest paid employees appear at the top of the list.

9. Two new students have just enrolled in the daycare. Create a columnar form named *Students* that includes all of the fields in the Students table. Make sure the student's first name field appears before the last name field and that the guardian's first name field appears before the last name field. Enter the new records shown in Table CS.4.

TABLE CS.4	DATA FOR STUDENTS FORM					
Student ID	Student Name	Birth Date	Class ID	Guardian	Guardian Phone	Allergies/ Special Needs
27	Gabrielle March	1/30/00	1	Sally March	(402) 555-4002	
28	Darren Finch	6/2/99	2	Ron Finch	(402) 555-9977	

10. Re-sort the form in ascending order by student last name.

11. The daycare is considering the startup of a field trip program for some of the older students. Create a query that lists students born before June 15, 1997. For each student, include the student's name, birth date, class name, room number, and teacher's last name. Save the query as *Students Eligible for Field Trips.*

12. The daycare director would like a list of students, grouped by the classes in which they are enrolled. Generate a report that includes each student's name, birth date, class name, and weekly fee. Group the report by classes and sum the fee field. Save the report as *Class Lists.* Preview and print it. Look at the report to determine the total weekly fees generated by the Toddler 2 class. What are the total fees generated by all classes?

13. Create a data access page that shows all of the fields from the Classes table. Do not group the records, but sort them in ascending order by class ID. Add the heading *Tiny Tots Daycare: Available Classes.* Save the data access page as *Tiny Tots Classes* in the *Projects* folder on your Student Data Disk.

14. Compact the database and then close it.

APPENDICES

CONTENTS

Portfolio Builder

WHAT IS A PORTFOLIO?

A **portfolio** is an organized collection of your work that demonstrates skills and knowledge acquired from one or more courses. The materials included in a portfolio should pertain to a specific educational or career goal. In addition to actual assignments, a portfolio should contain your self-reflection or comments on each piece of work as well as an overall statement introducing the portfolio.

Two types of portfolios exist. The first, which shows progress toward a goal over a period of time, is called a **developmental portfolio.** Developmental portfolios help you become more aware of your strengths and weaknesses and assist you in improving your abilities. The second type, called a **representational portfolio,** displays a variety of your best work. You can show a representational portfolio as evidence of your skills and knowledge. While you may use either type of portfolio when you are seeking employment, a representational portfolio is more effective.

WHY USE PORTFOLIOS?

Portfolios offer great advantages to you, your instructor, and potential employers. They allow you to reevaluate the work you have created, by determining which assignments should be included in the portfolio and analyzing how you can improve future assignments. If the goal of the portfolio is career related, portfolios also help you connect classroom activities with practical applications. A wide variety of genuine work is captured in a portfolio, rather than a snapshot of knowledge at a specific time under particular circumstances. Presenting a portfolio of your work to your instructor and potential employers gives them the opportunity to evaluate your overall skills and performance more accurately.

CREATING A PORTFOLIO

Creating a portfolio involves three steps—planning, selecting work to include, and providing comments about your work. First, you should plan the overall purpose and organization of the portfolio. After you plan your portfolio, you can begin selecting pieces of work to include in it. Ideally, you should select the work as you complete each document; however, you can review prior work to include as well. Table A.1 recommends some databases that you may want to consider for inclusion in your portfolio; however, you should also choose additional pieces of work of which you are proud.

TABLE A.1	POSSIBLE DOCUMENTS TO INCLUDE IN YOUR PORTFOLIO
File Name	**Activity**
Be Fruitful, Lesson 2	Lesson 2
Smyth Business College, Lesson 3	Skills Review, Lesson 3
Payton Properties, Lesson 4	Lesson Applications, Lesson 4
Electro Shop, Lesson 5	Projects, Lesson 5
Tiny Tots Daycare	Case Study

Create a list or log that provides a summary of the contents of your portfolio. (Your instructor may provide a preformatted log that you can complete.) The log can include columns in which you can list the file name, description of the file, when and by whom the file was reviewed, whether the file was revised, and the grade you received on the assignment.

Lastly, you should prepare comments for each piece of work included in the portfolio. As you add work to your portfolio, generate comments about each piece. You may want to reflect on the skills used to create the database or object, or you can explain how the database or object is applicable to a specific job for which you are interviewing. Your instructor may provide you with a preformatted comments form or you may type your comments using word processing software.

HANDS On

Building Your Portfolio

In this activity, you will plan your portfolio, select the Access database objects to include in the portfolio, and prepare written comments about each piece of work included in the portfolio.

1. Using word processing software, answer the following questions to help you plan your portfolio:

   ■ What is the purpose of your portfolio?

   ■ What criteria will you use in selecting work to be included in the portfolio?

   ■ What is the overall goal that your portfolio will meet?

   ■ How will you organize your portfolio?

2. Using either Access or word processing software, create a log that provides a summary of the contents of your portfolio. Follow the guidelines given by your instructor or provided in this appendix.

3. Remember the purpose and goal of your portfolio and select and print one database object that you have completed to include in your portfolio. Enter information about the object in your log.

4. Prepare comments about the selected database and attach them to the printout.

5. Repeat steps 3 and 4 to select and prepare comments for other databases to include in your portfolio.

6. Using word processing software, write a paragraph or two introducing your portfolio. Include some of the information considered in step 1.

7. Gather the documents to include in your portfolio and place them in a binder, folder, or other container in an organized manner.

FEATURE	BUTTON	MOUSE ACTION	KEYBOARD ACTION
Basic Skills			
Close a dialog box	✕	Click Cancel or Close	Esc
Close a menu		Click menu name on menu bar or anywhere outside of menu	Esc, Esc
Close any window	✕	Click the window's Close button	Ctrl + F4
Create a new database		Click File, New	Ctrl + N
Exit Access	✕	Click File, Exit or click Access's Close button	Alt + F4
Open a database		Click File, Open	Ctrl + O
Open a menu		Click menu name on menu bar	Press Alt in combination with underlined letter in menu name
Start Access	Start	Click the Start button, move to Programs, click Microsoft Access	
Undo previous action	↺	Click Edit, Undo	Ctrl + Z
Create a Data Access Page			
Create a data access page using a wizard		Click Pages in Objects bar, double-click Create data access page by using wizard	Alt + I, P
Open a data access page	Open	Double-click name of data access page	Select name and press Enter
View a data access page in the Web browser		Open page, click File, Web Page Preview	Alt + F, B

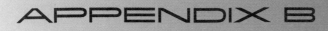

APPENDIX B

COMMAND SUMMARY

FEATURE	BUTTON	MOUSE ACTION	KEYBOARD ACTION
Filters			
Apply filter		Click Records, Apply Filter/Sort	Alt + R, Y
Apply Filter By Selection		Select text to filter, click Records, Filter, Filter By Selection	Alt + R, F, S
Apply Filter For Input		Right-click field, click Filter For, type text, press Enter	
Clear selection criteria		Click Edit, Clear Grid	Alt + E, A
Open Advanced Filter/Sort window		Click Records, Filter, Advanced Filter/Sort	Alt + R, F, A
Open Filter By Form window		Click Records, Filter, Filter By Form	Alt + R, F, F
Remove filter		Click Records, Remove Filter/Sort	Alt + R, R
Forms			
Add new record to form		Click Insert, New Record	Alt + I, W
Close Print Preview	Close	Click View, Form View	Alt + V, F
Create AutoForm		Click Insert, AutoForm	Alt + I, O
Create form with Form Wizard		Click Forms in Objects bar, double-click Create form by using wizard	
Move to first record		Click Edit, Go To, First	Ctrl + Home
Move to last record		Click Edit, Go To, Last	Ctrl + End
Move to next record		Click Edit, Go To, Next	Ctrl + PgDn
Move to previous record		Click Edit, Go To, Previous	Ctrl + PgUp
Move to specific record		Highlight current record number, type new record number, and press Enter	F5, type new record number, press Enter

FEATURE	BUTTON	MOUSE ACTION	KEYBOARD ACTION
Preview form		Click File, Print Preview	Alt + F, V
Print form		Click File, Print	Ctrl + P
Save form		Click File, Save	Ctrl + S
Switch to Datasheet view		Click View, Datasheet View	Alt + V, S
Switch to Design view		Click View, Design View	Alt + V, D
Switch to Form view		Click View, Form View	Alt + V, F

Help

FEATURE	BUTTON	MOUSE ACTION	KEYBOARD ACTION
Display Help topics		With Help window open, click the Show button and click Contents tab	With Help window open, Alt + C
Display ScreenTips		Click Help, What's This?	Shift + F1
Exit Help system		Click Close button	Esc
Open the Answer Wizard		With Help window open, click the Show button and click the Answer Wizard tab	With Help window open, Alt + A
Search for Help topics		With Help window open, click Show button and click Index tab	With Help window open, Alt + I
Use the Office Assistant		Click Help, Microsoft Access Help or click the Office Assistant	F1

Hyperlinks and the Web

FEATURE	BUTTON	MOUSE ACTION	KEYBOARD ACTION
Create hyperlink		Click Insert, Hyperlink	Alt + I, I
Display Web toolbar		Click View, Toolbars, Web	Alt + V, T, select Web
Go to a bookmark or favorite place		On the Web toolbar, click Favorites, click name of favorite place or bookmark from drop-down list	

COMMAND SUMMARY

FEATURE	BUTTON	MOUSE ACTION	KEYBOARD ACTION
Go to a Web site		On the Web toolbar, click Go, Open	Alt + G, O
Go to the Search Page		On the Web toolbar, click Go, Search the Web	Alt + G,W
Go to the Start Page		On the Web toolbar, click Go, Start Page	Alt + G, S
Set a bookmark or favorite place		On the Web toolbar, click Favorites, Add to Favorites	
Stop current connection			

Queries

Add tables to existing query		Click Query, Show Table	Alt + Q, T
Create query in Design view		Click Queries in Objects bar, double-click Create query in Design view	Alt + I, Q
Create query using Query Wizard		Click Queries in Objects bar, double-click Create query by using wizard	Alt + I, Q
Delete join		Click join line and press Delete	
Join tables		Drag common field from one Field list to the other	
Open existing query	Open	Double-click name of query	Select name and press Enter
Run query		Click Query, Run	Alt + Q, R
Save query		Click File, Save	Ctrl + S
Save query under new name		Click File, Save As	F12
Switch to Datasheet view		Click View, Datasheet View	Alt + V, S
Switch to Query Design view		Click View, Design View	Alt + V, D

FEATURE	BUTTON	MOUSE ACTION	KEYBOARD ACTION

Relationships among Tables

| Edit table relationships | | Double-click the join line | |
| Set table relationships | | Click Tools, Relationships | Alt + T, R |

Reports

Close report in Print Preview	Close	Click Close button	Ctrl + F4
Create a report with the Report Wizard		Click Reports in the Objects bar, double-click Create report by using wizard	Alt + I, R
Create AutoReport		Click Insert, AutoReport	Alt + I, E
Move to specific page		Double-click current page number, type new page number, and press Enter←	F5, type new page number, and press Enter←
Open a report	Preview	Double-click name of report	Select name of report and press Enter←
Print report		Click File, Print	Ctrl + P
Save report		Click File, Save	Ctrl + S
View report in Design view		Click View, Design View	Alt + V, D
View report in Print Preview		Click View, Print Preview	Alt + V, V
Zoom display in or out		Click on report	Alt + V, Z

Tables and Databases

| Create a new database | | Click File, New | Ctrl + N |
| Create a table in Design view | | Click Tables in the Objects bar, double-click Create table in Design view | Alt + I, T |

APPENDIX B

COMMAND SUMMARY

FEATURE	BUTTON	MOUSE ACTION	KEYBOARD ACTION
Create a table with the Table Wizard		Click Tables in the Objects bar, double-click Create table by using wizard	Alt + I, T
Display table objects		Click Tables in the Objects bar	Alt + V, J, T
Import a table		Click File, Get External Data, Import	Alt + F, G, I
Open a database		Click File, Open	Ctrl + O
Open a table	Open	Select table name, click Open button in Database window	Select table name in Database window, Alt + O

Tables—Datasheet View

Add new record		Click Insert, New Record	Alt + I, W
Close a subdatasheet		Click expand indicator (-)	
Close all subdatasheets		Click Format, Subdatasheet, Collapse All	
Copy data to Clipboard		Click Edit, Copy	Ctrl + C
Delete character to left of insertion point			Backspace
Delete character to right of insertion point			Delete
Delete record		Click Edit, Delete Record	Select record, Delete
Display Zoom window for adding or editing text			Shift + F2
Duplicate value in current field from previous record			Ctrl + '
Freeze columns		Click Format, Freeze Columns	Alt + O, Z
Hide columns		Click Format, Hide Columns	Alt + O, H

FEATURE	BUTTON	MOUSE ACTION	KEYBOARD ACTION
Increase or decrease row height		Drag any border between record selectors or choose Format, Row Height	Alt + O, R
Move one or more columns		Select column(s) and drag column selector	
Move to first field in current record		Click in column	Home
Move to first field in first record		Click in column	Ctrl + Home
Move to first record	◄|	Click Edit, Go To, First	Ctrl + ↑
Move to last field in current record		Click in column	End
Move to last field in last record		Click in column	Ctrl + End
Move to last record	►|	Click Edit, Go To, Last	Ctrl + ↓
Move to next field		Click in column	Tab or Enter
Move to next record	►	Click Edit, Go To, Next	↓
Move to previous field		Click in column	Shift + Tab
Move to previous record	◄	Click Edit, Go To, Previous	↑
Move to specific record		Double-click current record number, type new record number, press Enter	F5, type new record number, press Enter
Narrow or widen column		Drag column's left border or choose Format, Column Width	Alt + O, C
Open a subdatasheet		Click expand indicator (+)	
Open all subdatasheets		Click Format, Subdatasheet, Expand All	
Open Find dialog box	🔍	Click Edit, Find	Ctrl + F

COMMAND SUMMARY

FEATURE	BUTTON	MOUSE ACTION	KEYBOARD ACTION
Open Replace dialog box		Click Edit, Replace	`Ctrl` + H
Open Unhide Columns dialog box		Click Format, Unhide Columns	`Alt` + O, U
Paste append records from Clipboard into open table		Click Edit, Paste Append	`Alt` + E, N
Select all records		Click Edit, Select All Records	`Ctrl` + A
Select column		Click column selector	`Ctrl` + `Spacebar` (toggle)
Select record		Click record selector	`⇧ Shift` + `Spacebar` (toggle)
Switch between navigating and editing			`F2`
Undo changes to current field	↺	Click Edit, Undo	`Esc`
Undo changes to current record	↺	Click Edit, Undo	`Esc`
Undo most recent change	↺	Click Edit, Undo	`Ctrl` + Z
Unfreeze columns		Click Format, Unfreeze All Columns	`Alt` + O, A

Tables—Design View

FEATURE	BUTTON	MOUSE ACTION	KEYBOARD ACTION
Delete row (field)	⊟	Select row, click Edit, Delete	`Delete`
Insert row (field)	⊟	Select row, click Insert, Rows	`Alt` + I, R
Move to next column		Click in desired column	`Tab`
Move to previous column		Click in desired column	`⇧ Shift` + `Tab`
Open a table in Design view	Design	Select table name, click Design button in Database window	Select table name in Database window, `Alt` + D
Save table design	💾	Click File, Save	`Ctrl` + S

FEATURE	BUTTON	MOUSE ACTION	KEYBOARD ACTION
Save table design under new name		Click File, Save As	F12
Select field (row)		Click field selector	
Set primary key		Select field or fields, click Edit, Primary Key	Alt + E, K
Switch to and from Field Properties area		Click in desired area of Table Design window	F6

Sorting and Selecting Records

FEATURE	BUTTON	MOUSE ACTION	KEYBOARD ACTION
Sort fields in ascending order		Click Records, Sort, Sort Ascending	Alt + R, S, A
Sort fields in descending order		Click Records, Sort, Sort Descending	Alt + R, S, C

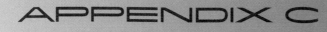

TOOLBAR SUMMARY

Database Toolbar

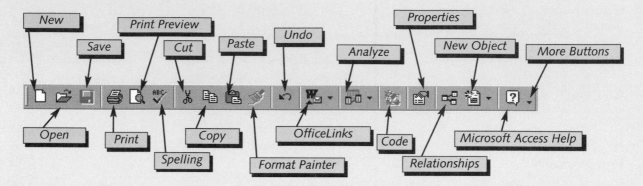

Form Design Toolbar

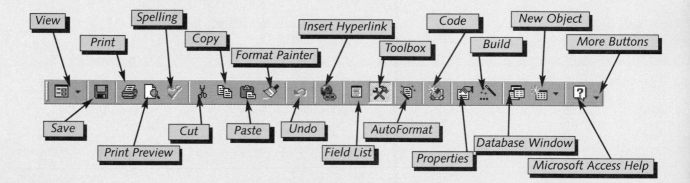

Formatting (Datasheet) Toolbar

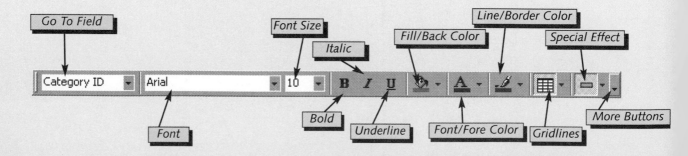

Query Design Toolbar

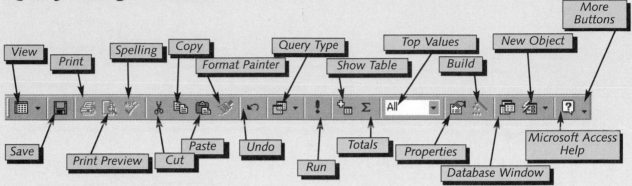

View • Print • Spelling • Copy • Format Painter • Query Type • Show Table • Top Values • Build • New Object • More Buttons

Save • Print Preview • Cut • Paste • Undo • Run • Totals • Properties • Database Window • Microsoft Access Help

Report Design Toolbar

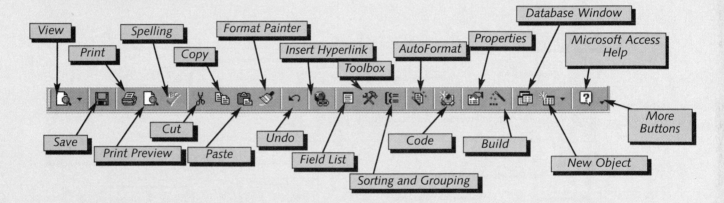

View • Print • Spelling • Copy • Format Painter • Insert Hyperlink • Toolbox • AutoFormat • Properties • Database Window • Microsoft Access Help

Save • Print Preview • Cut • Paste • Undo • Field List • Sorting and Grouping • Code • Build • New Object • More Buttons

Table Datasheet Toolbar

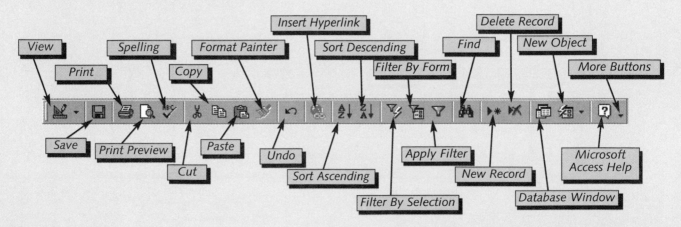

View • Print • Spelling • Copy • Format Painter • Insert Hyperlink • Sort Descending • Filter By Form • Find • Delete Record • New Object • More Buttons

Save • Print Preview • Cut • Paste • Undo • Sort Ascending • Filter By Selection • Apply Filter • New Record • Database Window • Microsoft Access Help

TOOLBAR SUMMARY

Table Design Toolbar

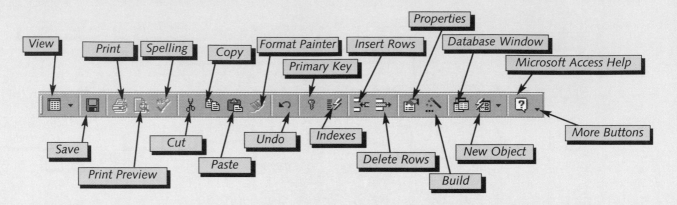

Toolbox

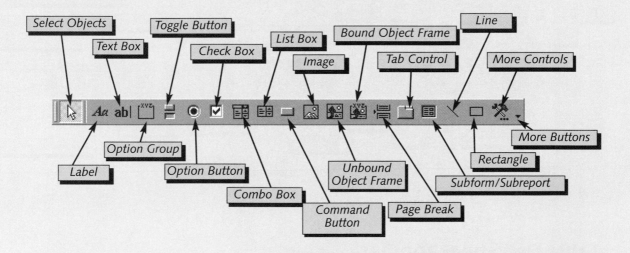

Web Toolbar

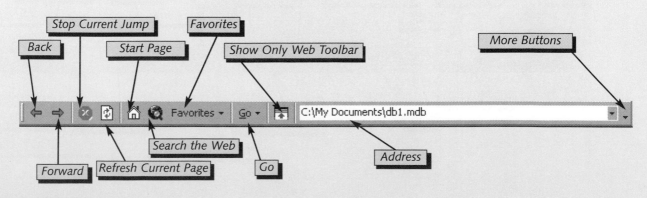

ANSWERS TO *Self* ✓CHECK

Lesson 1

1. b
2. d
3. e
4. c
5. a

Lesson 2

1. yes/no
2. hyperlink
3. default value
4. input mask
5. Captions

Lesson 3

1. importing
2. `⇧ Shift` + `Tab`
3. record selector, Delete Record
4. Zoom
5. `Ctrl` + '

Lesson 4

1. c
2. e
3. a
4. b
5. d

Lesson 5

1. T
2. F
3. T
4. T
5. F

Glossary

A

action An instruction or a command that you can combine with other instructions in a macro to automate a task.

adaptive menu A feature that allows each user to customize menus. When you select a less frequently used command from an expanded menu, you add that command to the short menu. Compare with *short menu* and *expanded menu*.

application Specialized software program for accomplishing a specific task, such as creating text, manipulating financial information, or tracking records.

application window A rectangle on the desktop containing the menus and document(s) for an application.

ascending sort A sort that arranges letters from A to Z, numbers from smallest to largest, and dates from earliest to most recent.

AutoForm A form that Access builds automatically; the AutoForm gathers the information it needs by examining the selected table or query.

AutoReport A report that Access builds automatically, based on the selected table or query.

B

bound control A control that is linked to a field in another table.

browser A software package that lets the user access the major components of the Internet, such as the World Wide Web, e-mail, and so on.

button A box labeled with words or pictures that you can click to select a setting or put a command into effect.

C

calculated control A control that uses an expression as the data source.

caption Words or phrases used to abbreviate or clarify field names. Captions are used as labels in forms and tables.

choose See *select*.

click The technique of quickly pressing and releasing the left button on a mouse or trackball.

Clipboard A temporary storage area for information that is used by all Windows applications.

close To remove a file from the window and the computer's memory.

columnar form A form that displays each field on a separate line with field labels or captions to their left as identifiers.

columnar report A report that displays all fields in a single column with field labels or captions to their left as identifiers.

commands Instructions that you issue to the computer, usually by choosing from a menu, clicking a button, or pressing a combination of keys on the keyboard.

common field A field that has the same name and data type as a field in one or more other tables. You need to set up common fields in preparation for sharing data between tables. The common field is what lets Access find matching data in different tables.

compact To rearrange how a fragmented database is stored on disk, improving performance and reducing size.

comparison operator A symbol that is used to compare a value or text in the table to characters that you enter.

controls Objects that display raw data, perform the actions upon the data, and allow you to format the data.

current record The record that is active. In Datasheet view, the current record is the row that contains a triangle or pencil icon in the record selector.

customize Alter to include personal preferences.

D

data access page A database object designed to be viewed in a Web browser.

data type A designation that determines the type of data that can be entered into a field, such as text, numbers, and dates.

database An organized collection of data about similar entities—such as employees, customers, or inventory items. In Access, a database also means a collection of objects—such as reports, forms, tables, queries, and data access pages—associated with a particular topic.

Database window A window that lets you gain access to all the objects (tables, forms, reports, and so on) in a particular database.

datasheet A tabular layout of rows and columns that allows you to add, edit, and view data in a table immediately.

DBMS (database management system) A system for storing and manipulating the data in a database.

descending sort A sort that arranges letters from Z to A, numbers from largest to smallest, and dates from most recent to the earliest.

deselect To return an object to the original color or turn off an option, indicating that an item will not be affected by the next action you take or that an option will no longer be in effect.

Design view A view that permits you to set up and modify the structure and appearance of database objects.

desktop The working area of the screen that displays many Windows 98 tools and the background for your computer work.

detail All the raw data or calculations derived from the raw data, on a form or report.

developmental portfolio A portfolio that shows your progress toward a goal over a period of time.

dialog box A rectangle containing a set of options that appears when the application requires more information from the user to perform a requested operation.

ditto key The ⎡Ctrl⎤ + ' key combination, which repeats the value from the same field in the previous record.

double-click The technique of rapidly pressing and releasing the left button on a mouse or trackball twice when the mouse pointer on screen is pointing to an object.

drag See *drag-and-drop.*

drag-and-drop The technique of moving an object on screen by pointing to the object, pressing and holding the left mouse button, moving the mouse to the new location, and then releasing the button. Also called *dragging.*

E

expanded menu A list of all the commands available when you select a menu name on the menu bar. The expanded menu appears if you click the double arrow at the bottom of a short menu. Compare with *short menu.*

expression A combination of field names, values, and comparison operators that can be evaluated as criteria for most types of filters.

F

field A column in a table that contains a category of data.

Field list A small window that lists all of the fields in a table or query. You can select fields to include in a filter or query from the Field list.

field properties Field settings that control the way a field looks and behaves.

filter A way to display your data to see only a selected portion of it.

footer Text that appears at the bottom of each printed page.

foreign key A field in a related table that has the same name and data type as the primary key in the primary table.

form Windows that present a custom layout for your data, enabling you to view, edit, and enter data.

freeze An option that lets you keep columns visible on the screen, even when you scroll.

Glossary

G

glossary term   An underlined word or phrase that, when clicked, displays a definition.

groups   Categories of information from the table or query that you can use to arrange records and show subtotals in a report.

H

header   Text that appears at the top of each printed page.

home page   The first of several pages at a Web site.

hyperlink   Text or a graphic inserted in a Help frame, a document, or a Web page that links to another frame, a document, an Internet address, a Web page on the World Wide Web, or an HTML page on an intranet.

Hypertext Markup Language (HTML)   The language used to tag a document with codes so the document can be viewed on the World Wide Web. HTML includes the capability that enables Web page creators to insert hyperlinks into their documents.

I

icon   A small image that represents a device, program, file, or folder.

import   The operation in which data from outside the database is brought into the database.

insertion point   The flashing, vertical line within a document that indicates where text will appear when typing begins.

Internet   A worldwide system of interconnected computer networks, allowing users to exchange digital information in the form of text, graphics, and other media.

J

join   A method of notifying Access how to match up records from one table with the appropriate records from any other tables.

joystick   An input device used to control the onscreen pointer; a small joystick is often found in the middle of keyboards on laptop computers.

K

keyboard shortcut   A way to use the keyboard to execute a command without going through the menu system. Usually a combination of Ctrl or Alt plus one letter keystroke.

keyword   Word or phrase used to define or narrow a search.

L

landscape orientation   A method of printing a report across the length of the page or horizontally.

M

macro   A series of stored commands that you can play back all at once by issuing a single command.

mailing labels   Sets of names and addresses or other information that you can gather from tables or queries and print for mass mailings.

many-to-many relationship   A relationship between tables in which each record in each table may have many matches in the other table.

menu   A list of items on the screen from which you can choose; menu usually refers to a list of commands or options.

menu bar   An area below the title bar of all application windows containing the names of menus, which, when clicked, displays a list of commands.

module   A set of programmed statements that are stored together as a unit; a module is used to automate a task.

mouse   A hand-held, button-activated input device that, when rolled along a flat surface directs an indicator to move correspondingly about a computer screen, allowing the operator to move the indicator freely, to select operations or manipulate data or graphics.

mouse pointer   See *pointer*.

O

objects The major components of an Access database, including tables, queries, forms, reports, data access pages, macros, and modules.

Office Assistant An animated character that can answer specific questions, offer tips, and provide help.

one-to-many relationship A relationship between two tables in which each record in the primary table can have no records, one record, or many matching records in the related table, but every record in the related table has one—and only one—associated record in the primary table.

one-to-one relationship A relationship between two tables in which every record in each table can have either no matching records or only a single matching record in the other table.

online The status of a printer when it is ready to accept output from your computer.

online Help system A window that opens to provide contextual assistance and other learning aids.

open To copy a file from disk into the computer's memory.

operating system A collection of programs that allows you to work with a computer by managing the flow of data between input devices, the computer's memory, storage devices, and output devices.

P

pointer An arrow or other onscreen image that moves in relation to the movement of a mouse or trackball. Also called a *mouse pointer*.

pointing Moving the mouse pointer to position it over an onscreen object.

portrait orientation A method of printing a report across the width of the page or vertically.

primary key A field or set of fields that uniquely identifies each record in the table.

primary table A table in a one-to-many relationship that can have zero, one, or many matching records in the related table; but every record in the related table has exactly one matching record in the primary table. You can think of a primary table as the "one" side in a one-to-many relationship.

print preview An accurate image of the printed output—including headers, footers, page breaks, and print titles—displayed on the screen. A print preview lets you see on the screen what you will be printing before you send the output to the printer.

properties The characteristics of a particular field, table, or database.

Q

query A question to the database, asking for a set of records from one or more tables or other queries that meets specific criteria.

query design grid The grid in the Query Design view window that you use to make decisions about how to sort and select your data and which fields to include in the recordset.

R

record A row in a table that contains the set of fields for one particular entity.

record selector The box in Datasheet view to the left of a record. You can click the record selector to highlight the entire record.

recordset A subset of your data sorted and selected as specified by a query. Recordsets change to reflect modifications to the data in your tables, and you can often make changes to recordsets that are reflected in the underlying table(s).

referential integrity A set of rules that Access can enforce to preserve the defined relationship between tables.

related table A table in a one-to-many relationship in which every record has exactly one matching record in the primary table. Also known as the *foreign table*.

Glossary

relational database   A database program that lets you link, or relate, two or more tables to share data between them.

relationship   The connection between two or more tables. If tables contain a common field, they can be linked through this field. When tables are related in this way, reports and other objects created can combine data from both tables.

report   Database objects that permit you to produce polished printed output of the data from tables or queries. Some Access reports automatically generate totals of the values in particular fields.

representational portfolio   A portfolio that displays a variety of your best work.

reverse video   White text against a dark background.

right-click   The technique of quickly pressing and releasing the right button on a mouse or trackball.

root folder   The top level of a disk icon, which contains files and folders that are not nested within any other folder.

row selector   A small box to the left of a field (in Table Design view) that you can click to select the entire field.

S

save   To take information from your computer's memory and store it on a more permanent medium—usually a floppy disk or a hard drive.

ScreenTip   Text which appears when you point to a tool and which provides information about the tool.

scroll bar   A rectangular bar that appears along the right or bottom side of a window when not all the contents of the window are visible, and which is used to bring the contents into view.

search engine   An Internet tool that allows you to look for information on a particular topic.

Search Page   The Web page used as a starting point for an Internet search.

select   To designate or highlight (typically by clicking an item with the mouse) where the next action will take place, which command will be executed next, or which option will be put into effect. To extract specified subsets of data based on criteria that you define.

selection criteria   Instructions that tell Access exactly which records you want to extract from the database.

select query   A query that you can use to sort, select, and view records from one or more tables.

short menu   A list of the most commonly used commands that appears when you click a menu name on the menu bar. Compare with *expanded menu.*

sort   To rearrange records into alphabetical, numerical, or chronological order.

subdatasheet   A datasheet within a datasheet that allows you to view and edit related or joined data in another table.

subform   A form within a form that displays related records.

T

table   A receptacle for data organized into a series of fields (columns) and records (rows).

tabular form   A form that displays all the fields for a single record in one row, field names or captions as column headings, and data in the table or query as a tabular arrangement of rows and columns.

tabular report   A report that displays the fields for a single record in one row, field names or captions as column headings, and all data in the table or query as a tabular arrangement of rows and columns.

taskbar   An area on the Windows 98 Desktop which displays a button for the Start menu, icons for commonly used Windows 98 features, an icon for any applications that are currently running, and a button for the clock.

toggle key   A key that turns on and off.

toolbar   A row of graphical buttons used to execute commands quickly.

touch-sensitive pad   An input device used to control the onscreen pointer by pressing a flat surface with your finger; usually found on laptop computers.

trackball   An input device that functions like an upside-down mouse, containing a ball that is rolled by the thumb or fingers to move the onscreen pointer.

U

unbound control   A control that does not have a data source and is used to display information or graphical elements such as lines, rectangles, or pictures.

URL (Uniform Resource Locator)   The address of a Web site. A URL can be made up of letters, numbers, and special symbols that are understood by the Internet.

W

Web page   A parcel of information located on the World Wide Web. The terms *Web page* and *Web site* are often used interchangeably. Also called *page.*

Web site   A specific place on the World Wide Web that contains Web pages. The terms *Web site* and *Web page* are often used interchangeably. Also called *site.*

wildcard character   A character used in searches and filters to find a variable string of characters. For instance, *we** would find all words that start with *we,* such as *weather, well,* and *weekday.*

wizard   An interactive help utility that guides a user through an operation step by step.

World Wide Web   An Internet service that allows users to view documents containing jumps to other documents anywhere on the Internet. The graphical documents are controlled by companies, organizations, and individuals with a special interest to share. Also referred to as the *Web* or *WWW.*

WYSIWYG   An acronym for *What you see is what you get,* a GUI characteristic in which documents appear on screen much as they will appear on a printed page.

Index

A

Access, 5
    exploring, 10–18
    introducing, 6–7
    starting, 8–10
Access Initial dialog box, *illus.,* 10
Access window, table of features, 11
Action, *def.,* 28, 290
Adaptive menu, *def.,* 12, 290
Add All Fields button, 215
Add field, 82–84
    in Query Design view, 181–182
Address button, 41
Adjacent fields, selecting, 82
Advanced filter/sort
    setting up, 175–176, *illus.,* 177
    using, 173–174
Align Left button, 17
Align Right button, 17
Alta Vista, 143
Analyze button, 16
Answer Wizard, using, 31–32
Anti–virus software, 108
Apple Macintosh computer, 7
Application(s), *def.,* 7, 290
Application window, *def.,* 10, 290
Ascending sort, *def.,* 164, 290, *illus.,* 165
AutoForm, *def.,* 210, 290
    creating an, 210–212
    saving an, 211
AutoNumber data type, 72
AutoReport, *def.,* 225, 290
    columnar, 226, *illus.,* 226
    creating, 225–228

B

Back button, 41
Backing up, database, 36
Between values, 174
Blank data, querying for, 186–187
Bold button, 17
Bookmark button, 188
Bound control, *def.,* 208, 290
Bound Object Frame button, 209
Browser, *def.,* 40, 290
Bullets button, 17
Busy pointer, 8
Buttons, *def.,* 7, 290
Byte number type, 74

C

Calculated control, *def.,* 208, 290
    creating a, 220–222
Calculated field, creating, 239–241
Calculations, 69
Caption(s), *def.,* 81, 290
    adding, to fields, 81–82
    table of, 86
Caption field property, 76

Categories, determining, 58–59
    See also Fields.
Center button, 17
Changes, canceling, to datasheet, 135
Check box, 15
Check Box button, 209
Choose, *def.,* 7
Click, *def.,* 7, 290
Clipboard, *def.,* 110, 290
Clipboard warning, *illus.,* 112
Close, *def.,* 290
Close database, *def.,* 38, 38–39
Code button, 16
Column
    changing, width, 130–131
    freezing, 134–135, *illus.,* 135
    hiding, 132–134, *illus.,* 134
    moving, *illus.,* 132
Columnar AutoReport, 226, *illus.,* 226
Columnar form, *def.,* 212, 290, *illus.,* 26
    creating, with Form Wizard, 212–214
Columnar report, *def.,* 228, 290
    creating, 228–230
Combo Box button, 209
Command(s), *def.,* 22, 290
    summary of, 277–285
Command button, 15, 209
Common field, *def.,* 60, 290
Compact, *def.,* 290
Compacting a database, 37–38, *def.,* 37, *illus.,* 87
Comparison operator, *def.,* 174, 290
Computer virus, 108
Contents tab, *illus.,* 32
    using, 32
Control(s), 208–209, *def.,* 208, 290
    creating a calculated, 220–222, 241
    modifying
        in forms, 218–223
        in reports, 238–243
    moving, *illus.,* 235
Control icon, 11
Control toolbox, 208
    table of, 209
Control Wizards button, 209
Copy button, 16
Copy, data in a table, 112–114
Criteria, selecting, 185–186
    with Filter by Form, *illus.,* 169
Crosshair pointer, 8
Currency data type, 72
Current record, *def.,* 290
Customer lists, 6
Customize, *def.,* 10, 290
Customize dialog box, *illus.,* 14
Cut button, 16

D

Data
    adding, *illus.,* 108
        using forms and subforms in, 216–218
    copying, in a table, 112–114
    editing, *illus.,* 22
        in query, 182
        using forms and subforms in, 216–218

Index

Index

Index

Index

Toolbar(s), *def.*, 15, 295
    exploring the Web, 40–43
    features of, 16
    moving, 15
    Web, *illus.*, 40
    working with, 15–18
Toolbar button, 11
Toolbox, control, 208
Toolbox toolbar, *illus.*, 219, 288
Tools menu, 13
Totals, creating, in reports, 235–238
Touch–sensitive pad, *def.*, 7, 295
Trackballs, *def.*, 7, 295

U

Unavailable pointer, 8
Unbound control, *def.*, 208, 295
Unbound Object Frame button, 209
Underline button, 17
Undo, 120–123, *illus.*, 122
    changes in saved record, 122–123
Undo button, 16
Undo command, 130
Unhide Columns dialog box, *illus.*, 133
Uniform Resource Locator, *def.*, 191, 295
URL. *See* Uniform Resource Locator.

V

Values
    filtering for, 170–171
    finding, in a table, 126
    replacing, in a table, 128
Vertical resize pointer, 8
View
    adding a record in Form, 25–27
    Query, 24–25
    Query Design, 179, *illus.*, 179
    records in datasheet, 116–125
Viewing, table, 20–22
    design, 22–23
View menu, 13
Virus, computer, 108

W

Web browser, def., 40
Web page, *def.*, 40, 295
    creating a, 246–249
Web site(s), *def.*, 40, 295
    business, 225
    navigating, 88–89
Web toolbar, *illus.*, 40, 288
    exploring the, 40–43
Widths, changing column, 130–131
Wildcard character, *def.*, 295
Window, database, *def.*, 20, *illus.*, 20
Window menu, 13
Windows 95, 7, 8
Windows 98, 7, 8
Windows desktop, *illus.*, 9
Wizard, *def.*, 63, 295
    Form, *def.*, 208
    Query, 183
    Report, 228–235
Word
    converting to Microsoft, 115
Working in background pointer, 8
Worksheet, importing a, 115–116
World Wide Web, *def.*, 40, 117, 295
    job–searching on, 173
WYSIWYG, *def.*, 295

Y

Yes/No data type, 72

Z

Zoom feature, 244
Zoom window, *illus.*, 124
    editing in, 124–125